Winter, Miriam
Therese.

Out of the depths.

$19.95

DATE		

BAKER & TAYLOR

OUT OF THE
DEPTHS

OUT OF THE
DEPTHS

THE STORY OF LUDMILA JAVOROVA
ORDAINED ROMAN CATHOLIC PRIEST

MIRIAM THERESE WINTER

A Crossroad Book
The Crossroad Publishing Company
New York

The Crossroad Publishing Company
481 Eighth Avenue, New York, NY 10001

Cover illustration: *Young Girl Sketch* 1896, pencil and chalk, by Moravian artist Alphonse Mucha, New York Museums, Alphonse Mucha Gallery. Photography by Javier Ortega, New York.

Back cover photograph, Ludmila Javorova in her apartment in Brno, 2000, photograph by Dolly Pomerleau.

Library of Congress Cataloging-in-Publication Data

Winter, Miriam Therese.
    Out of the depths : the story of Ludmila Javorova, ordained Roman Catholic priest / Miriam Therese Winter.
        p. cm.
    Includes bibliographical references.
    ISBN 0-8245-1889-6
    1. Javorova, Ludmila. 2. Priests – Czech Republic – Biography.
3. Women priests – Czech Republic – Biography. 4. Catholic Church – Czech Republic – Clergy – Biography. I. Title.
BX4705.J379 2001
282′.092–dc21

2001000361

1   2   3   4   5   6   7   8   9   10   06   05   04   03   02   01

To all my close and distant friends,
who contribute to the realization of God's gifts,
especially the priestly charism;
to our church community,
without which I would never have known
the beauty and the meaning
of life's unfolding;
to all who,
after the public disclosure of my ordination,
showed so cordial a togetherness
from all corners of the world;
to women and men who knowingly participate
in the work of God
without seeking credit:
to all of you I dedicate my story.

— LUDMILA JAVOROVA —

Brno–Zidenice
February 2, 2001
Feast of the Presentation of Jesus

Out of the depths
I cry to You,
O God.
Hear my voice.
Listen
to my supplications.
Listen
to my prayer.
I wait for You.
My soul waits,
more than sentinels watch
for morning,
more than death awaits
the dawn,
I wait,
and in Your word
I hope,
for in You
is unconditional love
and power
to redeem.
Out of the depths
I cry,
O God.
Lead me
out of the depths.

– Psalm 130 –

PROLOGUE

The black brocade looked stunning. It was the perfect dress for a night such as this. She slipped silently out of the house into December darkness, so she would not have to explain to her parents why she was in her party clothes leaving home at such an hour. She would not have been able to tell them, in fact, could never tell them what it was that awaited her. Tonight would change her forever, but in what way was a secret, and she would never tell.

She melted into the shadows to be certain not to be seen. Wariness was a way of life. She knew the bushes and trees had eyes, but tonight no one was watching. She walked the short distance to his house filled with anticipation. O blessed night. O beckoning night. In a way, she had been preparing for this for all of her thirty-eight years.

Once inside she did not hesitate. Felix was waiting for her upstairs. Everything was ready. The ancient ritual began. At the threshold of decision, before he laid his hands on her, he asked her once again, "Do you want to receive it?" She answered, "Yes, I do." With his brother Leo as witness, in the Moravian city of Brno in Czechoslovakia, Bishop Felix Maria Davidek ordained Ludmila Javorova a Roman Catholic priest.

In no time at all it was over, the transforming touch of the Eternal. Yet grace had made its mark on her, and on the level of essential being, what had happened would never end. Her First Mass, her first blessing, and then it was time to be heading home. She arrived after midnight and into a new day dawning. The familiar sights of her neighborhood evoked in her a pastoral response as she lifted all who were living there into the mercy of God.

At home a little child was crying. Her niece, part of the ex-

9

tended family that lived with her parents, had awakened in the night. She whispered to her from a distance. "If only my arm were long enough, I would comfort you and bless you. Hush, my child. Don't cry. Listen. I will give you a blessing, my new priestly blessing." And she did. Although it happened a generation ago, Ludmila remembers the moment as though it were yesterday. "I had such a desire to say those words, to comfort her and bless her. I lay awake for a long, long time, blessing everyone. I blessed my parents, my family, my friends. I blessed the whole world, the whole universe, with the blessing of a priest."

ONE

When I was being formed in secret,
taking shape in the depths of the earth,
in Your book were recorded all of my days
before any of them existed.

Psalm 139:15–16

There are two levels to the story of Ludmila Javorova. The first tells of external events. The second reveals an inner world that accompanied and made possible fidelity to the first. Here a deeply reflective woman met with God her Beloved to wrestle with the facts of her life, struggling to make sense of it all as she probed its depths for meaning. In this sacred sanctuary, Ludmila found refuge for her spirit and the strength to embrace her call. Her story, one of unwavering faith up against insurmountable odds, is told here as a legacy of hope and courage for our times.

✛

The story begins long, long ago in the home of her ancestors, deep in the heart of Moravia in Czechoslovakia. In September of 1898, in the village of Hvozdna, Ludmila's grandmother, Frantiska Vrlova, gave birth to Ludmila's mother. She and her husband, Pavel, named their daughter Ludmila, after a ninth-century saint and martyr from neighboring Bohemia, a name that the little girl would one day give to her own little girl who would grow up to be a priest. But that's later on in the story. Long before people spoke of such things, before anyone could imagine change in the traditions of the church, the seeds of a living faith were sown in the heart of a child. The Catholic religion's sacramental life and devout personal piety that defined its many believers had been

11

passed on intact to the next generation and eventually to the next, and so it would be again.

As soon as she was old enough, Ludmila went to Mass at the village church and learned to say the rosary. She spoke to the Virgin Mary, and sometimes to Jesus on the cross, lit candles by their statues, said her prayers before falling asleep, and placed wildflowers at makeshift shrines that interrupted meadows and fields or marked a place in the forest. When she was six, her carefree life was suddenly and irrevocably changed. Her sister Frantiska, who was seven, was watching her father load his gun as he prepared to go hunting, when the gunpowder exploded in the little girl's eyes, leaving her permanently blind. That same year, her mother died, and Ludmila turned to the mother of God to fill the void within her.

A maternal uncle, their mother's brother, priest and prior of Holy Mountain Redemptorist Monastery, came to console the distraught widower, who was left to care for three little girls and a toddler son named Jan. He knew of a woman, he said to Pavel, a very good woman who lived near the monastery. She said she was willing to help out with the children in the difficult days ahead. She was a woman of considerable wealth, with servants and staff, a large house and horses. Why not entrust the girls to her while he adjusted to the change? It seemed a sensible suggestion to the devastated Pavel. He sent six-year-old Ludmila and his eldest, Anezka, to Bohemia, left Frantiska at a school for the blind to learn how to be self-sufficient, and kept Jan at home with him.

Ludmila and Anezka went to live in a big house in the Bohemian town of Pribram. It was a long way from home. A fine house it was, but the woman who had been so highly praised was strict and often abusive. If the girls were late getting home from school, she would punish them by beating them or by letting them go hungry. Anezka threatened to tell her father. To prevent her, the woman took her to Prague to an institute for girls. It was a fortuitous move for Anezka. She was given an opportunity to live and mature in a nurturing environment. She would go on to complete university studies and enter the congregation of English Virgins founded by Mary Ward.

Her little sister, however, was far less fortunate. The two girls really loved each other, but now Ludmila was left all alone in a strange place with a domineering woman she could not seem to satisfy. She endured untold hardship until she was twelve years old, when she was sent to a school for girls run by the School Sisters of Notre Dame in Horazdovice in Bohemia. Further studies prepared her to be a kindergarten teacher. She had decided to remain with the sisters when her father sent for her. He had married again, and during the intervening years, there had been other children. He asked her to return to Hvozdna to help out in his household. Ludmila obeyed.

Frantisek Javora, Ludmila Javorova's father, was also born in Hvozdna in 1898. His father was a man of means, a tough, hardworking individual. Frantisek, the eldest of five children who bore his father's name, was destined to inherit the family farm, but he had no interest in property. Inclined to literature and the arts, he went off to study in Kromeriz. He was an avid reader, just like his grandmother, who owned a mill in Myslocovice. The only one in her village who could read, she had, it was said, a mill full of books. "Frantisek," she would say to her grandson, "I would give these books only to you," which eventually she did.

Frantisek Javora and Ludmila Vrlova met and decided to marry. Frantisek did not want to be burdened with property handed down through generations or bound by expectations he had no desire to fulfill, so he relinquished his right of inheritance and walked away unencumbered. His mother, Veronika, supported his decision, because she understood him, but his father did not. Forfeit one's inheritance? It simply wasn't done. The eldest son stayed home. This was their tradition. Inspired by the biblical Abraham, who had once set out on paths unknown, Frantisek would start a new tradition. With pioneering courage and with faith in God and in each other, the determined couple married in May of 1924 and then left familiar ways behind to begin life anew in the metropolitan city of Brno.

Brno, the largest city in Moravia, is situated 120 miles southeast of Prague. It lies in a wide valley above the confluence of two rivers, the Svratka and Svitava. Hills hover protectively on three sides and forested areas, even now, are sanctuary for songbirds and plant and animal life. When Czechoslovakia declared itself an independent republic on October 28, 1918, a flurry of economic growth changed the landscape of Brno in ways that were advantageous for development. It was a good place to settle. Here one could find a job in industry or in trade, a critical step toward securing a house and raising a family. The city had also become a cultural and educational center, good news to one who preferred books to financial security and wanted better opportunities for educating his children. The newly married couple bought an old house in the section of Brno known as Kralovo Pole and began life together there. One of the first things the young couple did was to order the construction of a bookcase large enough to hold all of Frantisek's books, those already in his possession and the many more he would eventually acquire.

On January 31, 1932, Ludmila Javorova was born. It was Sunday around noon when she came into the world at home, and all the bells were ringing. What a memorable moment for Frantisek Javora and Ludmila Javorova.* They rejoiced at the birth of a girl and the sound of the church bells welcoming her into their family. This child was not their firstborn. Four others had preceded her. All of them were boys. Little Frantisek had arrived in 1927, followed by Jan, Alois, and Stanislav, one right after the other. Now, at last, a daughter.

The house in Brno was situated near the place where Frantisek

---

*In the Czech language, males in this family have the surname Javora; females use Javorova.

worked. He had planned to live there permanently, but as the family grew in size, he knew a change was necessary. Sometime before Ludmila's birth, he sold that house and bought another on the outskirts of the city and went heavily into debt. Like most people with mortgages, they paid for it in installments, which continued for many years. The new house in Chrlice had a little garden. It was a medium-size house, but there was sufficient room for the family to expand.

As soon as he was able, Frantisek Javora went to Turany, the district next to Chrlice on the outer edge of Brno, to introduce himself to the pastor as his new parishioner. The priest spoke harshly to him because he had not come during office hours. Frantisek was hurt, but he was not resentful. In church he met a family from his previous parish in Kralovo Pole. The father was unemployed. Frantisek went home and partitioned his new house from the basement all the way up to the roof and gave half of it to that family. They had one child when they moved in. They would add four more. Ludmila and Frantisek had five more children in the years that followed. There were four sons—Vaclav, Josef, Vojtech, and Pavel—before another daughter. Maria, the tenth and final child, was born in 1942 when her mother was forty-four. The space the family had first occupied became home to twenty people—fifteen children, four parents, and an auntie. They survived the war together, spending six weeks in an underground shelter as the front passed through Brno. That experience strengthened their bonds even more, so that the children were heartbroken at their postwar parting. "Both families grew up in this medium-size house," recalls the younger Ludmila, "and until I was nearly an adult, I did not know they were not our relatives." The two families lived there together until the end of the war.

Ludmila shares some childhood memories about her mother, who was organized and efficient, filled with faith in God, and devoted to her ten children. "In the evening there were several little piles of clothes, all handmade by *maminka,** who would check them and replace what was necessary. She would be ironing and sewing late into the night. We children slept in two rooms, except for the small ones, who slept with my parents.

"She woke us all at the same time in the morning. When we went for Mass we got up at six. She always felt sorry for us when it was cold. In winter she would say, 'It's so nice and warm in there. I know you children would like to sleep in.' Then she would pull away the covers from the boys so they would not stay in bed too long. We would dress quickly in winter. I vividly remember starting the day. I would hear the sound of my mother's voice singing Marian songs in the kitchen and I would smell the aroma of coffee. Sometimes she invited beggars to come and have breakfast with us, poor men who earned their money by repairing pots and other household things.

"Breakfast always ended with a prayer to the Holy Spirit, and then she would walk us to the door. We had to leave for school all together, and when we returned, she was waiting for us. In the winter, when it was cold, she sat us down and warmed our hands. I remember the smell of the kitchen. It was always so welcoming.

"We had a routine for ending the day. Usually *tatinek* was with us. Sometimes *maminka* was. We all knelt down in the bedroom, and together we said our prayers: Our Father, Hail Mary, the Ten Commandments, and a prayer to the Holy Spirit. Then we examined our conscience. When papa closed the day with us, he always said: 'Children, the best examination of conscience is made when your eyes are closed.' So he had us all lie down on the floor, propped up on our elbows, with our fingers over our eyes. We would lie there prostrate in silence. We looked forward to this moment with him. We were already anticipating it as we prayed the Hail Mary. We were supposed to look back and remember the day. He would never suggest our transgressions. He hoped

---

Maminka: Mama; *Tatinek:* Papa.

we would remember them on our own. Myself, I wouldn't try to remember anything. I would lie there and wait until he ended the silence with the words, 'Get up and let us pray a penitence prayer.' We would also pray for those who had died. Mama did it differently. She began by saying, "Don't lie on the floor,' and 'Well, children, how was the morning?' Then she would name our faults, especially with the boys, pointing out those who did not obey. So we felt sorry, but only after she had stirred our conscience. She would say, 'Tell everything to Jesus, and let us repent over our misdeeds, because we don't know if we will wake up in the morning. It is war time. But always remember this: when you are leaving the house in the morning, always say, we will all meet again. Don't be sad or anxious. Now let us pray for the ones who died this day because of the war."

Their blind aunt Frantiska was part of the family. Her sister asked her to come live with them and help care for their children. She was an integral and much loved member of their household until her death.

"Auntie was a wonderful woman, very kind. She was also very cheerful. We received so much from her. What *maminka* couldn't give us because she did not have the time, this auntie could and did. For instance, when Mother was working in the evening, Auntie would have us gather around her, and she would tell us stories. She was excellent in telling fairytales, which she herself created, and she knew so many songs. She often played with us. She was spontaneous and imaginative and she had great empathy for us. We could share just about anything with her, and we usually did.

"With this auntie we would go to the institute for the blind and spend time with her former schoolmates. Those visits were very meaningful for us. We would go on Sunday afternoons, and we would read to the residents there. Papa went to the men's quarters, and we children would visit the women. We got to know some wonderful people. This put us in touch with the realities of life."

Opposites are often attracted to one another and, in the ensu-ing relationship, contribute diverse gifts toward a fuller experience of life. This was certainly true for the parents of this family. The mother was a woman of order and consistency, valuable traits for managing a rambunctious brood of ten. She was economical and adept at making limited resources last. She was organized and ob-jective, and she had a way of rationalizing why things had to be done a certain way. Once when her daughter objected, she replied: "There are more boys here, and boys need it this way." She worked very hard and into the night. There were always heaps of socks to be mended and all those clothes to wash without a washing machine. On one thing she was unyielding: everything had to be ironed. When asked by her little girl, "When do you pray?" she responded simply and sincerely. "Ludmila, my morning prayer is in the songs I sing. That is all I can manage, because I have a lot of duties." Especially remarkable in this simple woman was the tenacity of her trust in God. Her deep faith and her courage enveloped all in the family and formed the subtext of their lives.

Frantisek Javora, on the other hand, was helpless with the housework. He simply was not practical. This is evident from the stories his daughter Ludmila tells. "My father was meticulous. Whenever he washed the dishes, it was so carefully and precisely. My mother used to say to him, 'Oh, *tatinek*, we are not in a lab-oratory,' which is where he worked. When he washed a cup, he would look at it with the same precision he used in the lab. We didn't like to do dishes with him.

"He did not know how to cook. My mom would laugh about it, because when she was in labor, she had to tell him everything. There she was, lying in the bed, and in between contractions, she was telling him what to do.

"He had a lyrical and expansive spirit. He would tell us about the stars and about the world beyond us. He loved to go for walks with me. I was a good listener. Because I did not say very much, he liked to share things with me. He would always be telling me about the places he would visit after the war. He loved space, the mountains, the sea, even though he never visited the sea. He knew geography. He knew the whole continent. He was interested in literature, and he was very well read. He built a major library by buying books in second-hand book shops and binding them himself. He would read to us at bedtime. He tried to open up the world to his children through his books. He also knew theology, and priests would often come to the house to engage in theological discussions.

"My father was not equipped for the rough situations of life, and my mother understood that. She knew instinctively what he could do and never degraded or humiliated him for the things that he could not. When she saw that the demands were too great for him, she intervened to remove them or tactfully collaborated with him to find some solution that would preserve his self-esteem. This meant sometimes she had to do the work that men usually do.

"My father loved flowers. He planted them everywhere, inside and outside the house. My mother was worried that the children would be injured because there were cactuses all over the place. She would ask him again and again, 'When will you stop growing cactuses?' He would always answer, 'But they are so beautiful.' He loved nature and animals, and he was fond of trees." Maria, the youngest, shares in the memory. "When I hear trees whispering in the wind, I always imagine my father pruning his beloved trees. He did it so carefully. He would look from all sides at the little branch, deciding whether or not to cut it."

"My father loved singing." This is Ludmila speaking. "Both of them loved singing, but perhaps most of all my father loved books—books on philosophy, psychology, gardening, languages, everything. He always went to bed with four or five books, and they covered the top of his desk. He carried some with him whenever he traveled, and he traveled often because of his job, especially during the war. On Sunday he would open his bookcase, which was right next to his bed, bury himself in his books, and be transported to another world. One by one, like a prince with his trophies, he would take a volume, caress its cover, flip through its pages, put it back, and pull out another one. He would remain there for hours."

By all accounts the father of the family was a kind and honest man and a conscientious provider. He worked as a laboratory assistant in a research institute in Brno. He insisted that his children be prepared for the realities of life. "One day," says Ludmila, "he took me to an orphanage in the suburbs, and he asked the superior to give us someone who could show us around the institution, so that I could see the environment of children who had no parents. This experience contributed to the deepening of my social awareness."

The parents formed a partnership that was a model for their children. "I felt secure in my mother's faith and in her simple trust," says Ludmila. "My father deepened my thirst for knowledge. Those formative years sowed the seeds I would harvest for a lifetime."

Czechoslovakia, which borders Germany on the west, suffered under Nazi occupation throughout World War II. During the war there was an allotment of food, which meant there was never enough available for Ludmila's family. She remembers clearly. "German soldiers were everywhere and nobody was allowed to give food to anyone without the allotment vouchers. When the situation was desperate and my mother had nothing to give us to eat, she would simply say: 'Children, I don't know what I am going to cook tomorrow. Let us entrust it to God. Let us give God our worries.' Sometimes she would kneel with us for a short prayer. Then all afternoon I would hear her singing, 'Mighty Creator of Heaven and Earth,' a song that expresses a deep trust in God. And somehow, some way, we had enough to eat the following morning.

"I remember one winter, when my sister Maria was still in the pram. My mother had acquired an unauthorized sack of wheat. We had to take it to a mill so it could be ground into flour. She had gotten the grain in the summer and had kept it for an emergency, an act that was punishable by deportation to a concentration camp. She put the bag in the baby's pram, laid my sister on it, and off we went to the mill. German soldiers were everywhere, and I was terrified. We waited at the railway crossing. There were SS soldiers on guard there. She told me, 'Ludmila, take the pram. Go straight ahead into the mill. Do not look at anyone. Ring the bell. The lady will know what to do. Let her have the pram. And don't be afraid, my little one. I'll be praying for you and waiting for you here. The souls in purgatory have never let us down. There is no other way.' I took the pram and went into the mill. I was so scared, I shook inside. As a child, I was frightened of SS soldiers, frightened of the Gestapo, because I knew we were being watched and that my parents were in danger. No matter how scared I was, when *maminka* would tell me, don't be afraid, I felt I could go even into hell, that when the moment came to do so, my courage would not fail. And indeed I went through hell that day, carried along by her trust in God and strengthened by her faith in me. I was a child with very little courage, but her courage would encourage me.

"It was a daily struggle to find food to eat, and no matter how difficult the situation, my mother trusted that God would provide. Once when there was no food to cook and eight hungry boys in the house, she said, 'Children, tomorrow I have nothing to give you,' and she began to sing the words of her favorite hymn. "I will not be afraid of want, because You are taking care of me," resounded through the house. That evening she gathered the children to pray, and in the morning behind our door she found a three-kilo bag of flour. Nobody knows who put it there, even to this day."

Ludmila struggled as a girl growing up in the middle of eight brothers. "Always I would come to my mother. '*Maminka*, they do not want to play with me.' And she would ask, 'And what are they playing?' 'They are playing that they are cars.' Then my mother would say, 'So, come with me.' And she would welcome me into her own separate world. She always offered her presence to me if the boys sent me away. I was content just to be with her, the sole object of her attention, for this was something special that did not happen every day.

"Alois, who was three years older than me, liked to play with dolls. He played so carefully as if he were a girl, not a boy. He would find pretty clothes and then he would build a little room for the doll. Why, I do not know. And my mother was so unhappy about this. She told him, 'If this girl would be playing like this, I would say nothing, but you!' I did not play with dolls very often, because I had so many children around me who were alive. They were the children of my imagination. I would open the door of the bookcase with its beautiful blue curtains, and I imagined that I was the mother superior or the director of an orphanage. I gave commands as I played with these invisible children. Then in the evening I closed my orphanage and went out to the kitchen to *maminka*.

"Once when the catechist came to our house, he put his biretta, that funny little hat, on the edge of the table, like he always did. Oh, how I wanted to hold it in my hand, and maybe even try it on. So I whispered in my mother's ear, '*Maminka*, can I touch this thing?' The catechist overheard me. He looked at me sternly and said, 'Girls cannot touch this.' I hid behind my mother, and when he wasn't looking, I reached out and touched it anyway.

"Every Sunday my brothers played at pretending they were priests. They would celebrate 'Mass.' My mom would make little vestments for them. They had a bowl and pestle for a bell and they made a lot of noise with that. When it was time to do the preaching, they stood on a tiny chair, which was turned around with its back to the invisible congregation, so that it looked like a pulpit. The younger ones had to be altar boys. The older ones were the priests. But I was out of this. Not only was I not allowed to play, they didn't even want me among them, especially the older ones. So I went to tell my mother, because they had been tormenting me. 'Remain here with me,' she said. Then she tried to explain to me that girls couldn't be 'Reverend Fathers.' I was not content with this, so I went to find my father. He was by his bookcase, absorbed in his reading. I asked him, *'Tatinek,* why can't girls be Reverend Fathers?' Without even looking at me, my father responded: 'So you can pray for it, and maybe one day it will happen.' And he continued to read. I don't think he knew what he was saying. You would have to know my father. When he was reading, he was so deep in concentration that he did not notice anything. Even if the house fell down around him, he would continue to read. No matter how much noise my brothers made, he was not disturbed. However, I liked his answer, and I went away satisfied."

The family prayed together every day. In a sense they were like a mini-parish, a "domestic edition" of the church. They celebrated everyone's baptism and First Communion days and were introduced daily into the liturgical feasts and seasons. They always knew the evening before what the Mass would be tomorrow, whether it was a feast or a commemoration, and they knew which saint was being venerated on any given day. Their mother would tell the children all about the saints whose lives were celebrated and explain why the church remembered them and why it chose to honor them. Whenever possible the children participated in the Mass. They went to the chapel near their home, which was located in the institute for the blind, because it was closer than the parish church. They would take their blind auntie along. Their parents did not go with them, but they participated spiritually. There were many devotional practices that enriched family life. "For example," Ludmila recalls, "there was the daily sprinkling with holy water, and when we were not at home, before she went to sleep, my mother would bless us anyway, sprinkling holy water in the direction where we were. On the feast of the Epiphany, which stands at the threshold of the new year, the entire house was cleansed and blessed as we moved from room to room." Common prayer, spiritual discussion, sharing, reading, blessing the children, the keeping of special feasts, as well as family celebrations, both planned and spontaneous, were part of the fabric of their life. They anticipated many of the changes recommended by Vatican II. Always the church hierarchy was regarded with great respect.

Even though they had their differences, the children got along remarkably well. They really liked each other, and because they had one another, there was always someone to talk to, a sibling or two to play with or to turn to in distress. They were never idle. There were always chores to be done. They had to prepare the wood for heating, help out in the kitchen, polish all the shoes. Ludmila's job, for instance, was to take care of the younger ones, especially Maria, the baby, who sometimes felt like she was her sister's child. It was also Ludmila's duty to be helpful to *maminka*. For her brothers, it was the garden and collecting and chopping wood. The boys always had to be busy. That was one of the rules of the house. Their mother would have it no other way. When it came to Ludmila, however, she was more lenient.

Like any large family, theirs was fairly self-sufficient. They learned responsibility early on, learned how to share, how to listen to others. These qualities were often put to use beyond the confines of the home. They were generally helpful to others. They ran errands for elderly neighbors and brought them coal for heating. Sometimes Ludmila would go with her mother when one of their friends had died. "We are going to say goodbye," her mother said. On the way she would tell her something about the deceased person's life, and they would pray together. Her mother never thought that she was too small to be part of such a thing. Those were very special times. She never took the boys with her. Because of this, Ludmila grew up never knowing a fear of dead people, which was common among many of her contemporaries then, and perhaps even now.

To the children of the occupation, war had been around forever.

It was bound to influence their behavior. Ludmila liked to play soldiers. In the evening, in the garden, she would climb into the holes that had been dug for trees, and yell and cheer and declare victory as she ran around with her brothers. She did not know how to climb trees or how to get up on the roof, which put her at a disadvantage. "Once my older brother put me on the roof so we could watch football on the other side. Our parents did not like football, and they would not allow us to play it. My brother liked it a lot. So when our parents were not at home, he said, 'Come, let's go up on the roof.' I enjoyed being there on top of the world, but then I did not know how to get down. I was so afraid, and my brother was too, that our parents would find me up there. So he gave me instructions and helped me down, and I never did that again. I was sorry I could not climb trees, because trees were my companions. I often sat under trees in the meadow and listened to the sound of the wind whistling through the branches. I would be there alone, but never alone, for I had a whole world within me."

When Ludmila was a child she was afraid of the war, afraid of the bombs, afraid of losing the ones she loved. There was good reason to be frightened. She grew up in the crossfire of opposing forces during World War II. Between 1934 and 1939 the city of Brno had become one of the largest producers of arms in the world. After the Nazi Reich took control of the country in March of 1939, it was a tempting target. German soldiers were everywhere. Czechoslovakia remained under German occupation until the end of the war. The sound of exploding shrapnel could be heard throughout the greater part of Ludmila's formative years.

"Some days we would crawl back home from school because there were planes flying overhead, and they were shooting above us. And the boys would run away from me. My brothers would run and leave me behind. They were scared, like me, and they wanted to hide. Once there was a great bombing, and I had my baby sister with me. We lived not far from the airport. They were bombing the airport, and I was so scared. I had Maria on my back and I was running, running back home, but I could not breathe, I could not swallow. All the boys ran ahead—everybody—and I was out there all alone. There was no saliva in my mouth. I could not say anything, could not call out to them to tell them to wait for me. And when I came home, *maminka* embraced me. She held me close to her and said, 'Why are you so frightened? What is it you are scared of?' That was such a balm to me. Her words still live inside me. She said, 'All of us will meet anyway, even if they kill you.' There was such a strength for me in those moments when I was still a child. Through my mother's calm, unshakeable faith, God came to comfort me."

There were other experiences that left an indelible mark on the young girl's spirit. Ludmila tells of the time when she was sent away from home to the village of Hvozdna at the request of her father's father.

"I was ten years old, it was during the war, and my father decided that I would go to live with my grandfather. I would even go to school there. I remember that as the only time my mother opposed my father. I heard them arguing during the night, but he had already promised it and would not go back on his word. How my *maminka* objected. Why not send one of the boys? There were certainly enough of them. And my father said—I was ten years old and I still remember this—my father said that the boys cannot interrupt their schooling. To all of my mother's objections he replied that he did not want to interrupt a son's education for such a length of time. And so I had to go. It was the first time in my life that I went on the train alone. I can see it like in a movie, this little child in a dark blue coat with big gold buttons on it. My parents went with me to the station, my suitcase in hand. They got on the train with me and entrusted me to the conductor. They told him where I was going and asked him to keep an eye on me. They reminded me that my guardian angel would be accompanying me, so I need not be afraid; then they left me and were gone. The journey was a new experience for me. I even liked it.

"When I reached my grandfather's village, my auntie came for me, and I went with her to my grandfather's house. It was an isolated place. There were no neighbors anywhere near, just a lot of big gardens, and a house there in the gardens. There were some relatives across the street and a lot of mercenary soldiers—guerillas—lurking in the woods. Auntie Cecilie did not have any children. I was sent to school the following day, but from the moment I arrived in that place, something in me shut down. It was as if I had died. I could not eat, barely spoke, and I could do nothing to change it. My auntie did not understand this, did not understand why I wouldn't eat. She would lead me to my bed, and I would hide all the food she gave me behind the fireplace. I was so terribly homesick.

"I had been there for maybe six weeks when I sent a letter home. This is what I wrote. 'If you will not come for me, I will surely die here.' The next day my father arrived. He appeared in my room in the night, in the dark, after I had gone to bed. I had such a big quilt piled on top of me, one that is full of feathers. I leaped several meters to embrace him. I said, 'I want to go home immediately.' And he said, 'But immediately, we cannot. Come and see how the moon is shining. But tomorrow, surely we go home.' The very next morning he took me home. I was already crying on the way home from the railway station. I cried so much that my poor mother was terribly upset. 'What happened to you? What happened?' But of course, nothing had happened to me. I simply could not stop crying. And it seemed to me that our house was transfigured—I can see it even today. I kept saying, '*Maminka*, why are the walls shining? There is so much sun in here.' And my mother responded, 'But we didn't paint the walls while you were away.' Then I couldn't speak about it any more. I had had a mystical experience on returning to my home and family and to my mother's arms. It was as if I had been transported into paradise. It made such a deep impression on me that I'll remember it for the rest of my life. Later on there were times when I would leave home, and whenever I was returning, I always wanted to cry. I expected the moment would repeat itself, that my home would be filled with this radiant light, but it never happened again."

Meanwhile, the war had intensified, and its consequences invaded every aspect of life. In the school there were many Russians held captive by the Germans. This site was chosen intentionally to use the children as shields. It proved to be more an incentive than a deterrent, because they often bombed the school. Classes were held in one half of the building. The other half was a prison. "In the morning when we went to school, the teacher would give us the program for the day, but every half hour someone had to go and listen to the radio. We all took turns at this. We had to listen to the news to find out if enemy forces were headed for the city. The alarm would always sound too late, when they were already flying above us. Then they dismissed us immediately and we would go running home. The bombing began when we were on our way, out there in the open. Nobody seemed to be interested in whether we managed to reach home or not." These harrowing experiences were part of the early years of the children. Surprisingly, their life returned to normal in between.

Despite all the difficulties caused by the war, Ludmila arrived at the point where she was ready to advance to the next level in school. She had completed her first four grades, but it was 1942, and Hitler had banned Czech children from automatically continuing on. Admission to the second stage of education fell under the control of the protector of the Reich, and only a very small percentage of students were permitted to advance. Ludmila was not among them.

Ludmila's mother had a dream before she embarked on her journey as a wife and a mother. "When I was getting married," she said, "I had a dream, a vision, of a huge cross right there in front of me." She would say later on, "It's real. This cross is real." The shadow of that cross would fall on her path twice before the end of the war and strike down two of her sons.

Vaclav, her fifth son, who arrived the year after Ludmila was born, had a debilitating accident on the day of his First Communion, when he was eight years old. He was walking happily along the road between his mother and his auntie, both hands held tightly in theirs, when a motorcycle went out of control and ran right into him. He was left severely injured. The doctor said, "Come back in a year, and if nothing happens, he will be okay." One year later he had his first epileptic attack, and from then on, his condition deteriorated. Eventually, he became paralyzed and was bedridden for the rest of his life. He lived until the age of thirty-seven and required total care, which his loving family provided. Vaclav spent most of the day in his armchair. "We all learned to be more sensitive," says Maria. "For instance, I was a lively child and very much on the go, especially as I grew older, yet I remember thinking when I got back home, I have to go to my brother. I need to talk to him, because he is there alone."

TWO

They ascended into the heavens,
they went down into the depths,
and their courage melted away.
They cried to God,
and when they were at the end of their endurance,
God delivered them from their distress.

Psalm 107:26–28

There was a family by the name of Davidek that lived at the other end of Chrlice, a section of Brno that never relinquished the characteristics of a village. Their son Felix, by all accounts, considered Frantisek Javora's household his second home. His mother taught music to Ludmila and her brothers. Frantisek and Vojtech were such talented musicians that their parents decided to add a piano to the harmonium they had at home. Ludmila took piano lessons for two or three years, and then she quit. Her mother always emphasized that she would not be needing it, because after she herself had married, she never played again. The boys of both families grew up together and remained lifelong friends. No one would ever have suspected then the role that the talented Felix would play in the life of Ludmila Javorova and in the life of the church.

Felix Maria Davidek was born on January 12, 1921. The family, well known in Chrlice and economically well connected, consisted of Felix, his sister, Debora, a brother, Leo, his father, Antonin, who directed the collection of taxes, and his mother, Gabriela. The mother of three was often ill. Because she was preoccupied with doctors and with treatments, a former nun from Romania, Andela Jezova, was hired as nanny for the children.

Two men who were influential in the young boy's development were his grandfather, Felix Styblo, the founder and headmaster of the school in Chrlice, and Dr. Bohumil Rejnart, the family doctor. Felix had contracted tuberculosis when he was still an infant, and they thought he was going to die. The doctor was deeply concerned, not only for the mother, but also for her son. He supervised the boy's treatments and rehabilitation through his early years, and because he had no children of his own, introduced the precocious child to the world of science and scholars and to the intricacies of medicine. He took him to visit his patients and allowed him to stay late into the night listening to adult conversations when visitors from some of the noble houses and universities came to call.

Felix had a remarkable memory and a variety of skills. He was playing the piano at the age of four and, as he grew older and went to school, became steeped in the natural sciences and read voraciously. Still plagued by tuberculosis, he completed his studies at a classical grammar school and then shocked his parents and everyone else by announcing he had chosen the priesthood. His family had not been particularly devout, nor had Felix been exceptionally pious. He was oriented toward medicine and knowledgeable in science, but he wanted to be a missionary, and he dreamed of going to South America once he was ordained. The path toward ordination, however, would not be an easy one.

After the Nazis had entered the country in 1939, all the universities and faculties were shut down, except for the theology department, which was allowed to remain open. Although educational opportunities were severely limited, Felix began his studies at the seminary in Brno. During the years he was enrolled as a student, from 1940 to 1942, he met with a dozen priests and theologians to plan for the establishment of a Catholic university in Moravia in the future. Throughout the remainder of the German occupation, Felix met with individuals who were unable to study formally and prepared them for continuing their education once the war was over. While it never did take root as envisioned at the time, the concept of a Catholic university was a fundamental part of Davidek's pedagogical vision and integral to his ministry.

As a seminarian, Felix had several conflicts with one of the spiritual directors, who later became a bishop. One of the issues concerned the fact that he was studying medicine, which Felix considered essential and his superior did not. Another involved his bringing some of his friends, who happened to be female, into the seminary house. Along with the standard curriculum, Felix also studied languages, for he still felt a call to the missions, and he was an accomplished poet. His literary attempts since grammar school, which consisted of poetry and even some prose, came to fruition in 1940 with the publication of a collection of his poems.

During the years he was in seminary, Felix was often at Ludmila's home, not to visit Ludmila, a little girl barely ten years old, but to spend time with her brothers, and especially her father. A friendship developed between the two men, strengthened by a mutual love of books and the many characteristics they shared. Both were politically astute and deeply involved in the life of the church. Both knew and loved theology, philosophy, languages, and the wider world. They had so many interests, a certain sense of adventure, a vision that lifted them beyond the narrow frame of the immediate, an insatiable thirst for knowledge, and a love for God and God's people. Their friendship would deepen and grow through the years and would last until the end of their lives. Felix once told Ludmila he considered her father his "second father."

When Ludmila was a little older, she liked to visit her father's bookcase and remain there among his books. "When my brothers were lazy and did not want to work, they also came to the bookcase to hide, and they would be reading there. It was our place of refuge. When the bookcase door was open, no one could see who was hidden behind it. The bookcase was also big enough for some of the boys to climb inside. However, they would soon be discovered, for Mother usually knew where her boys were and would come and pull them out. Once when Josef tore his clothes—he had been climbing a tree—he came and asked me to help him. My brothers turned to me for refuge when they fell out of favor with *maminka*. 'Please,' Josef pleaded, 'sew this for me, but do it secretly. I'll go and hide behind the bookcase door.' Not only was there a big hole in his pants, but his leg had been scraped and was bleeding. We had to move quickly, before our mother discovered us, because she had a sixth sense when it came to the boys." He kept the pants on as she made the repair, and when she was sewing the back of the leg, all twisted up around him, the door suddenly shifted and there was *maminka*. "What are you doing there, you two?" Josef slid under the bed, but she caught him anyway.

Once when she was perusing the bookcase, Ludmila picked up a magazine entitled *Hlasy svatohostynske* (Saint Hostyn Voices). In it she saw this question raised by a female student: "Why can't women be ordained priests?" The year may have been 1944, or perhaps 1945. Ludmila does not remember that, but she remembers this: "I was so joyful that someone else had asked this question. I read those magazines diligently after that, but never saw an answer. Even so, it was as if, in my innermost being, there was an open window through which fresh air was blowing. It awakened a desire that lay dormant down deep in my heart."

Toward the end of 1944, as the war was drawing to a close, the air raids grew more intense. Some of her brothers had jobs in the city. Several others were out there studying or doing something else. During the bombings the rest of the family waited to see who would come home or who, perhaps, would not. In March 1945, in anticipation of the destruction that lay ahead, they closed the schools in the vicinity of Brno and sent all the children home. People stopped going to work. Frantisek Javora, with the help of his sons, did what he could to secure their house. They covered the windows with wooden slats and moved everyone to a shelter. There they huddled, day after day, as the front passed through the city of Brno. Missiles and bombs fell relentlessly. Maria was still a toddler. The circumstances were extreme. They could not cook in the shelter. Food was a constant concern. "There were good people," recalls Ludmila, who was thirteen at the time. "For instance, the baker of the region secretly baked bread for everyone so we would not die of hunger. The children were so courageous. My brothers would go to the bakery, which was about a kilometer away. They would tie the loaves of bread to their backs and crawl all the way to the shelter, because planes were flying overhead and there was shooting everywhere. They did this several times." On April 26, Brno was liberated by troops of the Soviet Army. The city had suffered severe damage, but after six weeks of unmitigated terror, the people who emerged from the shelters were determined to begin again.

The front had passed, the fighting had ceased, but the threat to human life was not over. Unexploded hand grenades were literally everywhere. The dead lay where they had fallen. More than seventeen thousand Soviets were among the casualties. Over twelve hundred buildings had been destroyed, and thousands more, severely damaged, were perilously close to toppling over onto the unwary passerby. There was danger at every turn. "Even my brothers were conscripted to dig graves to bury the dead," says Ludmila. Parents were justifiably distrustful toward the Russian soldiers, especially with the girls. "When I was in the shelter, I was often told: do not go out alone—ever—when the Russians are around." Ludmila recalls this clearly. Then she voices the feelings that would come back to haunt her people. "But of course, when the front had passed and we had been liberated by the Russians, there was great euphoria. The city was all in pieces, but the people were so happy, because, finally, we were free."

THREE

In Your hand are the depths of the earth
and also the heights of the mountains.
Let us come into Your presence
with thanksgiving.

Psalm 95:2, 4

Felix Maria Davidek was ordained a Roman Catholic priest on
July 29, 1945, in Brno by Bishop Stanislav Zela, assistant bishop
of Olomouc. His ordination announcement read:

> You say there is no need of prayer, there is no need of priests?
> But who will gain a hope for you in such moments when
> humanly everything is lost? The last thing to die in a human
> being is hope, but don't believe that it would die in 99 cases
> out of 100 if there were a priest present with his love for
> God and for people.

After the ceremony was over, Father Felix Maria Davidek returned to his home district of Chrlice in a horse-drawn carriage.
Ludmila, who was only thirteen at the time, had been chosen by
the parish church to welcome him in their name. It was an honor
to be given such a role. The church, Virgin Mary in Thorns, was
in Turany, adjacent to Chrlice. It counted the residents of both
among its parishioners, because Chrlice had no church of its own.

The ordination of a local boy so soon after the end of the war
and the liberation of the city was cause for significant celebration.
The First Mass of the newly ordained is always a high point in
the life of the church. Ordinarily the parish does all the preparation. Felix, however, proceeded to organize the entire event
himself, and it was anything but typical. He chose to celebrate

his First Holy Mass on the grounds of "the chateau" in Chrlice one week after his ordination. He had the place decorated with the colors of the church. Strips of yellow and white cloth hung from the chateau's windows, moving gracefully in the wind. He had also chosen his own flower girl, which was something the parish had always done for a priest's First Mass. Ludmila was filled with awe as she watched him celebrate the Eucharist and give his first blessing to all. Father Felix Maria Davidek. Wise. Courageous. Preacher. Priest. He seemed so far above and beyond her. Afterward he organized a dance—a ball—for all who had helped prepare the celebration. This newly ordained priest came to the ball, which was so untypical. And that defines him precisely. Felix Maria Davidek was truly not typical—a free spirit, spontaneous, unpredictable, with a charismatic zest for life. As he demonstrated at the first event he would preside over as a priest, he intended to live out his priesthood independently, in his own way. It was really of no concern to him that what he felt was worth doing had never been done before.

Felix continued to visit the Javora men, especially the eldest brother. Frantisek, the leader in a line of ten, firstborn of a happy marriage, was the darling of the family. They had clipped and kept a lock of his hair and recorded everything about him—his first tooth, his first word, his first step on the path of life. His contagious smile leaped out at them from so many photographs. When he was in his fifth year at school, he wrote an essay saying that he wanted to be a priest. So many hopes were pinned to this child, so many dreams unrealized. He was an accomplished musician, the most talented of all the children, or so they said at the time. He directed the parish choir and played several instruments, especially the organ, even the one in the Brno cathedral, as well as the harmonium at home.

They were carrying bombs from the railway station to the airport on that fateful day. The war was not quite over. Brno was only partially liberated and the city was in turmoil. Russian soldiers were everywhere, overseeing the operation, making sure the munitions supplies got to where they needed to go. The bombs were much too heavy to be transported by hand. When Frantisek said this to the soldiers, they replied, "We are fighting to free you. If you will not cooperate with us, we will have to shoot you." As he struggled to meet their unreasonable demands, he felt something tear inside him. By the time he got home he was not feeling well. There was nothing they could do for him. Radiology and operating rooms were not functioning at the time. The entire city was under siege. Six months later, he died.

Dying in a family circle has a culture all its own. When death claims a vibrant spirit, it is as if the house itself undergoes a transformation. There is no way to prepare oneself for such existential loss.

When the short, dark days of January returned, they all knew Frantisek was dying. He could no longer leave his bed. He was in excruciating pain, yet up until a few days before, he refused to lay his books aside and continued to express an interest in what was happening in the world and in those who were around him. He knew he was coming to the end of his time. He would speak to them about his death, but he was not fixated on it

It was his father who led the prayers at the bedside of his dying son. As the young boy lay suspended between home and the valley of the shadow of death, his father explained to his brothers and sisters that even if his body were immobile and unable to manifest anything, his soul would be fully aware and attentive. Ludmila wanted to run away, and at one point she did escape to the garden to be alone with her pain. But she soon returned to her place within the family circle. She never forgot her father's face, the tears falling on a lifeless hand, nor his words that followed immediately after, bringing balm to their wounded spirits. "At this moment the church is praying Lauds. Children, he is already home!"

Felix came to tell them: Frantisek had given him a sign to

let him know he had died. "At 5:00 a.m. I was awakened by a noise. It was as if someone were letting iron balls fall on a marble floor. I jumped out of bed to see what could have caused such a sound. Then I remembered, and I said to myself, Frantisek must have died. So I went immediately to the church and celebrated a Requiem Mass." And in the end it was so. Frantisek died at 5:00 a.m. on January 13, 1946. He was not yet twenty years old when they laid his body to rest. It was bitterly cold and the wind was merciless. His mother knelt there at his grave, unwilling and unable to cut the cord that continued to bind her to him. After this terrible tragedy, she buried the pain within her and went on with her life.

The house slowly settled into a routine designed to do without him. Her father suggested to Ludmila that she might want to go and study, but her heart just wasn't in it. Soon enough she would take those steps that would prepare her for her future. She was more inclined now to be by herself, alone with her thoughts and feelings, to walk through that world inside her and find some meaning there.

FOUR

May you have the power to comprehend, with all the saints,
what is the breadth and length and height and depth,
and to know the love of Christ that surpasses knowledge,
so that you may be filled with all the fullness of God.

Ephesians 3:18–19

It was not an easy transition from childhood to adolescence for Ludmila Javorova. She recalls the turbulent feelings and the struggle for some serenity as she looks back on those days. "Whenever I was overcome with fear—when bombs were falling on Brno, when the SS were just outside my door—my mother's faith would sustain me and lead me through the terror to a point of inner calm." But now, on the verge of becoming a woman, she longed for some of her mother's down-to-earth spirituality for herself. She thought about her mother's compassionate heart, the way she had time for other people when she had no time for herself, her many hidden acts of mercy, how she handed everything over to God. "Her trust in God taught me to dig for a similar stream in myself, a stream that has long been the source of my faith and the wellspring of my being."

Ludmila was perched on the cusp of a spiritual awakening that would move her beyond the practice of religion to a deeper relationship with God. Her mother suggested she make a retreat. She had never done such a thing before and she was a little anxious about what to expect. The retreat master, a Jesuit priest whose name was Ferdinand Nesrovnal, stood up the first evening and shouted: "Whoever is not yet fifteen, go home. Leave immediately." Ludmila was just one month away from her fifteenth birthday. When he bellowed those words again, her friend from school got up and left. Ludmila had no intention of leaving. "It was so interesting what he was saying. Afterward I went to his room and said: 'I am not fifteen, but I have decided not to leave.' He asked me several questions. One was how many brothers and sisters were in our family. I told him I had eight brothers, and then he said to me with a smile, 'Stay here and come to me again later on in the retreat.' He told me, 'Only because you have eight brothers,' and he laughed wholeheartedly. Then he jumped up from his chair and said, 'You can remain here for the retreat.'"

That first retreat was a turning point. "From that moment on my spiritual life really began to develop. I was completely absorbed in it. I felt a flame burning deep within. At the tender age of fifteen, all that I had considered important had suddenly lost its value. My heart was on fire with a passion to go out and save the world. I made a personal decision not to miss any occasion for some spiritual nourishment. Opportunities were all around me. I started to search for contacts—sisters, monks, certain religious orders. For example, there were some sisters who organized the free time of children. They had circles of activities for girls of different ages where they could learn practical skills that would help them in raising a family. I started to go there. I was attracted to their spirituality and interested in their inner life. I began to feel and act a bit different from other girls my age. Up to now we had been similar. We had the same hopes, the same interests, but from this point on, I went my own way. Throughout the rest of my adolescent years, I was as a woman."

Ludmila had already developed a deep love for the church, strong social empathies, and a passionate desire for anything new, especially in the realm of the spirit. "I was ready to leave behind all that was familiar and safe in order to serve God in the world. That desire to serve has been a fire within that has never been extinguished by anything or anyone. Indeed, by the time I was fifteen, it was clear to me what I wanted to do and which way I wanted to go."

In the spring of 1947, Ludmila asked her mother for permission to enter a convent. She had made this decision at the retreat, but waited until she had turned fifteen before she would act upon it. She was unprepared for her mother's response. The woman whom Ludmila thought she knew looked at her child for a moment, and then she said calmly but firmly, "My daughter, at your age, nobody goes to a convent." Then seeing that Ludmila was hurt by her words, she said: "I waited for you for such a long time, and I need you so much." Ludmila looked at her speechless. The words, hanging in the silence between them, fell like a blow on her sensitive spirit. A wall went up within her, separating her from the very one she had hoped to emulate.

Ludmila could not bear the decision. That very day she went to the sisters of the congregation of Saints Cyril and Methodius and asked if she could stay with them. She wanted to live there in the convent. She would help them with their work, anything, if she could only remain with them. The sisters took her in. Ludmila herself has said that her relationship toward God at this time was as if it were her first love. "I was full of it day and night. Maybe you would laugh at this, but at that time I was writing letters, and I carried them to the tabernacle and I hid them behind the flowers there or sometimes behind the statues. I do not know who read them, or if anybody did, or who took them away at the end of the day. I was only concerned about one thing. I wanted to give myself completely to God. My desire was so strong."

A few days later, at seven in the morning, the mother superior came to Ludmila and took her to the parlor. There was her father waiting for her. "Ludmila," he said gently, "you have to come home. This is not the solution to your problem." So Ludmila went home with him. But she asked for and received permission to return to the sisters now and then. Whenever she had some free time, she would go back to them. Eventually, she asked the catechist to lend her a key to the chapel, and on Sundays, in the afternoon, she would go there to sit in the stillness and pray.

"Those were beautiful moments," she recalls, and the beginning of her heart's maturing.

Somewhere along the way, after the war and before the second wave of oppression, Ludmila finished school, completing the three-year program in a single year.

FIVE

The floods covered them.
They went down into the depths like a stone.

Exodus 15:5

By the time Germany had surrendered unconditionally to the Allied Forces in May 1945 to signal the end of World War II, a critical decision had been made regarding the future of Czechoslovakia. According to the Yalta Conference, the country would come under the Soviet "sphere of influence." The politically astute in this war-torn nation worried about the ominous implications of that phrase. The Communist Party's rise to power had been a concern for decades. A significant political party in Brno in 1925, it grew more prominent during the years leading up to the end of the war. Czechoslovakia had made a pact with the Soviet Union to protect it from Nazi incursion. When they freed the occupied territories, the Soviet armies could readily assume the guise of liberating heroes. Parliamentary elections in 1946 resulted in landslide victories for communists throughout the country. By banning acceptance of the economic assistance offered under the Marshall Plan in 1947, the Soviet Union further isolated the nation and tightened its control. Following the "communist coup" on February 25, 1948, all political power in Czechoslovakia was in the hands of the communists, resulting in four more decades of authoritarian governance with devastating results. By the end of that year most companies had been placed under communist control, and nearly all of the workforce were now considered employees of the state. For the next several years the systematic takeover affected all aspects of society, resulting in a totalitarian state known as "Totality."

An outcome of the communist takeover was the relentless and brutal persecution of the church. Karl Marx's assertion that "religion is the opiate of the masses" resulted in the imposition of a "scientific atheism" throughout Czechoslovakia. All denominations suffered. The Roman Catholic Church, with its tightly woven infrastructure and opposing philosophy, posed a particular threat to the communist regime. In 1949 Pope Pius XII issued a proclamation stating that any Roman Catholic who supported communism in any way would be excommunicated. The government retaliated by launching a full-fledged response aimed at totally destabilizing the church's institutional base. It took control of the seminaries, the theological faculties, and diocesan offices, it nationalized the schools, and it established the insidious Peace Committee of Catholic Clergy to divide the church from within. Religious orders were banned and their members sent to labor settlements in remote areas of the country. Bishops were either jailed or placed under house arrest. A majority of priests were conscripted into a type of military service and sent to army camps called PTP, which consisted of "hard labor technical squads" living under very difficult conditions. A number of priests were murdered. The church was placed under government supervision and church property was seized. This was the situation of the Roman Catholic Church at the start of the 1950s. Rumors of communist infiltration and priestly collaboration were already circulating and would only intensify. The lives of those who lived through those times need to be considered through this lens.

"After the elections in 1946, when we realized the communists had won, we were horrified," Ludmila recalls. "People were so unrealistic. They had the naïve idea that we cannot repeat the history, the terrible history in Russia. When we warned them not to vote for the communists, they said: 'Why not? What happened in Russia cannot possibly happen here.' Even Christians were electing communists. In fact the church did not believe those of us who were worried. My father was very politically active at the time, and we children helped him. We tried to go against the stream, tried to prevent the communists from winning in our district in Brno.

"In 1948 my parents still did not want me to go into the convent. It was a time of widespread uncertainty. They felt there was no future for religious life, but I insisted. I had turned sixteen, and for me, this was the only direction in which I was willing to go. We finally came to an agreement. I would go to study for one year in a school that ordinarily prepared girls for marriage. I would learn some practical skills that would be useful to me later on in life, like sewing, for example, and cooking."

After the year was over, Ludmila decided to continue her studies. The future of religious life was tenuous in the turbulent political climate. Her parents insisted this was not the time to be taking such a step. Since nursing was also considered a vocation, she decided to become a nurse. One had to be eighteen to enter the program. She did not meet that prerequisite. Once she was ready to enroll, she would have to leave home and live in a state-controlled boarding house while attending nursing school. It was a mandatory regulation imposed by the communist government, and of course, her parents objected. These so-called boarding schools governed by the state were under communist supervision. Students attending various schools shared a dormitory type of arrangement with a state-appointed overseer who regulated their free time and attempted to indoctrinate them in communist ideology. Ludmila remained at home while taking some preliminary steps. She began by working in a hospital to gain some practical experience, because it was recommended that one work in a related environment before enrolling in a particular school. She hoped that things might change politically, but nothing ever did. Eventually she left the hospital and the possibility of becoming a nurse.

Priests still came to Ludmila's house to visit with her father. "They would sit there talking to him," Ludmila says. "My mother was also in the room, but they paid no attention to her, other than the very basic exchange that social etiquette required. They did not treat her as an equal, and that really troubled me. She deserved something better than that. I was aware of this already as a child. I used to say to my mother, and I would say this in an emotional tone of voice: 'They just want to command you. They only give you bits of advice. They do not talk to you. They do not invite you to talk to them.' She did not like me to say such things. She had respect for the priests. She thought that as I matured I would grow out of this way of thinking, but I was already eighteen years old, and I still had not outgrown it."

As a result of communist party regulations, Ludmila could no longer go to the quiet convent chapel for solitude and prayer, because the sisters were gone. All convents and monasteries were closed. The sisters had been sent to live in designated areas far away from their religious houses and forced to work in factories or in labor camps. Ludmila's Auntie Anezka, who was with the English Virgins, was sent to an agricultural commune, where she and members of her congregation were put in a building without windows. They were all in there together. Choir sisters, who were well educated and had never done manual labor, now had to share hard agricultural work with extern sisters accustomed to housekeeping tasks. Religious orders were not separated into distinctive groups, which made life even more difficult. Each religious community longed to practice its own spirituality, but in the intermingling and confusion, this was impossible. Because there appeared to be no change in sight, Ludmila's dream of a formal religious life seemed destined to remain unfulfilled.

The communist government required everyone to have a job. Since it was against the law to be unemployed, Ludmila had to work somewhere. This marked the beginning of a series of work-related efforts for her, each one a step on the path to maturity, with no clear understanding of where God might be leading her, or if she were being led at all.

She went to work in a factory, where she had her first experience of communist brainwashing techniques. "All day long we
had to listen to these socialist-communist songs blaring from the
loudspeaker. You cannot imagine it. There was one woman who
was appointed to control us, to keep watch over us. We had to
use the word 'comrade' in our greeting in the morning. Teachers,
leaders, bosses, everyone...it was 'comrade this' and 'comrade
that.' If you asked for anything or needed anything, you had to
address the person as 'comrade.' It was absurd. We would only
address our supervisors this way, and then only because we had
to. Another communist expression was: 'Honor be to the work.' It
was like a communist greeting. Oh, how I hated this. Never in my
life did I let this greeting come out of my mouth. I remember how
unhappy my mother was about where I was working and what I
was doing. Many times when I came back from my job, I found
her at home praying. She would say: 'I have been so worried about
you. I'm unable to go to sleep.' Then one day people started to
rebel, and shortly after there was a strike. For the first time in my
life I could see what it meant to resist an oppressive regime and
then to be struck down by it. Many were imprisoned. My brother
Jan lost his job. I was sent to another factory, where I started all
over again."

Her new job was in a factory that manufactured carpets.
Ludmila was supposed to learn how to manipulate the massive
machinery that wove commercial carpets on industrial-size looms.
"The environment was so depressing. I had never seen such a
place in my life. It was a real working-class factory. We started
work at six in the morning, which was normal here, especially in
factories. I had to travel to get there, which meant getting up before 4:00 a.m. so I could go to daily Mass at 5:15 a.m. Arriving in
the hall with the big machines at that early hour meant one might
see anything, even the most intimate moments between a woman
and a man. It was an environment that was morally corrupt. I
was very stressed by what I saw. They led me to a big machine. I

was eager to learn how to do this work as quickly as possible, so I would not have to depend on anybody, or be around some of them any longer than was necessary. Later on I understood the reasons for their moral impoverishment and felt the urge to help others like them."

That first day on the job Ludmila was introduced to her new boss. The next day he said to her: "This kind of work is not for you. This environment is not good for you. Come with me. You will work in my office." He gave her some clerical tasks to do, and at the end of the day, he said: "You will do the same tomorrow. Do not go to the machine. You will be coming here." She remembers him with gratitude. He was a good man and kind to her. She was sent for some basic training, a course in secretarial skills, such as typing and general administration. Still, it was not easy for her. She was responsible for counting the money for the workers and paying their salaries, which brought her in touch with ordinary people, some of whom were quite rough. "It was a part of life I had not been prepared for. I had no idea of such things before."

She was propositioned often. "I got so many bad offers from old men there. I didn't even understand what they wanted from me. I had a certain intuition, of course, that warned me to be careful. My parents were so afraid for me, concerned about what I was getting into, the kind of influences shaping me at such a tender age. I was nineteen, a young woman now, and it was a dangerous world for someone like me." She stayed in that job for some time, enduring the relentless tactics of an oppressive regime. "The forces of communism tried to control our entire existence. It began to devour us bit by bit, consuming us from the inside, penetrating us through and through. We didn't know how to handle it or how to protect ourselves."

After he was ordained, Felix was appointed chaplain of the church in Horni Stepanov, a small village in a remote area far from any city or town. It was a distant outpost in the diocese of

Brno. There was no electricity. He himself would say that he was given this appointment because there was a cow at the parish house. His health had always been delicate, and having fresh milk every day would help to strengthen him.

Even though the diocesan consistory of Brno did not permit attendance at secular universities, Felix had finished his medical studies and graduated from medical school in 1947, prior to the communist coup. He began working as a physician while he was chaplain in Stepanov. There was no resident doctor in this tiny highland village so soon after the war, so he set up his medical practice with the permission of the district physician, who was an elderly man. The territory was much too large for one person. He was grateful for Davidek's help. Felix continued to pursue his studies in philosophy and psychology and in the natural sciences and had earned his doctoral degree in psychology by 1948. However, the communists were already in control, and the doctorate could be awarded only with the National Committee's consent. He knew he would never get it, so he figured out how to acquire it himself. He got the appropriate documentation surreptitiously and received the degree in Brno. During this period he published a book called *Christian World View* and two collections of poems.

The idea of founding a Catholic university had remained with Davidek after the war was over. The group that affirmed the idea earlier now felt they should focus on supporting the state system of education. Davidek felt otherwise. After the communist takeover in 1948, he decided to implement his vision of establishing a university, even though he was certain his superiors would not understand. He had an intuitive sense of where the future was heading and refused to face it unprepared. He would say that to stand with hands folded was the same, for him, as ceasing to live. Preparatory work essential to founding a university had already been completed prior to the coup. Official transcripts and diplomas had been designed and printed. He established a philo-

sophical faculty and named his new university Catholic Atheneum
Chrlice.

Soon after arriving in Stepanov, Davidek proceeded to gather
around him young men and women who were willing to study
with him. He gave lectures and prepared his students for taking
their exams at official institutions. He was in contact with the
university at Olomouc and with a grammar school in Brno. There
were also other teachers who lectured on a variety of subjects.
Frantisek Javora loaned part of his library to him. The Catholic
Atheneum continued in existence from 1948 until 1950, when
Davidek was apprehended by the secret police.

Stepanov was a village in the Drahany highlands. There was no
train or bus. In winter, when there was snow, most people traveled
on skis, but Felix never learned to ski. He decided he would learn
how to ride a motorcycle, and eventually he did, but after he killed
several hens he abandoned the idea. He would travel part of the
way on foot from Stepanov to either Olomouc or Brno.

Davidek was a problematic priest for the diocesan consistory.
His bishop did not approve of either his Atheneum or his acting
as a physician. The bishop disagreed on principle, but he was also
worried about a possible intervention from the state. So-called
"church secretaries," always hard-line communists, had been appointed as overseers when the state took control of the church.
Everything had to be submitted to them and was subject to their
approval. Neither the church nor the state thought it appropriate
for students to come to a priest to study something unrelated to
ministerial services. The church secretaries insisted the bishop do
something with this renegade priest. Whether or not the bishop
submitted to this external pressure or whether it was simply coincidence cannot be said for certain, but the fact is that Father
Davidek was suddenly reassigned. He was moved to Petrovice on
the other side of the diocese. Because of the political climate and
the growing alienation between his bishop and himself, Davidek
could not protest the decision. He simply had to obey.

Separated from his students and from the faculty he had established and for whom he was responsible, Davidek began to travel from Petrovice to Stepanov and back. For at least part of the way, he was able to take the train. Then one day a letter from his bishop demanded, under church obedience, that Davidek cease his activities with regard to the Atheneum and stay away from Stepanov. This ordinance Davidek refused to obey. He was convinced that his most important task was to continue the work he had started for as long as it would be possible to survive the communist assault on religion and society, leaving an avenue open for the preparation of future priests.

The clandestine activities of Davidek's Atheneum were becoming a threat to those involved. The climate had grown more oppressive. Priests had been thrown into prisons or dispatched to labor camps. Spies were everywhere. On April 22, 1950, on his way to the railway station in Sebetov, Felix was arrested by the StB,* the dreaded secret police who were Czechoslovakia's counterpart to Russia's KGB. He was taken to the police station in Boskovice, near Stepanov, a building that had once been a school. After a period of time, Felix asked his guard to allow him to go to the toilet, which was on the ground floor. When he did not return, the guard told a boy to go and see why he was taking so long. He looked in the bathroom. There was nobody there. Davidek had jumped out the window. The boy delayed returning in order to give the fugitive more time. Davidek ran toward the railway station and then into the woods. When they realized their prisoner had escaped, they took the dogs and went after him, but he managed to get away. They had the place surrounded, but as they continued to search for him, it began to rain, and they lost all trace of him.

Davidek spent half a year in hiding. During that time he continued to keep in touch with Atheneum contacts in clandestine

---

*Statni Bezpecnost, state security.

ways. He wore various disguises whenever they agreed to meet. At times he would appear as a woman walking down the street. He had known for some time that he and his cohorts had to leave the country. It was much too dangerous to remain where they were. He could not hide forever. If captured, he would be sent to prison and the others would be charged with him. For months he had been carefully organizing their escape. The borders were heavily guarded and surrounded by barbed wire charged with electricity. The only place he felt they could succeed was south of Brno, somewhere along the Dyje river, which meant they had to swim to freedom, all the way across. Davidek hoped to make it to Vienna, and from there to continue on to South America to serve as a missionary priest. It took a lot of meticulous planning before an attempt was made. Lay supporters and religious sisters assisted in the preparations, endangering their own personal safety. On the first leg of the journey, several of Davidek's students took him in the trunk of a car from the place where he had been hiding to a second secure location. At the appointed time they headed south, only to discover they had been betrayed by a communist collaborator, the very person who had organized their escape. Only one of three separate groups made it safely out of the country. Those who were traveling with Davidek were captured along the Austrian border. No one got away.

Davidek was apprehended in the vicinity of Breclav and detained for eleven months in Uherske Hradiste, a maximum security prison in which the inmates were chained, and then moved to Valdice in northern Bohemia. These two institutions were among the harshest facilities in the country. He was brought to trial together with his students and some priests who did not belong to his group. According to the accusation, all of them together formed an illegal entity. They were charged with plotting against the state to undermine its educational system, with founding the university where Davidek trained students to turn against the state, and with conspiracy. They were accused of being enemies of the people's democracy, and to the list of Davidek's charges was added his attempted escape. He was sentenced to twenty-four years in prison, plus the loss of all his assets and his civil rights. He also had to pay a fine. When he was apprehended, police had gone to the parish house and confiscated everything, including all his books.

SIX

Out of the depths I cry to You.
O God, hear my voice.

Psalm 130:1–2

When the news reached Chrlice, the people were devastated. Family, friends, the parish, the school, all went into mourning. Ludmila's father prayed for Felix until he was released. She says, "We felt as if a member of our family circle had left us, and we filled the empty place with our prayers. It was difficult for all of us, but it strengthened our faith and increased our antipathy toward such a violent regime."

Ludmila quit her job in the factory. "I can't remember the precise date. Once again I wanted to study, so I tried some evening classes at the nearby grammar school, but I was being watched, closely, by those in charge of the school. The secret police started following me. They knew I was aware of it. One of their members had suddenly appeared in our classroom and asked the girl sitting next to me to let him take her place. He said he wanted to sit with me, but from his questions I knew immediately who he was. Later my suspicion was confirmed. They already knew all about me, that I wanted to enter a convent, that my auntie was in a convent. They knew my activities; they knew my friends." There were a number of reasons why Ludmila might be under surveillance. Her father was a deeply religious man and that automatically put him in opposition to the state. Her brothers were considered troublemakers. They too had to be watched. They were friends with certain people, for instance, Davidek, and others already in prison. Ludmila recalls a series of events that reveal what is was like to live in such circumstances.

Rajhrad, a Benedictine monastery near Brno, had a beautiful library, a very ancient library filled with precious books. Agents of the state came and took all the books outside, threw them into piles, and left them there in the rain. "My father lamented when he saw something so barbarian. He went there several times and tried to take some books, but it was not possible. They were closely guarded by the militia. Later on my friend and I learned that some of the books had been taken to old empty barns just outside the town. We went there together at night, in the dark, and we filled several boxes, as much as we were able to carry. We could not use a flashlight, so we had no way of choosing the more valuable manuscripts. We took what we could and hurried off when the soldier went away. The boxes were so heavy, it was hard to carry them. When we sorted the books, we tried to determine what kind of book it was from how the book was bound. The rare books we hid under the staircase in the tower of the church. Later on we carried all the books to our home. Once one of the boxes broke open in front of the railway station and everything fell out. I prayed I would not be discovered, because if I had been caught, I would have gone straight to prison. We hid the books until 1968, when we gave them to the Jesuits."

Ludmila tells of another encounter with the StB at school. "One of my schoolmates offered to show me the place where books from monasteries were taken. I considered his offer suspicious. Why should he want to take me there? I didn't believe him. The state secret police, who wore regular clothes, also had assistants called 'narks.' They were ordinary people and they were everywhere. I knew this person was one of them. Still, I was interested in seeing where they had put the books. I thought perhaps I could salvage some, until I saw that it was impossible. He took me down to the old cellars beneath the town pawnshop where those precious books had been dumped in piles and lay there like heaps of coal. He told me to choose some for myself. He would help me carry them home. Without giving him a reason, I refused to do it and left. I knew this was provocation, that I was being set up. He never showed up at school again. However, another StB schoolmate came who expressed an interest in convents, but I already knew this was a trap and I did not fall for it.

"I decided to leave the school. I thought, if I went away from there, they would not be interested in me anymore. So I went to learn how to embroider carpet designs, something that has to be done by hand. I worked at this for several years, always expecting that something would change and I could finally do what I wanted. Then those in charge of the enterprise sent me to do office work again, and that is where I remained. I was able to study along with the work. I attended secondary school and studied economics, where the atmosphere was a bit more relaxed."

One day Ludmila heard that the Jesuit priest who had led the retreat when she was not quite fifteen had been killed and tossed from a train. There was danger everywhere. It hovered just outside their door, and then the fear hit home. Her brother Stanislav had been arrested. They had thrown him in jail like a common criminal because he had taken the homilies of the priests and made copies of them on his typewriter, which was of course illegal.

"My brother was apprehended on August 13. That same day the StB came to inspect our house, confiscated some of my father's books, and left the rest in disarray. When I arrived home from work, I went to the Palace of Justice, and I found a lawyer who said to me, after he had heard my story: 'If you want to get out of this with your life, just turn around and disappear and never come back here again.' I paused outside to consider whether or not to pursue this. One brother was already in prison. What would it do to my parents if I should find myself there as well? I went home to think it over and to discuss it with my father. He told me he would take care of it. On August 15, the Virgin Mary's day, the whole family went to Mass in the evening and tried to keep from crying as we sang the Marian hymns. The next day my father went to Bohunice, the prison in Brno, to inquire about my brother and to find out why they had taken his books. He asked that the books be returned to him. They said it would all be settled after his son's trial, for Stanislav had not yet been convicted. So he returned home to wait.

"It was six months before Stanislav came to trial. On the day of his court appearance, we were all present there. We waited outside the building to catch a glimpse of him. We had to stand quite far away. When he saw us, we tried to encourage him with a little wave of our hand. He looked at us and smiled. Stanislav was convicted, of course. He was sentenced to three years in prison for collaborating with priests.

"Stanislav was imprisoned in Il'ava. The town is a remote medieval fortress in Slovakia, far from our home. My parents were allowed to visit him just once. The time of the visit was set to make it extremely difficult for them. It was early in the morning. Public transport did not go to that town and there was nowhere to sleep overnight. My parents traveled together. It took them two days to get there. Only my mother got in to see him. She was allowed fifteen minutes with him. It was such a traumatic experience for her, seeing her son in that prison and having to leave him there.

"I was allowed to visit him once as well, after he was moved to Valdice. I too traveled the whole night to get there. I entered a large room with a counter in the middle that divided the area in two. The counter went all the way down to the floor so that our legs could not touch. First they seated all the visitors on one side in a long line. Then two guards escorted each prisoner and had them sit on the other side. We could visit face to face, but people were all around us and all the guards remained. Stanislav sat across from me with two guards on either side of him. We had only twenty minutes, but there was nothing much to say.

"It was chaos. Everyone was talking. It was impossible to speak, because there was no privacy. We were allowed to give a parcel weighing no more than half a kilo that we had to open in front of the guards. They chose what he could keep and returned what he could not. No bread. There might be something hidden inside. Just fruit, and a few other things. I had put a lemon in the box. They handed it back to me. They refused to let him have it. Because of some ridiculous regulation, I thought, and I got very angry. 'Why can't he have this lemon?' I asked? 'Because he can't. It's an order. We don't have to explain to you.' I demanded to see the prison commander. They said he wasn't there, but I absolutely insisted, and I refused to leave. I waited a long time to see him, through at least one change of the guard. But I did manage to persuade him to give Stanislav that lemon. I had been so furious. I wanted to tear them all to pieces.

"Our home had been under surveillance for nearly a year, but now activities intensified. Someone was watching us day and night, taking note of who was entering and leaving the house and reporting to the secret police on what we did and how we lived. We knew who it was. There were also others who spied on our privacy. Some of them were women. It was one more form of harassment.

"We talked about Stanislav every day. I once asked my mother: 'What do you think they are doing to him? Is he being beaten?' She replied: 'We mustn't let those images arise. We must trust he will come back healthy.' We prayed for him constantly." Stanislav did have a serious illness once, something involving the liver, but he got over it. Three years later he was released and returned to his family. The same cannot be said for Frantisek Javora's books. Not all of them made it home.

Ludmila was admitted to a hospital for spinal surgery when she was twenty-five. It was a traumatic experience. Hospitals throughout the country had deteriorated under the regime. The more highly skilled physicians and surgeons had been sent to work in factories, and those who remained, though competent, were often less qualified. "Dr. Lukes," Ludmila says, "was an exception. He was as a doctor should be. From the moment I met him, he was healing for my soul." The surgical procedure to correct an injury to her spine, which she received from a fall on the ice, was rarely performed at the time. She was given local anesthesia. The operation was a success. However, within days, a nurse inadvertently gave her an enema with extremely hot water that was near the boiling point. She went into shock and her whole body suffered severe trauma. She spent two months in the hospital and six weeks recuperating in a convalescent home.

While she was in the hospital, Ludmila visited people, paying special attention to those who were isolated or depressed. "During Totality* hospital visits were limited to a two-hour period twice a week. Ambulatory patients spent this time in rooms where they were allowed to smoke or in corridors where they stood around chatting. I noticed a solitary middle-aged man who seemed remote and unresponsive. He would go for a walk when others were resting, and would enter the smoking room only when nobody else was there. He never said hello to anyone. His behavior caught my attention, and I interceded for him in my prayers. One day—it was the feast of the Epiphany—I smiled at him. He was standing by the window, and I asked him for permission to open the window for awhile so I could listen to the cathedral bells. He frowned at me and then exploded: 'I do not talk to women. I hate them. Leave me alone!' I said, 'You probably have a reason for feeling the way you do,' but I remained at the window. He left. I felt so sorry for him. Several days later, I was in the corridor with some other patients doing morning exercises when I saw this man approaching. I knew he was heading for the out-patient department, so I ordered everyone to move to the side so he could take the shortest route instead of going around us. I could tell he was not happy, and the other patients complained. I quieted them saying I disapproved of such behavior. That afternoon I entered the smoking room because I knew this man was in there, and despite the

---

*The period under communist control.

fact that I did not smoke, I lit a cigarette. He showed no aversion this time. We started to talk and he shared a painful part of his life with me.

"During the German occupation, he had participated in the resistance movement. He was married then to a woman whom he loved with all his heart. 'She was my everything,' he said. 'I risked my life for her. Nevertheless, she was demanding and I wanted to fulfill all her desires. I was able to keep her happy because I earned a lot of money. During the war, however, I was shot several times. I looked forward to returning home, but when my wife saw what had happened to me, she kicked me out of the house because, she said, she did not want to live with a cripple. She wanted a normal husband. I had nowhere to go, so I rented a flat in a town far away and took out my revenge on women. I would date a woman, abuse her, and then kick her out, over and over again. Those actions are the sores that seriously wound my soul.' He was critically ill with brain cancer and was scheduled to undergo surgery. As he was awaiting surgery alone in his room, he asked me to come and see him. I would sneak in at night so no one would see me and would find him screaming in pain. When he was able to speak, he begged me to marry him once he was well again. He did not want to live as he had lived before and he wanted me to help him. At first I did not comment, but he kept repeating his request every time I came to visit. Then one day, after much prayer, I felt in my heart that I would be willing to do anything for his salvation, so when he asked me again, I promised to marry him. He immediately fell asleep. Although he had a terminal illness, there was no certainty he would die, and I tried not to imagine what it would mean for me if he lived. I was determined to go to even this extreme for the salvation of another, but only because I knew I was not doing this alone and that I had not made this decision on my own. God was with me throughout my process of discernment. The day before his surgery, my brother Stanislav came to the hospital with a priest in disguise, who brought this man the Sacrament of Reconciliation. The next day, he died."

Ludmila had never told anyone other than her parents of her inclination to religious life. "Relatives and family friends often asked my parents and me why I remained unmarried when it is impossible to enter a convent and good families are what is needed. Only my parents knew the reason why, and they never pressured me. When I was between twenty-five and thirty years of age, a friend of ours returned from prison. He was a lawyer, but the communists had interrupted his studies, because he worked for the church. He showed an interest in me and all my friends were enthusiastic. I knew I had the skills for raising a family, but I also knew I could manage on my own. During this time I often prayed that while I did not want to change my decision, which was to enter a convent, I would not hesitate to do so if I knew this was what God wanted. Even if I were fifty years old, I would change everything in my life in order to be faithful to God. The young man and I continued to meet, but only for a short time. I knew he was becoming attracted to me, but I had other thoughts, and in my heart I resisted. I felt sorry for him. He had just re-turned from prison and was full of hope for the future, but my decision was obvious. I turned him down. Later on I had similar offers, but I let them pass me by. Again and again I was called upon to reconsider my future. I knew I had a choice, but I always ended up where I started."

Something had taken root in Ludmila long before she realized it. Even as a child she was often led in ways beyond her under-standing. From the moment of her spiritual awakening, she could feel the force of a direction, but lacked a destination. Her brief encounter with this sensitive young man had no real chance for permanence. Even if she had wanted this, it would not have been for her. "I thought, I will never go through this again. This is not for me. And that was when I realized that I could not change my commitment to God, who had been leading me for so long and would continue to lead me. I felt the intensity of a call, and although I did not know what I would do, I trusted that one day God would show me which way I should go."

When Ludmila was twenty-eight, she considered a job in social services. At least, that's what she said. Outwardly she spoke of children in need, while secretly she thought, "Finally, I am entering the convent." The sisters, many of them former professors, worked among children with mental disabilities. They had been assigned to do this work by the communist regime. They labored under extreme conditions with shortages of everything in a place that was not too accessible. The work was so demanding that they occasionally received permission to hire a civilian woman. This person of course had to meet with the approval of the regime. The sisters used this as a way of incorporating new members into their community without arousing the suspicion of the StB. They invited the woman to work among them. This was their arrangement with Ludmila. She would live with someone in some other location, but would spend the day with them. That was how their novitiate was presently being done. It was risky to prepare new members, however, even secretly. Yet ten years after the violent takeover of the monasteries and convents and the desecration of their sacred spaces, even as they were being watched, religious life was still around and the works of mercy flourished.

So Ludmila quit her job again and said goodbye to everyone. She bought her ticket for the train, packed her bags, and went to sleep that last night at home after receiving her parents' blessing. When she awoke in the morning, she said: "I am not going anywhere." She sent a telegram telling the sisters that she would not be coming. They were shocked by her decision. Ludmila never did communicate the reason for her sudden change of plans. Suffice it to say that in some matters the heart has its reasons, and God knows the reason why.

The obligation to work was mandatory. There was an opening on the National Committee, a governance agency, but all who worked there were communists controlled by the StB, so Ludmila did not pursue it. She found a job in a research institute in administration and remained there for many years.

When she did not leave for the convent, Ludmila looked for ways to develop spiritually on her own. In the process, she came in contact with young women who valued the same things she did. A group formed to pursue growth in the spirituality of Don Bosco, founder of the Salesians, whose educational methods promoted a Gospel lifestyle that led to holiness of life. They contacted members of the religious order and met often with some of the priests, but seldom found understanding. Ludmila thought it might be because the priests were living under such harsh conditions. They themselves may have been seeking direction in those difficult times. "The older priests told us that in order to protect our vocation we had to be different from other girls, that we should at least wear a kerchief. Our group was ambivalent. Some of us did not want to submit to those instructions. Others considered doing so, but I myself would not. Such suggestions were impractical and could not be carried out, yet still some felt they had to agree because it was said by a priest.

"Some of us were told we should marry, because the church needed good families and not people who were seeking something unrealistic. In some ways, this was true. The church did need good families, but the church also needed those who would devote their lives to different services, for there are many gifts given by the one Spirit. Comments such as those by the priest invoked storms inside me, and when such a storm came out even during the Sacrament of Reconciliation, I began to realize that not all priests have this understanding of the Spirit, so I no longer sought their approval.

"Women had very few spiritual opportunities before 1965. We were not considered independent. It was my misfortune not to have met priests who would have been able to help me understand my situation and could allow me greater freedom in my relationship with God. I was aware that while seeking spiritual independence I might be shaping my spiritual life according to what I wanted, yet that was not really a danger, because at the core of my being as a woman was the desire to give of myself and to sacrifice myself, even on a spiritual level. It was difficult for the priest to understand this. Our group grew more divided. We who were somewhat independent could not agree in principle with those who felt it was essential to do everything the priest advised. When we realized we were unable to resolve the differences among us, several of us left."

Ludmila's experience with this group of women had been interesting and challenging, but her hope for a spiritual community with a relevant spirituality remained unfulfilled. "Their spirituality was not right for me. Because it had no structure, I could not make it mine. It did not evoke that enthusiasm for the Spirit that was already within me." It was the early 1960s. Ludmila continued to search for something that would speak to her heart.

SEVEN

You have cast me into the depths of the pit,
like those forsaken among the dead.
I am shut in so I cannot escape.

Psalm 88:5, 6, 8

Felix was sent to Mirov, the dreaded medieval prison about 150 kilometers north of Brno, out in the middle of nowhere. He spent the greater part of his imprisonment in that desolate place, most of the time in solitary confinement, and still, he managed to survive.

Those solitary cells in the stone fortification were deep under ground, and consequently without windows. One meal a day consisted of a slice of bread and something hot that tasted like water. At least twelve hours of every day were spent walking, endlessly walking. At night he slept on a plank bed, a single sheet his only defense against the frigid winters, and sometimes, not even that. He earned those accommodations by verbally resisting unjust guards, by coming to the defense of others, and by absolving prisoners during walks. Whenever he was out of solitary, he would do something to tweak the system, and the cycle would begin again.

He organized a university, even there among the prisoners, constructing a system of education that was functionally unique. Priests, professors, anyone with the necessary skills shared responsibility in his pedagogical scheme. Each had to prepare a lecture in the area of his expertise and deliver that lecture to one or two other persons during outdoor exercise. Unless they had been told otherwise, prisoners would walk the radial paths in separated sections, from the center to the perimeter and back to the center again, three abreast or in pairs and in a line. When they were three together, the lecturer walked in the middle flanked by stu-

dents on either side, his lecture notes recorded on miniature slips
of paper in which cigarettes had been rolled. Those miniature bits
formed an archive to the human quest for learning, a testament
to the spirit and to the power of the mind.

It was a broad-based curriculum. They taught all kinds of
subjects in those barbed wire corridors—theology, philosophy, science, language—as long as someone was prepared to speak and
someone was willing to listen. They even lectured inside the cells
where the attendance was much larger. There were so many prisoners in dorm-like cells, they could only lie there on their beds,
which were stacked in layers and lined up in a row. They had
the time to listen. A certain core group of the faculty did more
than organize lectures. Some of them thought about the future of
the church, designing methods of pastoral work and strategies for
change. A group of them agreed to meet together after their release to see if what they had envisioned had any chance of coming
about. Given the length of his sentence, Davidek, the princi-
pal dreamer, entertained no illusions this would be happening
anytime soon.

Davidek, theologian and educator, was also Felix the poet. A
major portfolio of prison poems was produced by him during that
period, scribbled on snippets of paper with a small stub of a pencil in the dark hours of night. These clandestine activities—the
lecturing, writing, possession of contraband, such as pencils and
pieces of paper—were all strictly forbidden, which helps to explain
how he was able to accumulate so much solitary time. A number
of his infractions came from his practices as a priest, a doctor, a
concerned human being. Ministering to others was not permitted.
He took the risk and paid for it with confinement for months on
end. Davidek was incorrigible because of his unfailing spirit and
a compassionate heart.

One of his activities was celebrating Mass. This was only possible by accommodating to the conditions of his prison situation.
He had to choose the right time, like during the changing of the

guard, when there was less chance of being interrupted, and he also had to anticipate what he would do if he were discovered. One of the challenges lay in procuring the Eucharistic elements. Prisoners were allowed to receive a parcel at least once a year, so they would ask for raisins. Sometimes it was possible to buy raisins in the commissary. Davidek and other priests, for there were many at Mirov, would put the raisins in tiny glasses used for medication and cover them with water. In a very short time they had altar wine. They had no access to hosts, so they would take a roll from Sunday breakfast and hide it until it was needed. The dry roll would be laid on cigarette paper and all of it, including the paper, would be consumed at Mass. Instead of the cup there was a coffee spoon. The Mass was celebrated in secret. Some priests found it impossible to celebrate under such conditions and this was an additional suffering for them. Davidek and others never gave up their priestly role of celebrating Mass and ministering to others.

Because he was a physician, he would sometimes be consulted after incidents of self-mutilation and attempted suicide. They would also seek his advice with regard to mental patients, and he would be taken to see a prisoner in life-and-death situations. Occasionally he had access to others through his own illness. Twice his tuberculosis returned. When he was in the prison infirmary, he would minister to those who were there, usually young men in a deep depression because they had no hope for the future and had lost the will to live.

When a new prisoner came, Davidek made coffee for him. He prepared it in the toilet, which was just a hole in the ground. He would make a fire and boil water, which he had put into a small tin, and then he would brew the coffee in it. For the fire he used the *Rude Pravo*, a major communist newspaper the prisoners had to read. He would stuff its pages in the toilet and watch as the totalitarian propaganda all went up in smoke. Such satisfactions were few, however, for in the hellhole of Mirov the losses outnumbered the gains. A lot of things were confiscated during so-called *filcunk,* a slang word for prison raids. Guards rushed into a cell without warning and would strip search one of the prisoners, who were not allowed to have anything personal in their possession. Davidek lost all his lectures and all the poems he had written in prison during those raids.

The men who were incarcerated with him—bishops, priests, professors, ordinary people—never forgot all that Davidek did to help lift their spirits. One man tells of a Way of the Cross that Davidek had written. He asked Davidek to join him for the walk, and when he did, they prayed it together. It was so beautiful, he recalls, so difficult and so demanding, that he knew he would never forget it.

Some prisons also included a separate section for women. Mirov was not one of those places. Once, when Davidek was transferred for a while to a prison where there were also women, he boldly ministered to them. He knew there were women on the other side of the wall that enclosed the exercise area, even though he never saw them, never heard the sound of their voices. He would give absolution to them by bellowing over the wall. "*Ego te absolvo. . . .* In the name of the Father and of the Son and of the Holy Spirit." Davidek the priest would absolve the women of their sins in an ad hoc Sacrament of Penance, for they had no access to any sacraments, not even the Eucharist. Those who heard him understood and knew it was meant for them. He would be hauled into solitary immediately, but at his next opportunity, he would do it again. That men had access to the spiritual support of a sacramental life, while women in prison were denied this simply because of their gender, seemed to him unjust and contrary to the ways of the Spirit. If only the women had priests among them, like the men had, the harsh conditions of their present life would be easier to bear.

Time passed. Davidek had spent more than fourteen years locked away in a prison. Suddenly, one day, he was free.

EIGHT

You have shown me many calamities.
You who were with me through so many troubles
will bring me up from the depths of the earth
and will revive me again.

Psalm 71:20

Felix liked to say that he was literally kicked out of the prison, and in one sense perhaps he was. He had reached the midpoint of his sentence. The political climate had changed considerably. Most priests were already free. The authorities wanted him to ask for mercy. At least, that's how he described it. Write and ask for mercy, they told him, and then they would release him. Davidek refused. "Why should I ask for mercy?" he said. "I will never ask for mercy. I have not done anything to warrant imprisonment. I have stood my ground for all these years. I will not submit to you now." They knew the man, so they stopped insisting. One day, allowing no time to prepare, they put a suitcase in one of his hands and a ticket in the other and sent him on his way. It was February 1964. He stepped out into the sunshine, inhaled the air of freedom, and headed for the train. "They kicked me out of the prison with a ticket and a toothbrush." That was all that was in the suitcase. He could hear it rattling around.

He took the first thing that came along. The train was up to full speed when he realized it was going the wrong way. Brno was in the opposite direction. At the next station he crossed the tracks and took the train for home. Home. It had a strange sound to it. Where does a priest call home? He had no parish assignment. He was returning after so many years to the family he had left behind. Along the way his brother had married. He did not know his brother's wife. No one was expecting him. It was the middle of the night. As he approached the familiar landscape, he felt the stirring of memories and paused to savor them. The house, the corridor of chestnut trees opening their arms to welcome him, the jubilant face of his mother, older now yet still the same...yes, he had come home. After awhile the excitement settled into a serene relief.

Before he fell asleep, Felix let his best friends know he would visit them the following evening. Ludmila and her family were ecstatic. "I am unable to describe our joy," she says, "like the dawn after years of darkness. We could not wait for the moment when he would ring the doorbell and be with us again." It had been so long since she had seen him. The last firm memory she had of Felix was at her brother's funeral. He was in and out of their home after that, but never for long and never with her. She wondered what he looked like now. From the security of the surrounding shadows he finally emerged and burst into the room.

"He embraced all of us spontaneously," she recalls. "He greeted everyone and wanted to know what we had been doing the whole time he was gone and what we were doing now. I told him about my work. He asked about my literary and cultural life. He also wanted to know what had happened to those former seminarians who could no longer study theology."

After the communist takeover in 1948, church schools were closed and students were dismissed. Attendance at the state-controlled seminary, the only one in the region, was forbidden by the Vatican under threat of excommunication, because lecturers there, even priests, were loyal to the state. Those who did attend the seminary were excused from a type of mandatory military service in the so-called PTP labor camps. Many who refused to give in to the regime and walked away from studies in a "communist seminary" ended up in those work camps. Some of those men, now forty years old, were still devoted to their calling. Felix asked Ludmila to help him find the ones who still wanted to be priests.

"He wanted to know whether I knew of any men, personally or otherwise, who were willing to consider the priesthood. Of course I knew such people, although I was surprised—and pleased—to be asked. Until that moment almost no one outside of the StB had expressed an interest in me." It was a turning point for Ludmila. Here was this man, just out of prison, under surveillance by the secret police. He had spent fourteen years in jail for doing this very thing. She had not seen him for all those years and she felt he knew nothing at all about her, yet here he was inviting her into a partnership with him. No decisions were made that evening. The very next day he came again, and from that moment Ludmila's cooperation with Davidek began.

He asked her several questions, like, What was she reading? What did she do in her free time? Then he said, "I need you." "Need me for what?" "I can't tell you now," he said. She said, "Then I can't tell you I am at your disposal if you can't tell me what you want me to do." He paused for a moment. "The church needs you." Or perhaps it was, "The church needs it." Ludmila is not quite certain, but those were the words that struck her then and they have remained with her. "From the very beginning," she says, "we shared a love for the church. His had been developed. I inherited mine from my mother's milk." Felix was a man who did not delay when in pursuit of a goal. He would not take time to recover from the physical hardship of recent years. He would get to work immediately. Ludmila was the first of many to be invited to join with him.

Ludmila asked for a trial period. Experience had taught her that you don't jump into the river without first being sure you can swim. "Give me three months to try it out before I make up my mind. I'm meeting other women these days and I am really busy." He was all enthused. "That is what I like." The three-month trial period did not last for even a day. He came right back and was very persistent, as only Felix could be. He invited Ludmila to his place, and without hesitation, she accepted. That in itself was astonishing when one recalls the rules dictating behavior between women and men at the time. There was also a deep divide between parishioners and clergy. None of this occurred to Ludmila as she went with Felix that day. He immediately laid out the program. "Meanwhile," he said, "we are going to do philosophy together. You will come here every day after work." Ludmila sums it all up by saying, "And that's how we began." She was fully engaged right from the start. Nevertheless she gave herself three months to decide if she would dedicate herself to the work completely, which she did.

Felix was given a room at home. It was up under the eaves, and although it was simple and very small, compared to where he had been living, it was more than adequate. It had a tiny window in the corner where the walls met to form a triangle with the roof. A bed, a wardrobe, a table and chair left very little room for visitors, or for that matter, Felix himself.

It wasn't long before Ludmila's parents heard from their parish priest. "She is going to that Davidek's place. It is scandalizing." Frantisek Javora laughed, but her mother took it seriously. She told Ludmila to stop. She said, "He is coming over to our house, so that should be enough." Ludmila started to be more careful, made sure when she went that she wasn't seen. It did not matter to her who saw her, but it mattered to her mother, and she was sensitive to that. "So I continued coming to his place and he was coming to our place." Those lessons in philosophy from someone who had a goal in life and pursued it with a passion were a lifeline to her spirit and the renaissance of her soul. She had no intention of stopping what she had been searching for day after day, year after year, just when she had found it. The goal of this charismatic priest who had long been friend to her family was synonymous with her call: to bring people to God and God to people in the midst of the pervasive godlessness of a totalitarian state.

Philosophy would open up a whole new world to Ludmila Javorova. Conversations on essence and existence, on the world of being and the principles of knowing took place in the cramped and crowded quarters known as Felix's room. "When I came there for his lecture, he had to remove all the books from his chair so I would have a place to sit. He liked to serve coffee to his guests, even though there was no place to cook in his room. He would prepare it in his sister-in-law's kitchen on the other side of the house and then put the pot of coffee in his bed and bury it in the blankets. 'This is the prison way of keeping it warm,' was his explanation. When someone came to visit, he would take the coffee pot out of the bed, pour coffee into very small cups, and then return the pot to its warmer. The way he went about it was charming and unrepeatable. He would make a ritual of it." Little by little people learned that Felix Davidek had returned. Before long they began coming to him secretly to study.

Why take such a chance? Felix was on probation and would be for ten more years, the length of the sentence he should have served. To be caught would mean imprisonment all over again, this time perhaps for life. There is only one explanation. Davidek's commitment to preparing young men surreptitiously for ordained priesthood in Czechoslovakia had been a driving force within him for all of his priestly life. He was convinced that future priests needed a formation that differed from the traditional seminary program, one that was both spiritual and human. He believed what he did was essential for the survival of the church, and that the church was the visible expression of the love of Jesus Christ. He shared the apostle Paul's conviction that nothing— neither death, nor life, not even life in prison, neither totalitarian rulers nor their power to suppress, not present persecution or the terrifying threat of things to come—would be able to separate him from his responsibility to his call.

Then why choose Ludmila, inexperienced and a woman, for such an unprecedented venture? "He did not have much of a choice," she says, "because he did not know people. He had been gone for all those years. But he also had this rule, which remained integral to the project: to work with the material available. To proceed this way was a major art and also a major pain. He had such a capacity, such vision. I thought I could never begin to meet the expectations this required. He felt just the opposite. Felix judged people according to their attitude and their abilities, not by their credentials. How often I thought to myself, this is the same thing God does. We are unable to even conceive of God, yet God cooperates with us. God does not put us aside or throw us away or look for someone more competent than us, but takes us as we are." As it turned out, the one who was available to help in facilitating Davidek's mission was the person he needed to have. Ludmila's skills complemented his, and on the level of determination, the two of them were the same. "I was never able to do things halfway and then leave the task unfinished. I have always put my whole being into whatever I do. That's a quality both of us shared. Whatever job it was, at the moment when something was there to be done, I was able to do it and still be aware of the surrounding situation. In other words, I can tend to the specific without losing sight of the whole. I know this about myself, but on that day after Felix came home, when he invited me into his project, he could not know this about me, because when he left I was just a child fifteen years of age."

Felix outlined his program for a relevant expression of the local church in a paper entitled "The Reality of Being." It was the first paper he wrote after coming out of prison. He finished it within three months, while he was teaching Ludmila the elements of philosophical inquiry and while Ludmila was discreetly recruiting candidates to come and study with him. "At the time that I was meeting with the women, we wanted to begin something new even then, but we were too dependent on priests who did not share this vision. So I received Davidek's words with great joy and the real work began, the work of switching the terrain of the sacred to the immediacy of our world. Through my association with Felix, I came to understand that we are people of God. We are church in the midst of God's world, channels of grace in every situation, and when necessary, agents of the change that is inherent in the Gospels."

Davidek knew he was being watched from the moment he returned to Chrlice. In addition to lectures in philosophy, he gave Ludmila instructions on how to detect and evade surveillance by the secret police. "He taught me how to figure out in which intervals he and those he was meeting with were being watched, because it was only at certain times. I would walk casually around my own place and then around Davidek's place at those designated times, remembering the people I met along the way, especially those who appeared to be in no hurry to get anywhere, individuals who were just hanging around smoking a cigarette. I took note of their behavior and was aware of what they wore. This way we would know who to avoid and how to escape detection. I was already familiar with situations such as this. Before my brother's imprisonment, my family and my home were being watched day and night by the police. Even our neighbors were aware of it. They often identified the watchman assigned to spy on us. Once in the night my blind aunt said, 'There is somebody in the house.' And indeed there was somebody in the house. He had entered from the gardens. The surveillance of Felix by the secret police never ended. We were able to detect their presence nearby until the end of his life. At those times when the agents were circling the house, we could not go out or bring anybody in, but we had other ways of proceeding.

"Sometimes, especially in the beginning, it was difficult for me to leave our house and not tell anything to my parents, not even the time I would be back. They were very stressed and concerned that if anything should happen to me, they would not know about it. This had both advantages and disadvantages. The issue was not that they would not be able to keep a secret, but that it was safer for them if they did not know anything. I had to act against my feelings, for I had always shared everything with them. I chose now

to keep things to myself, because I did not want to lose them. It
was a way full of God's signs and favors, a way rich in experiences,
both positive and negative."

For reasons of security, Felix had decided that a woman from
his circle of friends should be his primary link to the outside world.
He assigned that role to Ludmila. Her first task was to find young
men who wanted to be priests and arrange their contact with
Felix. She realized she could not do this by herself. She needed
someone trustworthy to follow up on initial contact with potential
candidates. She felt that a man would be far more effective in this
particular position. Once that person was in place, in no time at all
a group of young men and older boys had been identified. Most of
them were former seminarians whose studies had been interrupted
and finally discontinued as a result of the communist takeover of
the seminaries and the church. Others had wanted to become
priests but had no way of doing so. The only seminary in the
region, which functioned with state approval, was full of professors
who had been appointed by the communists. No one could ever
be sure exactly who was collaborating with the regime. The state
also made the decision regarding who would be studying there.
That was all that was available to those who would be priests.
When offered an alternative, few could resist. The living spirit
of the church had been literally paralyzed under communism and
its institutional structures had been compromised. Here was an
opportunity to do something tangible to revitalize the church. In
order to protect the anonymity of Felix and others, people were
not told who it was that was trying to contact them, nor were
they given much information about what the program entailed.
Nevertheless, they wanted to be involved, even though they did
not know the full scope of the plan. Their incorporation followed
strict safety procedures, which were not always the same. Only in
a few cases was there direct contact with Davidek. Usually it was
mediated by at least two people who would report to Ludmila.
She would go to Davidek. Meetings were arranged at different

times and in a place that was always guarded. The visitor was instructed to arrive unseen. After the interview was over, he would be escorted away. Often he did not know the exact house he had just visited, especially when the meeting took place at night. Patrols of StB members and their neighborhood helpers operated around the clock. Sometimes it was extremely difficult for Davidek and the potential candidate to complete their conversations in time to leave so as not to be seen.

Davidek was eager to introduce his idea of the university again. He was very aware that the times had changed since the days of his Atheneum. It would be necessary to conceptualize and construct this university in a new way. He contacted Stanislav Kratky, a priest he knew in seminary who had also been in prison and was now secretly preparing men for the priesthood on his own. Together they began to search for ways to have those men ordained. Davidek told Kratky about his idea of a university. They worked out a program of study and the seminars began. The organization of those seminars was the core of Ludmila's work. She describes them in this way.

"The seminars took place only at night and often lasted until morning. Location was of prime importance. The place had to be secure. We looked for houses or apartments with a separate entry and exit, because we needed more than one way in. People who were willing to let us use a room in their house or flat, either in town or outside of town, put themselves at risk, for in every house was an undercover guard linked to the StB. Discretion meant we could not all show up at the same time, but would have to spread our arrivals over the course of several hours. We could never come all the way by car or even by public transportation. We always had to approach the meeting place on foot in order not to draw attention to ourselves. Local people were always walking in their neighborhoods. If anyone noticed anything unusual, it had to be reported. All were trained to be aware of suspicious persons and to note if someone was walking behind them or if they were being watched. If something seemed out of order, we never returned to that place again. The first seminars, in fact, most of them, met nearby at my brother Josef's apartment. The house was strategically located and ideal for our purposes. It was a corner house. His sister-in-law's mother lived on the ground floor, he and his family on the second floor, and another family lived in the flat above. There was an entry leading in from the park, another leading in from the street, and still another possibility of entering through the garage.

"The first lessons that were taught concerned security. It was difficult at first for some of the participants to grasp the necessary discipline and order that our security measures required. We stressed again and again that the safety of everyone depended on each individual. We were determined that no one in the program would be in excessive danger or need take unreasonable risks. We were not always sure about the neighbors, so precautions had to be taken." It was Ludmila's responsibility to see that Davidek was never alone, for his life was always endangered, whether at night or at noon. It was vital to know who he was talking to and, at least in general terms, what the meeting was about. Always two people were informed about his important meetings. They did not know about each other. Everything had to be remembered. Nothing could be written down. It was necessary to proceed this way, so that if someone happened to be jailed, everything would continue and information would still be passed on to the appropriate people. Felix was extremely wary because of past experiences. Ludmila adopted his strategies regarding security, but others were less cautious. Some saw no reason to be fearful. The regime was becoming less repressive. Some restrictions had been lifted. Their feeling could be summed up as, "The past is not the present. Let's not overreact." Felix, however, was disparaging of any communist attempt to placate the masses. He considered their efforts at improving the political climate a sham. He refused to let down his guard. He felt that the forces of evil would flare up again when the people least expected it. Once the fox was in the hen house, no one would be safe. It turned out that he was right. His attention to security matters would keep them safe. Felix had a wealth of knowledge about the techniques and strategies of the secret police, so he could undermine their system. His was a well organized operation. As a result of his safety procedures, they were not discovered by the StB for a very long time.

Occasionally, there were seminars every night, but not for everyone. For instance, Davidek would lecture in one place and then lecture again in another location for those who, for various reasons, could not attend the first one. The second lecture was not a rerun, because Davidek never repeated a lecture. He always said something new. His seminars were not limited to candidates for the priesthood, but were open to all who expressed an interest and were deemed to be trustworthy. Davidek did the security check on all new participants. Those who failed to meet the criteria for the safety of the program would not be informed of anything and all communications would cease. It was Ludmila's responsibility to follow through on this. Those who had studied with Kratky and were more advanced than the others did not follow the same schedule as those who were less prepared. The length of time spent in seminars depended on the individual. When the issue of ordination was finally resolved, each seminarian would follow a course of study designed to meet his needs and his opportunities for pastoral service. Those who successfully completed the program might serve as examiners to assess a student's understanding of a subject or mastery of the curriculum. Spiritual exercises took place during weekends, some ninety kilometers from Brno, in the house of Dr. Frantisek Mikes, who would eventually be ordained. "His mother cooked for all of us," Ludmila recalls with gratitude, "and we took turns participating, every weekend a different group. It was a risk to hide so many people and a sacrifice to feed us and house us overnight."

Ludmila gives this eyewitness account of a seminar session.

"Every seminar began with Mass. There were so many people in the beginning of the program, many had to sit on the floor. Often thirty or more persons would be huddled in a very small space. We were uncertain about the neighbors, so we had to be very quiet. Don't talk so loud, don't make so much noise: I would say this over and over. It was especially challenging when the group reacted spontaneously, which it so often did. The sudden burst of laughter, voices raised aloud in conversation could give us all away, but it was hard to keep the group quiet, especially during the breaks. There were other problems to be solved, namely, how to ventilate the room. Since we could not allow the light to spill out into the darkness, we covered all the windows to keep the light inside, cutting off our source of air. Despite everything, those were very joyful occasions, because at that time, nothing like this had ever happened anywhere in our vicinity.

"Davidek listened every night to foreign radio broadcasts and the broader exposure enriched us. Every seminar would begin with an analysis of the political situation and also the situation of the church all over the world. He taught us that we were responsible for the politics of our society, that we had to understand and critique our social-political reality, learn to think in political terms. He placed church-related instruction in the widest context possible, integrating with political science those aspects of theology, anthropology, philosophy, psychology, and even cybernetics that he understood so well. He was able to combine both theoretical and practical knowledge in the many seminar topics that he chose to address. Religious science, leadership, systematic theology, pastoral theology, moral theology, ethics, and biblical exegesis were some of the subjects he dealt with in preparing future priests.

"He especially stressed creativity. To Davidek it was vitally important to cultivate an ability to discern new forms of life in any given time. It was equally important not to leave things to spontaneity, but rather to direct them while still being open to the unknown, and to support new elements in society, especially in young people who were the future of the church and of the world. The criteria of good leadership, he said, are reflected in the capacity to simplify these processes and to hasten their arrival. He stressed the importance of creating a pedagogical program through which these new understandings can be taught in a form possible for others to receive them. Leadership as the art of guiding and managing is not a manipulation of power nor the exercise of control but a distribution of freedom that is created and developed in the space of an inner freedom within the person who creates it. This issue of leadership was so important to Davidek that he encouraged those of us associated with him to make it an integral part of our examination of conscience.

"He had a certain vision of the world, and he formed people around him according to this vision. He defended evolution and taught that it was not in contradiction to spiritual values. In this he was influenced by the writings of Teilhard de Chardin, which at the time were not acceptable to the institutional church.

"He spoke of the Sacrament of Reconciliation as a sacrament of compassion. He would say that it is a channel of sanctity that we do not appreciate enough. He would repeat again and again that we have not yet learned to work with the sacraments as we should, that we are not able to draw energy from them in the ways that God intends. Felix created for us guidelines for examining our conscience to assist us in understanding ourselves and the world around us and to help us deepen our relationship with God. These also helped us significantly in our approach to the Sacrament of Reconciliation. As we got to know ourselves better, we learned to be more responsible for our own way to sanctity. The sacrament, he said, should lead us to more independence and more responsibility in our own spiritual life.

"Those seminars with Dr. Davidek were the way he chose to implement his new university. Because it was under the totalitarian system, such activity was forbidden under penalty of imprisonment, so we studied in secret. We went underground, so to speak, and dealt with the disciplines most needed, not only in the ministry, but in life. We studied, not in a classical way, but at night, in very small groups, under very difficult conditions. When daylight came, we could not sleep. We had to go to work, because that was the law. It was very exhausting, yet very exhilarating, for we were like dried-out wells thirsting for this kind of knowledge.

"At first we were unable to write things down because we were told not to do so. Not all were able to study this way, at night, and with such a large amount of material on so many subjects taught in such a way. He would lecture by beginning with one remark, which he would place in a wider context. For two hours he would develop the idea in a free-flowing process consisting of lecture and commentary that was rooted in tradition yet oriented to new approaches, and then he would weave it all together and reconnect with his original remark. He often spoke spontaneously and always very quickly, making many diversions on the way to his main point, with a complex finish at the end. It was very difficult to hang on to the main thought of the lecture for two or three hours in the night after we had worked all day. A few people started taking notes, just so they could remember the main points of the talk. I had no trouble following him, but often I had to leave to check out security, so sometimes I lost the continuity between one thought and the next. Once the program was established, I was sleeping an average of only two or three hours a night, sometimes less than that.

"After Mass, the lecture, the discussion, and a lot of informal conversation, it would be the middle of the night or just before morning when we would finally leave, quickly, and in the dark, because we could not turn on a light. Sometimes someone would take the wrong shoes, for we always removed them on arrival and retrieved them when we left. Once, after all had left the seminar, somebody rang the doorbell. Who could that be at such an hour? It was four o'clock in the morning. We were more than a little concerned. It was strictly forbidden to return to the house once someone had left it. My brother Josef went to the door and opened it with caution—we were meeting at his house on Sevcikova Street—and there was one of the participants who stood nearly two meters tall. He had taken the shoes of another by mistake and had tried his best to walk home in them, but he simply could not do it. The shoes were so small, barely half his size, that he had to return and exchange them. Unfortunately, his own shoes were no longer there and we had no other pair to give him. We thought of the person walking home in his shoes and all we could do was laugh."

Ludmila was responsible for all organizational aspects of the seminars, their setup and implementation, the facilitation of the sessions, and issues of security. She also took it upon herself to make sure Davidek was understood. With his quick thinking and speaking, some people could not keep up with him, and others sometimes were lost within his conceptualizations and unable to give him feedback. At the break Ludmila would say to him, "Repeat this," or, "Clarify that." Eventually a form of dialogue emerged in the group that was not possible at the beginning. Ludmila encouraged and contributed to this spirited exchange. While she did many things in the early days of this new enterprise, Ludmila felt that organization and security were at the core of her involvement. She needed "to be always watching things, to be always a little bit in front." While the role itself was extremely stressful, she has said, "I didn't feel it as a stress, because I was just burning for this thing. There was nobody beforehand who had come with such a program, and then all of a sudden this way opened up and I gave myself totally to it."

Women had always been a part of Felix Davidek's programs. They were drawn to him because of his vision and his charismatic qualities, and because he treated them as equals. "Felix had a nice relationship with women." That is Ludmila's assessment, and her sister agrees. Maria participated from the very beginning. "I was always present at the seminars, whenever it was possible.

When I heard Dr. Davidek speak, something in me was awakened, something that was already there. It corresponded with my inner being. He talked a lot about time, about how we should be using our time, economizing our time. He spoke of 'micro-moments.' "

Maria's childhood friend Majka Luxova was never much interested in formal church structures, even within this new initiative, but participated in the lectures and seminars for years. "Davidek's lectures dealt with real life, concrete life, the specifics of life. I was never involved in the program of his church, the structure or the problems, because I am a person created for freedom. Felix was open to new ideas. I loved his attitude in religious things. In fact I believed that the things he taught had to come true one day. Listening to him was so natural. He created a new space for me within which I could really develop, a space of inner freedom. I flowed along with it. He had hope for everyone. In spite of all the difficulties we lived in, he always had hope. And he had profound respect for the church."

Those first participants were trained to be recruiters. Each one had a circle of friends and enthusiasm for the program. They were told how to evaluate prospects, how to approach individual persons, what to tell them about the seminars, how to invite them to join the project. No one came directly to Davidek, who always had the last word about who would be accepted. There was a probationary period, which provided an opportunity to test the various applicants for their suitability for the program. They had to be able to keep a secret and not be afraid of taking risks. Security was paramount. Many applied who were not chosen. Some could not be counted on to keep strict secrecy. Before long a diverse group had gathered around Davidek. Some came seeking ordination. Davidek did not wait until he had a group of men to prepare for priesthood together. Except for the lectures, which all the candidates attended along with other women and men, he worked with each one individually, addressing issues related to work, prayer, study, free time, and even personal problems.

Some who had been seminarians once were stuck in traditional approaches and disapproved of innovation. There were some who just could not handle working in partnership with women. In each of these cases Davidek would decide that the person was insufficiently prepared for the future of ministry and therefore not qualified to continue on with him in the company of others, but might do so individually. He would meet privately with those who felt called to priesthood, respecting their limitations in their ability to adapt. He did not want to lose anyone. Some candidates were much older, beyond an age when one might more easily discard stereotypes. He felt that each priest enriches the church. What was important was to cooperate with the charism that had been given to them. Davidek was looking for those candidates who, as he used to say, were sorted out and verified by life.

"Koinotes," derived from *koinonia,* a Greek word meaning community, was the name Felix gave to what was emerging under his leadership in partnership with Ludmila Javorova. It was more than just a program, far more than a course of study, and it was not restricted to seminarians nor oriented only to clergy. Furthermore, it was clear from the very beginning that it was not just for men. What Davidek envisioned was a way of being in the world, not alone, but as *ecclesia,* a community of believers, a genuine *koinonia,* which he called the local church. Vital to this understanding of church was finding a way to solve the problems of people and to combine this with the giving of hope and spiritual consolation to those in need.

"From the moment I began cooperating with him, he insisted that pastoral visits were essential to the program." Ludmila explains what these entailed. "He would tell me to find ill and lonesome people, those who are isolated from church and society, because they are part of Christ's body. It seems, he would say, as if their lives are simply set aside as no longer relevant. They are a vital presence in the church. They should be invited to participate in things. We must reach out to them. So right from the

start I began looking for such people. I would ask those who were
bedridden to offer their illness for the church, because the church
really needed it at that time. Then we began to ask a specific thing
from them. We would ask them to offer their illness for priests who
are not able to be ordained or for the security of this project. Such
visits became a regular part of the whole program. At the seminars
Davidek would always stress that we depend on the ill and the
suffering and must become more aware of them. He reminded us
that if they had not been praying and offering their suffering for
us, we would not be here. And so these two groups, Koinotes and
those who were suffering and alone, melded together spiritually. I
believe sick people gave us a lot." In the beginning Ludmila was
the only one who made these pastoral visits to the sick and the
infirm. Bit by bit other people started to identify with the idea.
Once ordained, a Koinotes priest was encouraged to look for ill
people to support him in his priesthood by offering their suffering
and their prayers for him. A number of priests did.

Unlike some other priests who had been released from prison,
Felix was not allowed to resume any official priestly work. This did
not surprise him. Still, he was a priest with a call to ministry, and
he was bound to minister, one way or another. Ludmila understood and supported him in this. What she did not understand
was his casual disregard of the mandatory work requirement. She
was afraid he would be arrested again. "He did not apply for a job,
not for a very long time. I kept telling him, they will imprison you
again. He said, 'I will not let them tell me what to do. I have to
be in charge of myself. And I have to have a job that would be
suitable for our project.' Eventually he found employment disin-
fecting bedding and other things at the local children's hospital.
The job offer came from a certain professor, who took a major
risk hiring someone like Davidek. There was also a person at the
hospital who cooperated with Felix in our new venture. Later on,
he became a priest."

Ludmila had another concern. Ordinarily, those released from prison took time for convalescing in order to focus on reintegrating body, mind, and spirit. Not Davidek. He immediately took up the task of being a priest again, but in a whole new way. He would say to Ludmila that the danger lies in the sudden removal of psychological tension after long years of suffering. The body is not ready for certain things, like the food you would now be eating and the complexities of daily life. A complete cessation of activity only complicates the process of returning to a normal life. As in everything Felix chose to do, he orchestrated his recovery from many brutal years in prison and his subsequent return to society in his own way. He began a new undertaking, and in the process, once again, he took control of his life.

One of his strategies for self-determination involved a high level of risk. Felix wanted to take a picture of the prison where he had spent so much time. Mirov was situated in an isolated wooded area that was closed to public access. It was dangerous to be caught trespassing there, yet he made up his mind to do it. Ludmila tells us how. "One day Felix said, 'We will go for a ride near the prison. You will get an attack of diarrhea and have to go into the woods. I, as a physician, will go with you. Since we cannot leave the driver all alone in the car, he will have to come with us. I will show him how the camera works, and he will take the picture.' That was the plan we followed.

"When we came to the place, I went into the woods and squatted behind a bush. Felix stood nearby, and next to him was the driver with the camera tucked into his trousers. Within moments, we were surrounded. Davidek yelled at the prison guards—he was known for his shouting: 'What is the matter with you? There is somebody here who is not feeling well. Why are you behaving like this?' They shouted back at him. Felix continued his verbal assault with such an intensity that the guards were absolutely astounded. Meanwhile, the driver had taken the picture, so we left the woods and drove away. Fortunately, they had not recognized Felix, or he might have been back in prison. By acting in this way, Felix took control of the situation. He had mastered this approach in Mirov, where he learned to attack with a volley of words in a threatening tone of voice. For example, I heard that when he was in prison, his clothes did not fit him. Everything was too big for him. He also hated to tie his shoelaces, so he would walk around with his shoes untied. Once one of the guards berated him. 'Davidek, look at you. Why do you walk around like that?' Felix shouted back at him. 'Is it my fault that I am here, that I have to wear clothes that are too big for me? Is it my fault you don't even know how to dress me?' He scared the guard with his verbal assault and was taken to the place where they issued the clothes and was given a more appropriate uniform, one that fit him better. So this became Felix's mode of defense. He would talk like a machine gun, staccato style. With prison guards, he was convinced, you always had to attack.

Sometime late in the summer following his February release, just as they had promised, Davidek and the other professors who had shared a prison ministry and had spent long hours discussing the future of the church came together to talk. It was startling to see how their ideas had changed and how much their opinions varied when revisited in freedom. Things on the outside differed from what they thought might be possible when looked at from within. Each of the priests had been released into a challenging situation where he had to go it alone. The consensus achieved in the context of a shared prison experience had changed under the influence of multiple realities. It was hard to maintain enthusiasm for an embryonic future in the face of all the fully developed demands of one's present life. They saw different needs, had different goals, envisioned the church in very different ways. In one sense Davidek had set too high an expectation. On the other hand, many disagreed with Davidek's understanding of future forms of church, and they did not feel that security was their highest priority. Perhaps this more than anything else led to a parting of the ways. Davidek did remain close to a Franciscan priest, Frantisek

Barta, whose ideas of the church and its future were harmonious with his own.

About a year after Felix's release from prison, a small, shabby parcel arrived in the mail. Felix brought it to Ludmila and said, "Look what came to me. I don't know who it is from." The name of the sender was missing. He removed the plain brown paper wrapping and there were his prison lectures and poems. Not all of them, but quite a few, written in tiny handwriting on toilet paper, various bits of waste paper, and scraps of wrapping paper. Most of what had been written on very small cigarette paper was lost to him forever. He had used an ordinary pencil, which becomes less legible with the passage of time, so some of it was hard to decipher. One of the prison guards, who seems to have been a decent human being, must have smuggled the confiscated papers out of the prison in his pockets, then stuffed them in a box, and sent them on to Davidek. Felix tried to discover the identity of the sender, but he never found out who it was.

Religious and cultural attitudes were reflected in how priests interacted with their female parishioners. As males and again as clergy, they had been programmed to respond in a way that would make it extremely difficult to relate to women as equals. In Koinotes, however, they would have to be able to cooperate with everyone, with women as well as with men. Seminarians preparing for a celibate life thought it would be better if they kept their distance from the opposite sex. Davidek wanted to teach them not to be afraid of women. "And that's why," Ludmila explains, "Davidek asked those who were having the most trouble to attend dancing lessons. And I had to go through this with them. I asked other women to join me. Most of them refused, but I was willing to do this for priests if it would make their task easier. I had a great respect for priests.

"We had a number of lessons. I attended every one. Some of those guys had a terrible time trying to learn what to do with themselves. They were unable to move, and I loved to dance. I would get so angry with them, because they would be holding me too tight and they were not able to lead me. Some who could not dance at all would dance with nobody but me. Sometimes I would just let them sit, and I would go to the man who was leading the lessons, someone who knew what he was doing, because I wanted to dance. Many of them had this fear of women, which they could not overcome with one brief course in dancing. They simply could not grasp the final teaching of every session, that they were to accompany a woman safely home when the evening was over. I would ask myself at the end of the session,'How can I tell them politely that they should be taking me home?' This is something so evident, I shouldn't have to ask them to do it. There was such a lack of social grace, such a lack of sensitivity in many of those men. These were difficult moments for me, because sometimes it made me so angry. I would try to put my feelings aside, but when I sensed the discomfort in my escort was just too overwhelming, I would stand there shocked and disappointed, but always compassionate. When I felt someone was able to cope with confronting his fear of women, I would say, 'It is dangerous for me to walk home alone. Do accompany me.' And I have to say, those guys, they learned. The education they had been given beforehand was limited and so rigid, yet they learned to move beyond it. I think if communism gave anything to us, it was in imposing an environment in which men had to deal with their fear of women, at least to some extent, by having to be in contact with them."

Davidek was determined that all those who graduated from his university, which included future priests, would have a broad cultural background, and skills and knowledge in various fields. He wanted all members of Koinotes to be well rounded and well read, and therefore he promoted studies beyond the core curriculum of the lectures and seminars that he taught. He encouraged his students to study languages, to cultivate an interest in archaeology and anthropology, in culture and film and travel, and "in the knowledge of the newest findings in cybernetics and computer technology," a statement he included in one of the foundational texts of Koinotes. He discussed and debated with individual students texts from a range of literary works in a variety of fields and guided their personal reading. He taught them to connect their academic learning to contemporary concerns in practical ways that would be beneficial to their everyday lives and to the life of the church. He wanted them to have a sense of responsibility for the future of both the church and the world. He insisted that seminarians develop a fully integrated spiritual life, one rooted in the realities of this world and not focused solely on the next. Ludmila recalls that her first impression of Felix on his return was of "a deeply spiritual man." Those who knew him well would agree. He seemed driven by God's agenda, although he expressed it in terms of his own. This had helped him maintain his focus through all those years in prison. He emerged from his confinement informed, decisive, fully functional, and feeling responsible for the present, with a hopeful eye toward the future. Over time he had given shape to a well thought out initiative called Koinotes, one that would integrate the strengths and the needs of the church in the midst of the world. At the core of the project, and of his life, was a deep trust in the Spirit as both innovator and guide. Says Ludmila, "All of this was new to me."

As Davidek was formally constituting his new university, which was in essence a continuation of his earlier initiative in Stepanov in 1948, he entered into an agreement with Professor Kratky regarding its constitution, its lecturers, and its program. Kratky would join Davidek in a single coordinated effort. Davidek would provide study books similar to the ones he had made for his Atheneum students. Because the university was firmly established, it was decided that an honorary title would be awarded to some people associated with the program, a doctorate *honoris causa.* Davidek proposed giving the title to Ludmila, and Kratky agreed. "Of course, I objected," Ludmila says. "I really hadn't done anything to warrant such an honor." Davidek explained that she had contributed a lot to the university's development. Ludmila continued to protest. "It was natural for me to do what I did. I never desired any honorific titles." Davidek insisted. "The decision belongs to Professor Kratky and to me. We give it to you anyway." And they did. For a long time afterward, Felix insisted that she sign her name with the title. He felt it was important for the university's status. "So when there was something of an official nature, I would use the title, but otherwise I did not. Then after awhile he could not persuade me to do it anymore."

Through the seminars and other elements of the program, Koinotes was able to prepare candidates for ordination, but there was no one to ordain them. Felix contacted several bishops under house arrest in the area, but they refused to do it. There were reasons for declining. First of all, the bishops were afraid of transgressing church regulations, and, secondly, they were fearful of doing anything not sanctioned by the state. Felix persisted in his search. It was difficult and even dangerous to travel to where the bishops were, for anywhere Felix went the StB would follow. Those who arranged the meetings for him were also being watched by the StB, so they avoided public transportation and went by motorcycle, traveling part of the way by day and the rest of the way at night in order to discourage police pursuit. Felix used various roundabout ways to confuse the enemy. He went by train, motorcycle, car, on foot. "I accompanied him on some of those journeys," Ludmila explains, "but the contacts and meetings were arranged by others. We never traveled directly to the destination where the meeting was arranged. We always got out several kilometers before our station when we traveled by train and we walked the rest of the way so we could see whether any one was following us. The bishops who were under house arrest were allowed short visits under certain conditions, for example, with visiting relatives who had come from a distance, and these visits were recorded. Important issues could not be discussed because someone might be listening. Key points were written down and read and immediately destroyed. The best conversations took place on walks, but that was not always possible. Davidek negotiated without me. I watched the neighborhood. When he had difficulty gaining access to the house, he would ask to use the toilet. Once inside, he spoke with the person who had made the arrangements. At that point he would either be told that the meeting was impossible or be taken in to see the bishop. I accompanied Davidek three times. No one was willing to ordain for us. They felt it was too risky. When one by one the bishops refused to collaborate in the project, it was clear that some other means of proceeding had to be explored. Some seminarians had been waiting to be ordained for approximately twenty years. After these unsuccessful visits to local bishops, Davidek said during one of the seminars: 'Even though the church has keys, it does not open anything. It only rattles them, just like a jailer in Mirov. That is a terrible responsibility. Things have to be opened up despite the possibility of making mistakes, which can arise. I say that even about myself.' He knew the bishops he had visited, and those who had refused to see him, could legitimately ordain priests for the underground church in circumstances such as this, because it was an emergency situation, but they refused to do it."

NINE

Was it not You, O God,
who dried up the waters of the deep,
who made the depths of the sea a way
for Your people to cross over?
Isaiah 51:10

Attention turned toward finding assistance in another country. This was not a simple solution. The borders were heavily guarded, and only a limited number of people were permitted to go abroad either for business or on tour, and only for one or two days. On their return they had to report to the police and sign a declaration disclosing with whom they had met and what they had spoken about. The search for a sympathetic bishop who would agree to ordain meant a commitment to achieve the impossible. Someone would have to travel to another country, find a willing bishop, and put into place a process for those who would follow after. Images of his arrest the first time he attempted to cross the border so many years ago were surely foremost in Felix's mind as he considered this option, yet nothing would discourage him—neither danger, nor fear, nor the threat of being imprisoned again. He was a man of action seeking to promote, by the grace of God, a vital apostolic work. Some members, particularly Inzenyr* Jan Blaha, could go to East Germany on business. Professor Stanislav Kratky had contacts among the exiles there. Those exiles would provide the impetus for Koinotes to move forward.

---

*Inzenyr is a professional title used by those who have earned their graduate degree in science.

94

They arranged a meeting with Bishop Gerhard Schaffran of the diocese of Görlitz in East Germany. Ludmila and Inzenyr Jiri Pojer traveled to East Germany as tourists to try to open up a way for their future priests. Bishop Schaffran was willing to do more than ordain for the underground church. He would also take on the responsibility of delivering to the Vatican Davidek's news about the situation of the Czechoslovakian church. Ludmila picks up the story.

"There were two of us, Jiri Pojer and I, playing the role of tourists. We went by an express night train from Brno to Prague and then on to Dresden. Before leaving Brno, Felix had given Jiri important news to deliver to Bishop Schaffran, who would send it to the Vatican. Felix had written the highlights of his report concerning the status of the church on very small, thin paper used for rolling cigarettes, just as he had done in prison. The paper was carefully folded and wrapped in aluminum foil. Our specific instructions were that Jiri would go into the toilet before the train stopped at the border and insert the bit of aluminum foil behind a tooth in his mouth. Otherwise we were not to leave our seats anywhere near the border, so as not to raise suspicion or draw attention to ourselves. We were not to talk too much, were to behave appropriately, and were told to follow the instructions of the customs officers. Our personal things had to be in perfect order and we had to be ready to answer any question relating to where we were going and why we were going there. We were to speak leisurely, briefly, and to the point. If we were apprehended, we were not to betray Bishop Schaffran. We were aware of what would happen if any information was extracted from us. We knew that many lives, as well as the work of the church, were contingent on us. We were accompanied by the prayers of all Koinotes members, and this continuity of the life of the church filled us with inexpressible courage and hope.

"We arrived in East Germany late at night and were given lodging in a private home. In Görlitz, in a series of evasive tactics, we visited a museum and walked around the town. Then we went into a church together, stayed for a while, and left separately. I waited in a nearby park while Jiri went on to the meeting place to speak with Bishop Schaffran. After giving the bishop the messages sent by Davidek, they settled on a date for the ordination, which would always be on a weekday, and an approximate time. Then they established a procedure to be followed by the ordinands. The bishop tore some pictures in half. One half was to be given to the candidate. Bishop Schaffran would keep the other half. These would serve as a means of identifying legitimate candidates." Bishop Schaffran, the first bishop who was willing to ordain Koinotes priests for the underground church, had reason to support Davidek's cause. He too had been arrested under the communist regime and had spent several years in prison in the Soviet Union. He agreed to cooperate.

Ludmila now knew from experience that it would be a complex process to go from Brno to Görlitz in order to be ordained. "To prepare for such a journey was very demanding and never straightforward. God's providence helped us a lot." First, the seminarian had to meet the criteria established by Davidek to assess a candidate's readiness. When that had been accomplished, Davidek gave the individual a letter verifying the person's readiness for ordination, along with half the picture that had been torn in two. Once the candidate had obtained a government permit to go abroad, he was given explicit instructions on the procedures designed to safeguard the entire enterprise. On arrival in Görlitz he presented his credentials and his half of the picture to Bishop Schaffran, who was able to verify that this was indeed a candidate sent by Davidek and not someone collaborating with the secret police. After writing down his biographical information in Latin and his vow of celibacy, which would be sent on to the Vatican with a personal message from the bishop, the two had a formal meeting. Bishop Schaffran always talked for a long time with each individual, because he was interested in what was happening in

Czechoslovakia. That same evening the candidate was ordained a deacon. The following day, he was ordained a priest. No documents were given to the one ordained. Written records would endanger not only the new priest and the ordaining bishop, but also the core of Koinotes and the evolving underground church. "I can remember how happy all of us who knew about it were when the new priest returned," says Ludmila. "It is impossible to describe the joy we felt as we received his blessing. How devoutly we prayed that all our seminarians would one day get their chance."

Bishop Schaffran began ordaining priests for Koinotes in the summer of 1967. He ordained the five candidates sent to him by Davidek before Koinotes adopted a new strategy later that year. Until 1971, he continued to be the communication link between Koinotes and Rome, sending news from Davidek directly to the Vatican. Ludmila remembers with gratitude "the great service he has given to us and to the church. In this way we kept the Vatican informed. That was very important to us. The reports about the situation here were very diligently done by Davidek, with precise and accurate information. We did not try to hide anything from the authorities in Rome."

While some of Davidek's seminarians were ordained as a result of the East German connection, it was clear from the start that this arrangement would not solve the overall problem of ordinations for Koinotes. Only a few had been able to travel outside the country. A more effective means had to be found. The obvious solution was one that was already under consideration. Koinotes needed a bishop of its own. There was precedent for such an action. Rome had already dealt with similar situations.

The precedent for secret consecrations and ordinations had been set in Mexico in the 1920s as a result of the virulent persecution of Catholicism that intensified after the revolution. To counteract the decimation of the clergy and the complete suppression of the church, Pope Pius XI provided the means of ensuring there would be leaders to function in secret. Special faculties were given to bishops, which allowed them to surreptitiously consecrate bishops and ordain priests for the survival of the Catholic faith and a continuation of the sacraments, in effect, giving rise to an underground church. These "emergency faculties" were later invoked, again with Vatican approval, in countries under communist control: in Russia, where secret consecrations took place in 1926 in Moscow, in Romania in the late 1940s and early 1950s, where the consecration of bishops occurred without government approval, and in Czechoslovakia.

As the totalitarian regime unleashed its brutal repression of the Catholic Church in Czechoslovakia in 1949, Pope Pius XII extended the provisional authority inherent in the "Mexican faculties" to include this latest crisis. These special faculties allowed for the consecration of a secret successor for every diocese, according to specific conditions. Each bishop could consecrate only one secret bishop, who could then ordain priests without notifying either the Vatican or the state. These secret bishops were not permitted to consecrate other bishops and could function only if the incumbent bishop were arrested. To safeguard the secrecy and security of all involved, no documentation exists to verify the application of this extraordinary permission. The underground church in Czechoslovakia—known also as the hidden church, the silent church, the secret church, the clandestine church, the second line—traces its claim of Vatican approval through the following series of events.

In January 1951 in Bratislava, Slovakia, Bishop Robert Pobozny secretly consecrated Pavel Hnilica, a young Jesuit priest. Almost immediately a warrant was issued for Hnilica's arrest, forcing him to seek asylum outside the country. In August of that same year Jan Korec, another Jesuit clergyman working as a manual laborer, was consecrated as his successor. He says, "I had already received the instruction direct from Rome that there should always be two bishops—*uno nascosto, uno attivo*—one hidden, one active."* On September 9, 1955, Bishop Korec, S.J., secretly consecrated Jesuit Father Dominik Kal'ata. On May 18, 1961, Bishop Kal'ata, S.J., consecrated Jesuit Father Peter Dubovsky, through whom the valid apostolic succession of Koinotes consecrations and ordinations would eventually be traced.

The decision had been made for Koinotes to acquire a bishop of its own, one from within the community, who would be able to ordain in apostolic succession. The most viable option was for someone from Koinotes to find a bishop outside the country willing to seek papal approval for a bishop for Koinotes. While Davidek was the logical choice to investigate this possibility, neither he nor Kratky were eligible because of their political past. Both had been imprisoned and were still being watched, so they would never be allowed to leave the country. Jan Blaha and Frantisek Mikes, who already had traveled abroad on business, were under consideration, even though neither one was ordained. In the end Davidek chose Blaha, a twenty-nine-year-old scientist with a degree in chemistry, who had recently come to Koinotes seeking ordination. For quite some time Davidek refused to consider Blaha because he did not meet his requirements. He was on record with the police over an incident in which he had been falsely accused of conspiring against the state, and his brother-in-law had been harassed by the regime. Only three people knew he was a contender: Ludmila, Mikes, and Kratky. Mikes, the other candidate, spoke in favor of Blaha. After his initial hesitation, Davidek decided on Blaha and immediately began to share with him essential information. Blaha's scientific and scholarly credentials were impeccable, his priestly vocation genuine, his academic readiness for ordination nearly complete, and he had a permit to go abroad. The plan was for him to travel to East Germany to be ordained a priest. The next step was uncertain. There was no guarantee that any bishop would be willing to try to obtain

---

*Catholic Digest, July 1991.

a mandate from the Vatican for an episcopal consecration, but it was worth a try.

Jan Blaha was scheduled to leave the country in July of 1967. During the intervening months, he continued his studies and prepared the paper that would be read at the professional seminar he planned to attend. He asked the authorities for an extension of his time abroad so he could take a holiday and his request was granted. Once he was in East Germany, he made contact with Josef Stimpfle, the bishop in Augsburg, who listened to Blaha's story and then read the testimony that had been written by Davidek in Latin and smuggled out of the country. After giving careful consideration to the request for ordination, he decided he would do it and ordained him a deacon. Then on July 12, 1967, Jan Blaha was ordained a priest by Bishop Josef Stimpfle in Augsburg. He returned to Czechoslovakia, and on October 28, 1967, four months after he had been ordained, Jan Blaha was consecrated bishop by Bishop Peter Dubovsky, S.J. The next day, October 29, Bishop Jan Blaha consecrated Felix Maria Davidek a bishop and delegated his episcopal faculties to him.

Ludmila understood from the beginning that approval for the consecrations of Blaha and Davidek, with the delegation of faculties from the one to the other, came directly from Pope Paul VI. She says: "I remember some general things, but not the details, because this was immediately sealed as 'super secret,' so that Blaha would not be liquidated." She says it is her understanding that contacts outside the country arranged for a personal meeting with the pope, that Blaha went to Italy for some conference related to his work, and that while he was there, the meeting took place via Slovak bishop Pavel Hnilica. There are others who say this is not the way it happened. Blaha has neither confirmed nor denied this sequence of events. However, he has always insisted that his consecration and that of Davidek were done using special papal norms with the knowledge and approval of Rome, specifically, Pope Paul VI, and with the understanding that Davidek would be the presiding bishop. "Both Blaha and Davidek agreed that only Felix would function as a bishop and carry out all the ordinations," Ludmila explains. Bishop Dubovsky was not aware of this arrangement before he consecrated Blaha, and when he learned of it later, Ludmila said, he was outraged. "Blaha did not consecrate other bishops, and no one outside the inner circle knew that he was a bishop for quite some time," she explains.

As for Davidek's consecration, Ludmila knew enough to be able to affirm that it was indeed valid, although she did not know the name of the person who witnessed it. She would be called upon countless times to give evidence of its validity. After Blaha had delegated his faculties to Davidek, he did not function as a bishop until later on in the 1970s and only in the inner circle of Koinotes. After Davidek died, Blaha assumed leadership of Koinotes. As with all members, even those in leadership positions, his knowledge was limited. It would take everyone sharing whatever they knew, and especially Ludmila, who knew more than anyone else, to understand the full extent of Koinotes and its contributions to the church.

As Ludmila would say, Felix was pragmatic. It had cost him so many prayers and sacrifices, so much effort and work, to arrive at this moment. There were many candidates awaiting ordination. He wanted no further delay. "The very next day I brought him a candidate to ordain. That first ordination took place on a cold and foggy autumn evening. At 9:00 p.m. I walked with the candidate through the gardens and surreptitiously led him to the back door and into Davidek's house before I went on patrol. I did not witness this first ordination because I had to be on guard to guarantee everyone's safety. Two or three ordinations took place in Davidek's house before we moved to my parents' house. Then it was my brother Josef's place, and then there were other locations." This strategy enabled them all to evade the secret police.

Although the site was unpredictable, the event itself followed a carefully crafted routine. The candidate, who wore ordinary clothes, had to promise to follow strict security instructions should he be discovered. He was taken into the house after dark. The ritual was the same one used for any other ordination. Before the laying on of hands, Bishop Davidek told the candidate what he was about to do and asked if he agreed to receiving the Sacrament of Holy Orders. The candidate had to clearly and verbally affirm that he did. Immediately after receiving the sacrament, the newly ordained priest celebrated his First Mass. Before being escorted away, he had to promise he would not tell anyone about his ordination, not even his parents. This was never easy, especially for older men, but it was a necessary precaution. Parents posed the biggest threat, for one could never be certain they would be able to keep such a secret. The very first things the new priest received were two small white cloths—a corporal to be used for covering the chalice and a purificator for drying the sacred vessels. "In the beginning I made them from delicate white linen napkins or from white handkerchiefs that had not been used," says Ludmila. "After 1970 they had to procure this 'trousseau' on their own."

Davidek ordained Frantisek Mikes and other candidates for the priesthood. Some had been waiting a number of years to receive the sacrament. Wherever possible, these newly ordained priests were to establish small clandestine communities, both spiritual and pastoral in nature, in the areas where they lived. By this was meant a very small circle of the priest's own friends, people he knew could be trusted. There was one strict rule with no exception. He had to exclude his family for the sake of security. The ministry of the newly ordained consisted of prayer, adoration, sacrifice, Mass, teaching catechism, and some pastoral work. It was easier for those who lived in towns than for those who came from villages, where everyone knew everyone else and secrecy was a challenge. Sometimes the priest would organize a trip so he might interact more freely with his people. In 1968 Davidek ordained twenty-one new priests. With each ordination Koinotes expanded into an ever-widening circle of small communities.

Davidek named a number of saints and saintly people as spe-
cial patrons of Koinotes. First of all there was the Blessed Virgin
Mary. Among the others were Teilhard de Chardin, the angels,
Saint Paul, Saint John the Evangelist, Saint Jude, Saints Cyril and
Methodius, Saint John Vianney, Pope Pius XII, Pope John XXIII,
Padre Pio, several Czechoslovakian bishops and priests, and all
who died in communist concentration camps, because they were
considered martyrs. These patrons were the special protectors of
Koinotes and were often invoked in prayer.

One day Davidek announced that he needed some letterhead
stationery with a coat of arms as emblem. "You cannot imagine,"
Ludmila recalls, "what it took to get this done. Under the totalitarian regime, everything was under very strict control." Davidek
already had his coat of arms. He had designed it soon after his
release from prison. He gave it to Brno artist Ludvik Kolek, who
set it in heraldic form and added the words Felix had chosen: *nasci
iamque non mori*—"to be born and not to die." Ludmila's brother
Alois, who was a bookbinder and a workshop manager, arranged
to have it printed, because he had friends in a print shop who
would do it secretly. Ludmila picked up the finished stationery
and envelopes after dark. She said to Felix: "Aren't we afraid to
write on these sheets of paper?" She was thinking of the StB.
He replied: "They know that I am a bishop because they interrogated me about it, so let them get used to it." The priest who
was always so secretive wrote all his official letters as bishop on
his personalized stationery.

Koinotes grew and gradually spread throughout Czechoslovakia. Each priest's group of close acquaintances became part of the
network, although none of them knew the extent of the movement or anything beyond what was happening in their immediate
circle. Groups differed in numbers and in other characteristics.
Size depended on what the individual priest was able to handle, for
he also had a daytime job. People gathered in one another's flats to
celebrate Eucharist. Hosts for consecration were acquired through

priests involved with official pastoral work. Wine for Mass, which differed from ordinary wine, could be purchased almost anywhere. An ordinary glass used exclusively for sacramental service was the chalice for the wine. Vladimir Veskrna, whose name in religion is Julius Eymard, offers this testimony: "I drove buses and was a secret priest for twenty-two years. We said Mass every day, sometimes alone, sometimes with a bunch of youngsters, sometimes with a dozen old women. We operated where the official priests couldn't reach."*

Koinotes evolved organically into a network of small domestic entities whose existence was well concealed. It consisted of pastoral ministries of women as well as men who ministered to each other and reached out to the sick who supported Christ's mission through their suffering and prayers. Davidek understood Koinotes to be the local church. He saw the church as a sacramental presence in the world, an understanding heavily influenced by the developments of Vatican II. He knew of the conciliar documents from foreign radio broadcasting, which he listened to at night, and also from foreign literature, most of it from Poland, which he was able to order through the local Soviet bookstore specializing in foreign literature, the only bookseller allowed to distribute that kind of material. The Council's expression of *aggiornamento* and its vision of the church affirmed his approach to ministry. He knew how to read the signs of the times, understood the importance of discerning the Spirit and the necessity of a relevant response. He saw the present situation as one of those signs and was moved to respond to it. For Felix this was *kairos* time, God's time. Ludmila recalls that "he emphasized to us that our 'local church' must be beneficial to the universal church. That meant we had obligations and responsibilities." She recalls hearing the following words, because she wrote them down. He said, "It is

---

*The Guardian (London), November 2, 1996.

necessary that every specific community perceive itself as a part of Christ's community, meaning the universal church. To count knowingly only on 'our own' is always against the Holy Spirit that was sent to us by Christ as Teacher and Comforter." Felix believed God's liberating Spirit was the driving force behind his initiatives. Those were the days of an inner freedom. There was a sense of well-being among Koinotes adherents, and the hint of a new and less oppressive environment all around.

The mid-1960s had witnessed a surprising shift in Czechoslovakia's political and cultural life. The heavy hand of communism suddenly adopted a lighter touch. A series of changes in the central government culminated in a wave of freedom known ever after as "Prague Spring." Alexander Dubcek, a Slovakian communist, assumed party leadership in January 1968. He appointed liberals to government posts, relaxed the rules of censorship, and promised economic and democratic reforms. Speaking in favor of human rights and human liberties and denouncing persecution on the basis of political convictions, Dubcek's government proceeded to introduce "socialism with a human face" as a "unique experiment in democratic communism." In this new climate of freedom, people began to be less afraid. Artistic aspects of culture flourished. Western imports were everywhere. Religion was affected in a number of positive ways. The Greek Catholic Church became legal again and the Roman Catholic Church was now less restricted. Religious communities reappeared. People went on pilgrimage. The only remaining Catholic newspaper published without being censored. The organization of so-called "peace priests" quietly went out of existence. Most bishops returned to their diocese. It was an interlude full of promise. Then in the night of August 21, tanks of the Soviet army invaded Czechoslovakia. Dubcek and other reformers were taken directly to Moscow, where they were forced to sign an agreement acquiescing to the ongoing presence of the Soviet army in Czechoslovakia. What followed was a twenty-year period of suppression and "normalization." The new government, directed by Moscow, was one of the most repressive in all of Eastern Europe.

Prior to August 1968, Koinotes members rejoiced in all of their newfound freedoms. They had high hopes for the future. As restrictive measures began to subside, many were convinced that things would be different. They felt they had nothing to fear. Davidek refused to believe it. His distrust of the communists and Dubcek led him to be even more cautious regarding security matters. He insisted that nothing had changed, that communist treachery and duplicity would reveal themselves in the end. Many were angry at his refusal to ease up on his strict policies when all else was more relaxed. Unfortunately, he was right, for their freedom was short-lived. Czechoslovakia sank even deeper into totalitarianism, dragging yet another generation into its oppressive mire. When the Soviet armies invaded, Davidek was convinced that the church was in peril, and he had good reason to think so. He received a message stating that the communists were preparing to undertake the complete liquidation of the church and that bishops and priests would again be subjected to arrests and imprisonment, and perhaps even deportation to the USSR. Davidek consecrated other bishops, but under the condition they would minister as bishops only if arrested or deported.

Before the end of 1970 Bishop Davidek had ordained approximately forty priests.

Bishop Eugen Kocis from the Greek Catholic Church ordained six married men within Koinotes. They had bi-ritual faculties, which meant they could celebrate Mass in either the Greek or the Latin rite. Both rites had coexisted in Moravia, Bohemia, and Slovakia long before the communists came. The privilege of celebrating in either one when "pastorally expedient" had been an established tradition until the Greek Catholic Church was suppressed by the totalitarian government and forced to join the Orthodox Church from 1950 to 1969. During those years of intense persecution, priests of the Greek Catholic Church and their families were deported to the Czech region from Slovakia, where their main eparchy was situated, and went underground. That caught the attention of Davidek. Collaboration between both covert movements provided a legitimate way of ordaining married priests within Koinotes. This would not only contribute to the restoration of the Greek Catholic Church in Czechoslovakia, but it was also advantageous for security reasons. The StB would not suspect that married men could be priests, and that guaranteed a larger pastoral sphere.

The first one among the married priests to be ordained within Koinotes was Ludmila's younger brother, Josef Javora. "I had the desire from childhood. I loved being around the altar, first as an altar boy and then later as sacristan. I played the organ faithfully for about twenty years. There was something about the Mass. It drew me, held me. I do not know how to explain it. The word that comes to mind is grace. When the occasion came with Father Felix, I accepted it with joy." It happened on February 26, 1969. Josef had been married to Bozena for seven years and they had two little boys when he began life as a priest. "It was beautiful. The children were sitting around the table and we had Mass. Often. Daily. It was beautiful."

As Koinotes expanded throughout Moravia, Bohemia, and into Slovakia, Felix made Ludmila his vicar general. She was already doing the work. The appointment recognized the reality in a visible, more structured way. It also made a statement. Koinotes would do more than preach and teach about women in ministry.

Ludmila accompanied Davidek as he traveled throughout the country on pastoral visitations to his priests, assisting him in the details of his administrative task. While others knew little if anything about the extent of his underground church, she in her role was aware of all aspects connected with the work of ministry. She witnessed most ordinations and consecrations and was present at all meetings involving issues of significance. One component of her ministry called for special preparation. During their pastoral visits to outlying villages, she and Davidek would often have to walk at night through the forest. "I am not a village child in the sense that I am comfortable in the countryside or that I have a sense of direction in the forest if I had to go by myself. I could never do it in the dark. But Davidek insisted, as a condition of my cooperation with him, that I had to be able to walk alone through the forest at night, in case we should get separated. It was a training I had to undergo, so I went twice and walked from Sebetov to Stepanov, which takes perhaps three hours, and I did it in the dark. The first time, I asked one of our bishops to please come with me. I said, 'Ivan, I cannot make it alone.' And so he went with me. I told him to walk half a kilometer in front of me, because I had the feeling that I would surely get lost in the forest. It was so cold, I couldn't feel my feet. He was far enough ahead that we couldn't see each other, so it felt like I was alone, but he was always listening for my steps to be sure I was still behind him."

While Felix was very methodical when it came to certain things he required of himself and others, he was also delightfully sponta- neous. Ludmila points out that "he was spontaneous with women, which was very atypical." Sometimes that spontaneity caused dif- ficulties for him. Ludmila recounts the following story to illustrate this point. "We went to visit a woman who was in the hospital. She had given birth to many children and at the age of fifty was experiencing great difficulties. When we came to the hospital, Felix asked me to find the woman for him while he waited some- where out of sight, for he had no official permission to function as a priest. I searched but could not find her. He insisted that she was definitely there, so eventually, in that huge hospital, I located a woman who had that name. I entered the ward and asked if a woman with that name was present, and yes, there she was, sur- rounded by her family, by her husband and her children. I told her I was bringing a visitor to see her. She gave me quite a startled look, but I paid no attention to that. I had fulfilled my assignment. I had found the woman I had been looking for and said what I was supposed to say, so I went to report to Felix. I said, 'Felix, that woman is right near the door. Her family is with her. Do whatever you need to do. I will wait out here for you.' With that, he barged through the door, and without looking either to the left or the right, he ran to the bed and gave her a brotherly embrace. Her husband stared at him in shock. Who was this man hugging his wife while she was lying in bed? He rose up like a rooster and shouted, 'You _____. I am going to report you!' And he continued to insult him. What I heard sounded very dangerous, so I hurried into the room and began to apologize to the woman's husband. I nudged Felix and said that he should leave. He had no idea what was going on, but when he heard me apologize and say that a mistake had been made, that there must have been two women in the hospital with the very same name, he turned and hurried away. You cannot imagine how much I laughed, once we were out of the hospital. Jan Blaha had driven us there from Brno, and he was waiting for us. I got in the car and laughed and laughed. I laughed the whole way home. Felix, however, did not. I said, 'Felix, you must allow me to tell this story for the rest of my life.' He was very upset. He would not answer me. The next day I said, 'So will you allow me to do this?' And he responded, 'Okay. Tell it wherever you wish.' So I tell this story to people whenever I want to laugh." And Ludmila laughed as she told it.

It was during their pastoral visits to the sisters in religious communities that Davidek's concern deepened regarding the unjust treatment of women and the absence of women priests. His memories of imprisoned women deprived of a sacramental ministry were echoed again and again in the stories told by the sisters and the concerns that they conveyed. Some of the women who had been in prison would confirm what Felix already knew, that the sisters in prison and those who had been sent to enforced labor camps had absolutely no spiritual help. Conditions were not only chaotic, but psychologically disruptive and a challenge to one's spiritual growth. What a variety of practices, customs, and traditions had been thrown together there. Members of different religious orders all experienced a discontinuity with the most meaningful aspects of life. The pain that Ludmila heard as she listened to their grieving was profound and personal, and she felt their deprivation as though it were her own. She went with Felix to visit them often out in the frontier areas. She had also gone on her own when he was still in prison, for she kept in touch with the order that she had wanted to join. They had been deposited in the most isolated parts of the country. Most were concentrated in the north along the border with Poland. The living conditions for these sisters were difficult and demanding. They had so many needs. It meant a lot when the bishop and his vicar took time to visit them.

Such visitations led Davidek to conclude that "society needs the service of women as a special instrument of the sanctification of humanity." His studies in church history and New Testament texts and his reading of works that had been published abroad provided the theological basis for his convictions concerning women. His thoughts were expressed in his lectures and in various seminars. In one particular lecture, which is thought to have been delivered in the summer of 1970, he gave a historical synthesis of how and why women had been excluded from the priesthood. He felt there was no dogmatic basis for continuing such a practice, particularly when the signs of the times revealed such a pressing need for women in ministry. He criticized the "Neolithic thinking" that was so degrading to women, and made it clear that this outmoded tradition left the whole church deprived.

TEN

You will again have compassion on us, O God.
You will cast all our sins into the depths of the sea.

Micah 7:19

In September 1970, Felix Davidek announced that he would convene a "Council of the People of God." This Council would include all the areas into which Koinotes had spread: Moravia, Bohemia, Slovakia, and the Czech parishes that had sprung up in Romania. Representatives of the people of God engaged in the mission of the church—priests, sisters, lay women and men, both young and old, plus the vicar general and a designated number of bishops—would gather to consider the concerns of the hidden church and, in particular, the place of women in the church. Attendance would not be limited to those within the Koinotes network. Because of the importance of what was to be discussed, Davidek would invite others who were trustworthy, open to new ideas, and capable of keeping a secret. He would also invite priests involved with official pastoral work.

Davidek went on to explain that the church in different localities had different problems, just like the New Testament churches, whose issues became the subject of debate between Peter and Paul. The purpose of a pastoral Council was to discern the appropriate practice for a particular place. The underground church in Czechoslovakia had specific needs distinct from most other countries. Koinotes, a local church with nonterritorial status, was similar in nature to the early church communities and had to discern how best to develop the path for salvation, as expressed through the universal church. One of the critical issues it faced concerned its ministry to women. It was urgent to address this question directly at this time. In this he felt led by the Spirit, for surely this was what was meant by the Vatican II directive to discern the signs of the times. Davidek's pastoral letter spoke of their being an "instrument of the Creator" and of his desire that "we do everything possible to ensure that the future stands before us as the Parousia and that we be nothing more than an instrument of its approach and its realization."

A preparatory commission met twice prior to the Council. Approximately twenty persons participated in those meetings: Felix, Ludmila, the bishops, representatives from among the lay and religious members of Koinotes, and priests, not only from Koinotes, but also from pastorates of the visible church. Both sessions opened with a concelebrated Mass. Those assembled were introduced to the topics and to the circumstances under which the need for a Council arose. Procedures for voting were established. One could vote "yes" or "no." Anyone who was present for at least three hours would be allowed to vote. The limited capacity of the meeting place meant that the number of delegates to the Council had to be limited. For reasons of security, only the inner circle of leaders would know who would not be attending but would be kept informed. Those who were absent would be allowed to submit their vote in writing. All members of the preparatory commission had to swear on the Bible that they agreed to having a Council, to the list of those invited to attend, and to the decision to discuss the issue of women's ordination. The Council discussion would focus, not on ordination itself, but on change in the church and precisely what changes were needed to respond to the signs of the times. Within that context delegates would decide whether to talk about women's ordination or not.

Everyone was told of the oral oath. They confirmed it by putting their right hand on the Sacred Scriptures while saying:

I swear on the Holy Scriptures that I agree to the topics that will be discussed. I make this oath to the Holy Gospel before the present witnesses that I agree to the calling together of the Council of God's people and to the suggested program about women's ordination and to the recommended participants, and that I will not inform anybody of this who is not directly involved.

The rule regarding secrecy was strict. Whoever said something to someone other than committee members had to report it. The subject of women's ordination was a delicate one. There were very few people in the country who would have been able to handle it. Religion and culture in Czechoslovakia related to women in traditional ways. Besides the potential for scandal, there was the danger that church authorities, not understanding the context within which the question had arisen, would respond with a heavy hand. Everyone agreed to take the oath. No one was forced to do it. The oath was taken again at the second preparatory session. The general atmosphere of both sessions was often joyful and very hopeful.

In addition to these meetings, several tasks were undertaken to support the discussion that would take place at the Council. Bishop Kratky was asked to do a dogmatic study on the subject of women's ordination and present it at the Council. Davidek's seminars at the time were concerned with nothing else but this, providing an opportunity for participants to engage in the issues and become familiar with the idea. Individuals were asked to translate articles from foreign magazines about the evolving role of women.

Davidek provided a framework for the Council of God's People that would focus the deliberation on some of the primary themes underlying the issue of women in the church and women's ordination. He proposed points for discussion:

1. The church is called to reflect *kairos* as a witness to how God comes to humanity and to God's people with new signs in new ways to form a new reality.

2. The pastoral and sociological situation speaks for the ordination of women under certain circumstances for specific needs.

3. The cultural-anthropological perspective reflects the changing role of women in culture and society and suggests that the evolutionary process implies internal change.

4. The ordination of women is derived from early church tradition that goes back to New Testament sources and evolves beyond the apostolic era into various ministries.

5. The Code of Canon law does not take into consideration all the circumstances and all the possibilities that could occur.

His proposal was accepted. All agreed that these were the areas that were to be discussed. It was expected that there would be a debate and that not everyone at the Council would accept the theoretical analysis or come to the conclusion that this was the appropriate time to move in this direction. On this basis the preparatory commission agreed to the agenda and confirmed it with an oath.

Besides the theoretical preparation, a massive amount of work went into the Council's organization. Ludmila was responsible for all the details which, in addition to her other duties, was a monumental task. Every single aspect had to be mapped out in advance. It was all done in between her job at the research institute and a lot more work at home, where she also spent some time each day with her paralyzed brother, Vaclav. Strategically, it was a nightmare, not only because of the size and scope of what they had undertaken, but because of security and safety concerns. Somehow they had to find a way to convene a number of individuals in one place at the same time and provide the necessary food and drink without arousing suspicion. Security also meant being careful not to leave a paper trail that could be discovered by the StB. Ludmila found this necessary rule particularly challenging. "I was never allowed to take notes. There was not a paper we could keep at the time. We had to remember everything. Some tasks had to be done really fast. At times there were so many things happening simultaneously, it was impossible to remember the details and the circumstances of them all. As I got more tired, I started to forget, so I began to take some coded notes. Later on, some of those notes were a big help to me. Others I could no longer decode, for too many years had gone by. After the Council, because it was during Totality when nothing was secure, I took those little pieces of paper to an old house in a village and I hid them in a well."

The dates for the Council were set for December 25 and 26, 1970. The holiday time meant delegates could meet without worrying about their jobs. It would take place in the parish house in Koberice, a small village southeast of Brno, where Father Josef Klusacek was pastor. He and Davidek were friends. The meeting place met all the conditions required for security. It had an entrance from the garden as well as from the front, and it was set back from the road. There were no neighboring houses. A detailed description of how and when the delegates were to assemble in Koberice was sent to them in advance.

Two days before the Council, Ludmila had a visitor. "On December 23, late in the night, one of the bishops came to our place. He patted my shoulder and said to me, 'Ludmila, I am just so glad this thing will be discussed. I guarantee to you, Felix will ordain you.' I said, 'Well, you cannot count on this.'" His comment had startled her. The possibility of being ordained was the furthest thing from her mind. Affirming the theological basis for the ordination of women was the first step in the process, and there was no absolute guarantee that the delegates would agree. It was nice that this bishop felt so positive, but now was not the time for idle speculation. There were too many last minute things to be done. She thought no more about it.

The following day something else occurred. Ludmila continues the narration. "On December 24 a priest came and asked me to

stop the Council from taking place. He pleaded with me to prevent it. I was astonished. I said, 'This is not possible. You will
have to tell me your reason for making such a request.' He said,
'I cannot give you the real reason, but what you are about to do
can lead to the founding of a new Czechoslovak Church.'* His
words warned of danger ahead, but I did not take him seriously.
There was no reason to think that we would be moving in that
direction. The bishops were part of the leadership group that affirmed discussing the question of women's ministry in the church.
Everything was in order. They had even spoken positively about
addressing the issue directly, and of course, I was enthused. I had
felt their support." On the surface Ludmila heard the priest out—
he was entitled to his opinion—but deep inside she felt the blow.
It hit with seismic force. His concerns had startled her, but it was
his intensity that came as such a shock. This was more than mere
opinion. She had a premonition that something was very wrong,
and later that night, as the sounds and symbols of Christmas Eve
were circulating all around, she was taken ill. A severe sore throat,
accompanied by chills and a high fever, upset her to the core, but
she was determined to hide it from others and, to some extent,
from herself. After all, she was in charge of logistics. The moment
they had been waiting for, the culmination of all their long hard
work, had finally arrived.

The next day, Christmas Day, Ludmila was not at all well, but
she was functioning. The Council was scheduled to begin after
dark, which was 5:00 p.m. that time of year. There would be sixty
participants. Not all of them would be present for the duration
of the Council, because there was not enough room at the site
to accommodate everyone at the same time. Most, but not all,
would be there at the start. Delegates arrived throughout the day
at various times and from different directions and proceeded to
the parish house. They came individually, not even in pairs, so as

---

*This was in reference to a breakaway church established early in the twentieth century.

not to draw attention to themselves. They entered the village on foot, for a car would have been too conspicuous. Those who had driven from a distance left their vehicles in neighboring villages and walked the several miles to Koberice. Felix and Ludmila were the last to arrive. This was according to the plan.

Ludmila picks up the narrative. "When we arrived at the parish house, before we had even come through the door, we saw three of our bishops in the foyer. They were awaiting our arrival. They stood in front of us. 'The Council is not to take place,' they said. Even today I am amazed at their audacity." Ludmila could not believe it. Here were her trusted colleagues, acting like total strangers. Among them was the bishop who had come to her two nights earlier to assure her she would be ordained. Felix was not intimidated. He said: "Let us go into the other room," for the delegates had already arrived.

The bishops had with them a woman who was strongly opposed to the ordination of women. They had invited her to be a guest at the Council in clear violation of the oath all three bishops had taken. They presented Felix Davidek with a nineteen-point memorandum in writing. All their complaints centered on the issue of women's ordination. Among their main objections were

- delegates do not have the training to fully understand what is involved

- opposing arguments have not been presented and we are lacking in expertise

- many of the delegates were not informed of the agenda in advance

- there has been insufficient psychological and sociological preparation

- it is impossible to separate theory from practice in discussion, as has been proposed

- it is against the current practice of the church and there must be sufficient reason to act contrary to church law

- more time is needed—one cannot ask for a decision on something heard for the first time

- it is not for the local church to decide: this is canon law

- we have yet to explore the potential of the "priesthood of all believers," which should precede any consideration of women's ordination

- security is a major concern—we doubt such a secret could be kept, and if not, this would threaten the hidden church, even beyond ourselves.

In their opinion, to proceed would be "a theological hazard, not a risk." They also made it clear that they were acting according to their conscience.

The bishops concluded by requesting that Davidek remove the issue of women's ordination from the Council agenda. Felix refused. He reminded them that they had been participating members of both preparatory sessions and that they had sworn an oath saying they were in agreement with the program as proposed. They had raised no objections earlier. Seminars on this issue had been held for approximately two years in advance of the Council. Specific studies that had been commissioned were introduced at the preparatory sessions. They had participated in the process and had expressed no concerns. This was neither the time nor the place for delivering ultimatums. As leaders they had a responsibility not to impede the Spirit and to allow the people of God an opportunity to voice their own opinions. It was not a matter of deciding, he insisted, but only of discussing the question. He wanted to know where the people stood and what they understood of the issue. It was time they began to talk about it, to consider the possibility. The second preparatory commission had agreed that "the matter will be dealt with by the whole people of God—*ecclesia tota,* God's community—in which the Holy Spirit is present. The Spirit is the soul of this community, and everything from so-called hierarchy to so-called laity is one flesh/body...." Davidek kept repeating: "We will not decide here about an actual ordination, but only discuss in general the question of the ordination of women." The bishops, however, refused to accept the approved agenda. There seemed to be no viable way to bridge the gap between them. The Council bishops were on sides that were diametrically opposed.

Felix came up with a way to move forward. He would delay opening the Council and instead call a meeting of the preparatory commission, which would decide whether or not the Council would proceed with its original agenda. This was the group that had already met twice to review and approve that agenda. Now they would vote on whether or not the discussion concerning the ordination of women would remain part of the program. Felix said he would abide by their vote. If the commission charged with approving the agenda decided not to continue with the discussion of women and ordination, he would remove it from the program. Ludmila was not happy. "This was dreadful, to delay the Council, because we had so little time. We had only the one night and several hours the following morning." But she knew it was the only way to proceed. So Bishop Davidek convened a meeting of the preparatory commission. The members withdrew to deliberate while the rest of the delegates waited. Approximately twenty minutes later, a vote was taken among commission members. The result of that secret ballot was to keep the discussion of women's ordination as part of the Council agenda.

The *Veni Creator* was sung to officially open the Council. After Davidek's initial comments, those members of the preparatory commission who asked that the question of women's ordination not be addressed came up with a new objection. They challenged the validity of the commission's vote affirming the original agenda. According to their understanding of the law, a vote cast only by members of the commission was not legally binding on all participants

of the Council. They also questioned the manner in which the
ballots were cast and called for a new way of voting. Ludmila recalls: "This was a nightmare." A rather raucous discussion ensued
before new ballots were distributed. This time, everyone would
vote on whether or not they agreed that the question of women's
ordination would be debated at the Council. Their choices:

_____ I agree
_____ I disagree
_____ I choose to abstain

There was the very real possibility that the whole issue of ordination would not be discussed any further, but when the people
voted, their answer was yes. They had affirmed the agenda.

By this time Felix and Ludmila realized that Bishop Stanislav
Kratky, who had been charged with providing the dogmatic expertise in support of ordaining women, was not going to appear
at the Council. And he would not appear because, they discovered, he had gone over to the other side. Felix felt that now, more
than ever, it was urgent to have some cogent arguments rooted
in tradition, so someone was sent by car that night to drive the
hundred kilometers to Bishop Kratky's residence and bring back
whatever he had prepared.

Meanwhile, the Council debate began. It was well after midnight. Progress had been delayed by the intermittent interruptions
of the dissenting bishops, and now they continued, time and again,
to try to disrupt the process. Ludmila remembers the quarreling,
although she would rather forget it. "Well, I have to say, it was a
fierce exchange of views. All I was aware of at the time was the
big cross on the wall of the room and absolutely nothing else."
They would say, "This is hazardous," over and over again. One of
their primary reasons against ordaining women was that "women
are not ready." They said they did not know a single woman who,
considering women's scientific knowledge and personal abilities,
could possibly accept the sacrament of priesthood. None were

suitable. Davidek kept repeating that they should abstain if in conscience they could not accept it or express their disagreement during voting, but at the moment it was important to proceed. His opponents continued to interrupt him, preventing him from saying what he wanted to say. They did not want to discuss the issue, let alone act on it. Besides believing that it was wrong, they were worried about what would happen when Rome found out about it.

Davidek proceeded to explain that there were two sides to the question. Sacramentally, it was not an issue. Legally, to ordain women was against canon law. The law, he said, does not cover all life situations, and this was one of the exceptions. Canon law must not infringe on God's law. "Life takes precedence over a codex. I am willing to take the risk." He spoke passionately to the assembly, saying: "The sign of the times comes from God and we are obliged to deal with it. God gives us the sign in our present situation, not through factual knowledge, but through psychological and sociological needs. It is time to deal with such a question. To accept it is something different. Those two issues are very different. This is our duty, and we have to fight for it, not force it, as some laws are forced upon us, for example, but to introduce it as our contribution to this time. In certain places society needs this service—women's ordination—as a special tool for the sanctification of the other half of humankind. I learned a lot about this while in prison. Afterward, women themselves told me about it.... It is insufficient today to keep only the male component. The people need the ordination of women. They are literally waiting for it and the church should not prevent it. If we have returned to the life-giving springs of early Christianity in everything else, then so shall it be in this."*

The discussion lasted deep into the night. The dissenters continued to try to take control of the process. They even threatened

---

*From the 1970 Council minutes.

the delegates with accusations of heresy. Finally Bishop Davidek told them to be quiet. The people were tired and hungry. Many had traveled long distances. They were sitting on the floor. The atmosphere was very tense. There was still much work to be done. By then not only were the bishops at variance, for two had stood with Davidek and four had gone against him, but the delegates had also been affected. One man, who was very gentle, turned to the women present and said, "No, girls, I would wish you this so much, but imagine what people would say to it." The entire group was divided and remained split until the end of the Council.

The vote with regard to ordaining women was taken just before daybreak. There were three possibilities in casting the secret ballot:

_____ I am for it
_____ I am against it
_____ I choose to abstain

The final result was inconclusive. Exactly half the delegates were for it and the other half against. When Ludmila heard the final count, she went out into the freezing night and wept with disappointment, as exhaustion and all the stress began to take its toll. Felix went out after her. He said: "Do not weep, Ludmila. I will do it anyway." She replied: "You mustn't do it." The brief encounter ended. They joined the others returning from break and went on with the Council program.

There was very little time left even to begin to address the concerns involving parish ministry, the only other item on the Council agenda, and a vitally important one. An attempt was made, but discussion continued to revert to the preceding question of women in ministry, for the debates and even the final vote had left many issues unresolved. Eventually, time ran out.

In his closing words to the Council, Bishop Davidek spoke to the underlying fear of schism that had filled the room. He said that for a schism to occur there were two essential requirements: "an agreement on both sides and a conscious separation from Rome." He assured those who had raised this concern that you have to want to break away from Rome, and both sides have to concur that this is indeed the intention. He said: "The Spirit speaks through the whole church." This was a fundamental premise of his episcopal leadership. The Council had been one way to give voice to the people of God. One of the sisters present expressed her thanks for being allowed to participate in the Council. She said with regard to women priests: "This question is not new to me. Already as a student I was asked by a priest to pray for it. It is not necessary at this time to consider the use of women priests in the front line [the visible church] in our circumstances. It is my opinion that a woman priest could only develop her activity fully within the second line [the underground church]. The question whether any woman feels ready for it or not is inappropriate. What man would say of himself that he is ready for this vocation?"

By noon the Council was officially over and the exodus began. Throughout the rest of the afternoon delegates started returning home, leaving the village the same way they had arrived the day before. The distance that some people had to travel, the limited size of the meeting place, and the occupations of the participants meant that some delegates arrived late, others had to leave early, and some did not get there at all. Those not in attendance had sent their ballots ahead with delegates who were attending, for they had thought about the issues and had made up their minds at home. When the Council finally came to an end, Ludmila was weary to the bone.

Davidek was also exhausted. "I had never seen him so tired," Ludmila recalls. It was as if the life force had been sucked out of him. The unanticipated betrayal by four of his bishops who were colleagues and friends and the divided vote on ordaining women had cut him to the core. Things had been so upbeat, so positive, so possible in the weeks before the Council, he had thought at one point the vote to ordain might be anything but close. He had been so convinced of its necessity and of its validity that he had not prepared himself in advance for what had just transpired. It was not the vote that disturbed him the most. It was the spirit of divisiveness that had seeped into the assembly, sowing seeds of discontent among those once of one accord. Yet he could not dismiss his convictions nor discount the need he knew was there. This was the real reason why he had acted the way he did and why he would do what he had to do before the week was out.

Eleven

When there were no depths
I was brought forth,
when there were no springs abounding with water.

Proverbs 8:24

Felix, Ludmila, and Jan Blaha were the last to leave Koberice. Ludmila went directly home. Late that evening, Felix came to see her. She tells of what transpired. "He told me to get ready. He asked me if I was willing to receive ordination from his hands. He was prepared to do it. He said the decision was mine, but not to take too long to decide or to delay in telling him. I wanted to know why he was in such a hurry. Why not wait with the ordination for maybe six months or a year? He replied: 'Believe me, I cannot delay it, because I do not know what will happen to me or what will happen with us.' The times were so uncertain. He felt the pressure of that intensely. Still, I persisted. Why this haste? What else was there behind it? He told me it was his burden, that he felt it was his duty, that I knew very well how it was with him, that it was 'a matter of conscience,' that we had already spoken about it at the Council. 'If we wait for a man to approve this,' he said, 'it will never happen, so we must go ahead without it.' 'But why have you chosen me?' He replied: 'It is natural. It is one minute to twelve.' By this he meant that the issue of women priests was urgent and could no longer be ignored. Later he told me that new things are not received with open arms, and that if we want them to be accepted, we have to make them present. And how would he inform the pope? 'It is my responsibility to inform the pope. I will investigate every possible way to inform him personally. Now let's pray to the Holy Spirit.'

"It is hard to identify the criteria whereby I made my decision. There was really no time to think much about it, because I had to work. At the same time I felt like I really did not have anything to think about. In my heart everything was clear. I guess one might say that some things are done on another level of being, one that is too deep, too transparent for words. I had one full day to live with the question. Then on the way home from work on December 28, I stopped in to see Felix, and I said, 'Yes, I will receive it.' It was all very simple. I said yes to it, to receiving everything associated with it, to all of the consequences connected to it. Of course I had no idea of the size and shape of the cross that was standing just ahead of me, that was out there awaiting me. I had no idea how to develop this charism, but I accepted it with faith, with a feeling of responsibility, and with love."

Around 10:00 p.m. that evening, Ludmila went to Felix's place ready to receive the sacrament reserved through the centuries for men. "Why did I not make a retreat before becoming ordained?" It may seem surprising that she spent no time at all preparing for such a significant step, but she was already prepared, had spent a lifetime getting ready, had heard every argument for and against, had felt the call again and again and had tucked it away in a room deep within, waiting for a time such as this. What more could she have said to God that had not already been spoken in words and silences? There would be the rest of her life in the fullness of priestly ministry to hear God speak to her. Ludmila would say more pragmatically, "There just wasn't time."

Prior to her priestly ordination, Ludmila was ordained a deacon. The liturgy for ordination to the priesthood was from the Rite of Ordination According to the Roman Pontifical, literally, word for word. Felix followed the same rite used from time immemorial to ordain men as priests:

> *Consecrare et sanctificare.* . . . Vouchsafe, O Lord, to conse-
> crate and sanctify these hands by this unction and by our

blessing. That whatsoever they shall bless may be blessed, and whatsoever they consecrate may be consecrated and sanctified in the name of our Lord Jesus Christ.

Accipe potestatem offere sacrificium Deo. . . . Receive power to offer sacrifice to God and to celebrate Mass, as well for the living as for the dead, in the name of the Lord.

As a member of Koinotes, the hidden church, local manifestation of the universal church, Ludmila Javorova was ordained a Roman Catholic priest in the late night hours of December 28, 1970, by Bishop Felix Maria Davidek in the presence of his brother, Leo, who witnessed the event. Following the rite of ordination, Ludmila celebrated her First Mass—simply, quietly, together with Felix and Leo Davidek, Mary the Mother of Jesus, and all the angels and saints of God.

As she walked back home around midnight, the awareness of what had just occurred reached her in all its fullness. "It is hard to describe the moment," she says. "A space was opened up for me and I entered into it. Its depths, its beauty are perceived without words. I go toward it. I do not know what it is, but I go." She also felt happy, she says, but this was a different kind of happiness than what we usually understand by the word. As she walked toward home that December night, she realized she was crying. Ludmila had spent a lifetime keeping her tears in check, had struggled to suppress her emotional response, to conceal the deep feelings within her. She did not like it when she cried. She had put up with it when she was young, but tonight? "I would always be holding my emotions back. I thought I would be over it by now. But in those first hours of priesthood, I can say I saw the beauty of God, at one moment I received the mercy of God, and I thought, I am crying. And I said, 'Get used to it. And let others get used to it. I am just going to cry!'" On entering her home, Ludmila smiled. Another little girl was crying, her niece, Bohumila. She remembered it was her name day—the name means "loved by God"—and she gifted the child with her blessing, the blessing of a brand new priest. She whispered, "You have such an important day for celebrating your name. When you are grown up, I will tell you about it, but for now, it is a secret."

Ludmila kept her secret. That was one of the conditions of her being ordained. She could tell no one about it. She did not tell her mother, nor did she tell her father. "A major problem for me at the time was, how would I celebrate Mass so that no one at home would see it? For the first few days, I went to Felix's place or Felix came to mine and we would celebrate together. Because he usually came every day, nobody was surprised or suspected any-thing. Later, I celebrated alone when everyone was sleeping. This secrecy was one of the many things I offered up for transformation during Mass.

"Felix always wished that the people would express aloud the words of consecration with the priest, so they would realize they too are celebrating the Mass. The priest is there as a servant. He is the one presiding, but they do everything together with him, and that's how a beautiful unity is formed. And so the Holy Mass becomes an act of salvation. Everything in this world is changing. There is nothing stable. People get used to its small acts and participate with joy. When the priest celebrates genuinely, he—or she—becomes attuned, and this helps to prevent the priest from becoming self-centered. Now that I was a priest and celebrating Mass together with him, I knew exactly what he meant and felt the same as he."

TWELVE

Now you are wrecked by the seas,
in the depths of the waters.

Ezekiel 27:34

Ludmila had little time to dwell on the fact that she was now a priest. During the days following her ordination, she anticipated repercussions from the Council and was attuned to all that was said and done. At daily Mass she was sick at heart whenever she thought of Koberice. "The Council was one of the most difficult moments of my entire life. It was a deep blow to my inner spirit. It is indescribable." The wisdom of hindsight would have been welcomed by her then. "Years later I understood I could not have expected anything else. New things are always accompanied by doubts, defense, and also the temptation to seek the security of law." What troubled her so profoundly was not the theoretical disagreement of the dissenting bishops. She could handle that. She could even accept their refusal to consider ordaining women as priests. It was the way they had gone about it. They had been her colleagues, her brothers in Christ with whom she had shared the Eucharist, who had worked side by side with her. They were invested with a certain authority, and she had respected them. "On the one hand, I understood them. On the other hand, I did not. I could not comprehend how they could swear to something they would so soon contradict. By bringing a woman to the Council who had not been previously approved, they violated their oath. They took an oath on the Bible, and within days they acted as if this oath had not occurred. Two days before the Council they congratulated me and expressed their joy that Davidek would soon ordain me; then during the Council they said they know of 'no-

body' among the women they knew who would be qualified to
accept the priesthood. I had trusted them completely. I felt like
I had been stabbed in the back, not by a stranger, but a friend."
After the Council Ludmila was told by some of the delegates that
they had been approached prior to the meeting and asked not
to attend it. The fact that the bishops had not been honest with
Felix or with her in the weeks preceding the Council is something
that still astounds her. It was her first experience of deceit within
an inner circle, and it would haunt her for years to come.

At the end of January 1971, Bishop Davidek convened a meeting to evaluate the Council. He accused the three opposing
bishops of breaking the promises they had made under oath, of
an abuse of trust, and of inappropriately interfering in the work of
the Holy Spirit. He gave them a personal letter eight pages long
in which he emphasized that he had full responsibility for this particular church, which was an expression of the whole church. He
criticized their disbelief in the concrete expression of Christ's mystical body, in the tangible impact of the Holy Spirit, in *kairos,* and
in the charisms of service. He accused them, by their behavior, of
driving out the Holy Spirit whom they were to await, of lacking
the courage to become a tool of the Spirit, and of refusing to accept the possibility of priesthood for women. "You didn't accept
the possibility and you didn't even want to take into account the
possibility of a vocation for women." They did not treat women
as equal partners, he said, but as persons who must still be led by
a man, as ones who they feel are not humanly mature in the natural order and therefore unable to carry the dignity of priesthood
through the supernatural order. "The glory of humility was not
demonstrated by humble abstention of the one who, at the moment, does not know." He also accused them of disorienting and
discouraging God's people and of preventing them from receiving even preliminary information according to the timetable that
had been established. "You disturbed the gathering's well-focused
prayer. You influenced, or at least you tried to influence, those

whom in humility you are to serve, to whom you are required to take the joy of the Gospel, whom you should always be liberating from the law to the freedom of the children of God." Davidek reproached the bishops for not showing the courage that was needed to take risks and to enter the darkness where God continues to call us into an unknown land, together with Abraham, Moses, and others. However, he wrote, "even these are unmistakable signs of the church," for "in the church we cannot see only its bright and lucid side," but "we have to see even the dark side," and the consequences are that "its supernatural mission is for ordinary human eyes sometimes very problematic." His final responsibility in this regard, he said, was an evaluation of the Council. "I myself am immensely obliged to the Holy Spirit for the gift of enabling us to see the concrete status and structure of Koinotes." In the end he would conclude, "The Council fulfilled its purpose."

There was a very heated discussion concerning the letter and its accusations. Davidek finally ended it. They would meet again, he said, but when he called them two months later, the bishops did not come, although one did send a substitute. Davidek discovered that they had begun developing their own program and were acting in ways that went beyond the scope of their faculties, thereby putting Koinotes at risk, for the distinction between the two groups was not really clear to others. Bishop Jiri Pojer, Davidek's liaison to Rome through Bishop Schaffran in East Germany, was one of the dissenting bishops. He and his colleagues had developed their own way of reporting their concerns to Rome. Davidek thereby lost his channel of communications to the Vatican, for Schaffran had agreed to a covert arrangement with one person only and nobody else. Later that same year, Pojer left the country for good and eventually married. In April Davidek ordained the last candidate who had been prepared by Bishop Kratky, with the bishop in attendance. The new priest was part of the dissident group. Then Davidek revoked the faculties of the three opposing bishops and banned them from continuing their work. He reminded the three bishops of the conditions of their episcopal consecrations. They were not authorized to exercise their faculties independently except in conditions of extreme emergency, such as imprisonment or deportation. The loss of their specific jurisdictions did not affect their consecration, he said, but if they wanted to continue their episcopal functions, they would have to go to Rome and arrange for that on their own. Although Bishop Stanislav Kratky also stood with the opposition, Davidek took no action against him. After these events had transpired, both the collaboration and the friendship, which had been an inseparable part of the work, were never the same again. Neither partnership nor contact with bishops and priests associated with the breakaway group would ever be restored. Ludmila states with conviction: "I can testify that Davidek prayed for it forever."

Bishop Stanislav Kratky and three of his former students—all of them bishops—left the Koinotes fellowship with others who had affiliated with them and founded their own branch of the underground church, which they also called Koinotes. It would evolve independently of Davidek. The decision of the breakaway group to retain the same name as Koinotes and their refusal to admit openly that they had severed their ties to Davidek would make it very difficult for future analysts to determine which group had performed what actions. They recruited members from among the Koinotes communities. Those opposed to women's ordination transferred their allegiance. Some who had not been informed of the conflict and were unaware of the distinctions between this new group and Davidek's group, to which they already belonged, also affiliated with them. Ludmila wanted to visit the outlying areas and update Koinotes members on what had happened and why. "Felix forbade me to carry out those visitations at that time. This was hard for me to accept, and I was angry with Felix. Today I realize, that under the circumstances, it would not have been a wise thing to do. I began to notice that certain priests were keeping their distance from me. Some treated me coldly, while others ignored me completely. At first I did not understand why they were doing this. The reason, of course, was clear. They suspected that Davidek would ordain me. If I happened to meet one of them on the street, more often than not I would be asked whether Felix had already ordained me. I did not want to deny it, but I could not tell them the truth. I always said something quite general, like, 'In this Felix acts very wisely.' I tried to encourage the individual to come back to the community. I could not force anyone into partnership, but I wanted to try to straighten things out. Whenever I made a suggestion regarding reconciliation, I was always given an answer that sounded as if it had been learned by rote, that I should not worry, that everything is okay. How I wished that this were true. These persons had and still have a place in my heart."

Developments following the Council were very stressful for Ludmila. "I had entered into the Koinotes fellowship with my whole being, because I could not do it any other way. When it split because of me, a woman, that was such a blow to me. After the Council I started to inform my parents more and more about some of my activities, but always only the most necessary things. They were not always happy about my partnership with Davidek, because they could see how demanding and dangerous to me and my health the whole thing was. They wanted me to reduce my workload. Davidek left our home daily after midnight, if there was no seminar. We always received visitors and held tutorial sessions at night."

Events leading up to the Council had also affected Ludmila deeply. "In 1970, the year of the Council, my paralyzed brother Vaclav died. So did my blind auntie. With every death the family loses something irreplaceable and immensely dear. During the night hours, Vaclav had stayed awake and prayed for priests and for the church. That was the very essence of his life." Physical exhaustion, lack of sleep, and constant stress finally had an impact. "I knew my body was responding to the pain of this experience," she says. "My psychic strength remained intact but my physical energy was depleted. I am one of those people who need silence and opportunities to be alone, because that is a source of energy for me. But during those difficult times, what I needed most was simply not available. I had so many duties to fulfill. I did not know what leisure time was. My body gave out and my spirit weakened. I fell ill, and for several years the doctors could not determine the cause. I could only say I was exhausted, but I could not tell them why. They thought one of the reasons was the fact that I was still single and that I was sorry about it, an erroneous conclusion many sick women have to endure. How little they knew about women like me. Eventually, when I fell into a coma, they diagnosed Addison's disease, but until that time I kept on working and lived only by the strength of my will. It was a serious illness. Before they found the cause, my eyesight deteriorated, and it was hard for me to see. Eventually I had to quit my outside job, but I continued to work for Koinotes. Many years would pass before I returned to outside work again."

Ludmila went through several jobs as the circumstances surrounding her changed. She realized that her physical condition, often invisible and unknown to others, was something she would have to deal with for the rest of her life. "My duties did not allow me to surrender to illness. I kept seeking help in God's providence. I saw the poverty of my humanity and I accepted it. This learning is irreplaceable, for I came to know what human weakness is and how we need to be indulgent at times. When we are not feeling well, we seem to do what we do not want to do, even though we are aware of it, because we lack the strength to do differently. I had to depend on the love of God. It was a purifying process for me and my greatest benefit of those troubled years."

*Wedding photo of
Ludmila's parents, 1924.*

*Ludmila,
at a very young age.*

Ludmila (on the right), her parents, her blind auntie (behind her), and seven brothers on Stanislav's First Communion Day.

Ludmila Javorova in 1940 on the day of her First Communion.

Ludmila (left), age fifteen, with two friends, on the feast of Corpus Christi.

Ludmila in her teens.

Ludmila in her teens.

Ludmila at work in a carpet factory in Brno during the early years of the communist era.

Bishop Felix Maria Davidek, founder of Koinotes.
Above: The bishop's coat of arms, "To be born and not to die."

Bishop Felix Maria Davidek with two of Ludmila's nieces, Bohumila (right) and her sister, Barbora.

*Ludmila
with her niece Barbora
in the early 1970s.*

*Ludmila
at her parish church,
where she is a catechist,
with one of the children
she helped prepare for
First Holy Communion.*

Ludmila Javorova (right) with Dr. Magda Zahorska, an ordained deacon, during their visit to the United States in 1997.

Ludmila in Cleveland, 1997.

Ludmila (second from right) with her sister Maria (left), their friend Majka, and their brother Josef, a married priest, in her apartment in Brno.

Ludmila (center) with her brother, Stanislav, his wife, Milada (right), their daughter, Barbora, and the author, Miriam Therese (second from right) outside their family residence in Chrlice, Ludmila's childhood home and the site of numerous Koinotes events.

Thirteen

These things God has revealed to us
through the Spirit,
for the Spirit searches everything,
even the depths of God.

1 Corinthians 2:10

There were many things that Ludmila had to carry silently within her. In the time of Totality, secrets had to be kept. Felix told her not to talk about her ordination, so she did not tell anyone, which meant she could not practice her priesthood openly, even within Koinotes. His experience at the Council had convinced Davidek that they had to proceed with caution, for even those who were affirming might not really understand. So Ludmila carried the burden and the blessing of her calling down deep within her and lived her unfolding ministry unsupported and alone. Every aspect of this new path, this challenging new reality she had to process and interpret internally on her own.

"My only concern was how I would practice my priesthood. How would I develop it? I did not have a clue. However, I did not mind. In the beginning the whole of my priesthood lay in celebrating Mass. Even though I did not have any of God's people around me, I had the community of saints and angels, God's mother, and our patron saints. Every Mass helps form the universe. This sense was strong in me. I felt connected to others who were also celebrating at home. During Totality, Masses were celebrated not only in churches but also in houses. This helped strengthen a sense of unity among us and within the church. We saw ourselves and the world beyond us all united with Christ." In addition to celebrating Mass on her own, Ludmila secretly concelebrated at the liturgies of Koinotes. During the consecration, she kept her hands hidden under the table where no one else could see them and would extend them over the Eucharistic elements of bread and wine as she silently repeated the words of consecration with the other priests.

"After my ordination, everything around me was lifted to a new dimension in my heart. I started to see everything pastorally. I talked to Christ about my attitude toward my pastoral work, my other tasks, and those things that troubled me, and in the evening I evaluated it all and placed in on the paten to offer to God for transformation. I believed—and I still believe—that Christ will complete all that is missing and will bring all things to fullness. I began to be even more dependent on Christ who, with me and through me, transformed not only the bread and the wine but my entire day.

"Because of all that I had to do, I became distant from my colleagues at work. I just did not have the time to share in their recreational activities. It was our custom to throw a party or go somewhere for a treat now and then, but I was always too busy. At first I missed these opportunities for friendship and relaxation. I love people and was close to some individuals with whom I worked. But then even when I went to a party or to some celebration, it would leave me with an emptiness so deep I felt it physically. It was after one of these parties that a man approached me and said, 'I could not measure up to you, even if I tried.' I wanted to know why. 'Because you are too pure a being and I'm too big a sinner.' He was an interesting person, an artist. He came to my office a number of times after that first encounter, although he knew nothing about me. Next to my table was a cupboard with doors. He would tell me, 'Open the cupboard door, and I will sit here in the corner and feel like I've gone to confession.' He said, 'I know you can handle it, and I have to tell these things to someone. I am terribly weak. I was unfaithful again. I don't want to do it, but I do.'

"And this happened many times. One Sunday morning, one of

my colleagues telephoned me and asked if that man was there with me, and I said no, he wasn't. My colleague said, 'He was looking for you with a terrible urgency, asking, where does she stay? He said he needed you desperately.' Well, he did not find me, and that evening he committed suicide, together with his wife. In his hand he held a letter in which he said goodbye. His wife had cancer, and she had been afraid for the future. He wrote that he wanted to end his life as a reparation to her for all the evil things he had done to her as an unfaithful husband. I think he may have been looking for me so that he could make his confession. I have never forgotten that man.

"There were many situations similar to this, instances when I was invited to share in another's personal life. People came to me with their problems. I had no idea who they were. I did not know who had sent them or how they had heard of me. They would speak in such a natural way about their difficulties. Sometimes I felt it was unbearable, what they were telling me. I could identify then with the priest who has to sit in the confessional and listen endlessly to the darker side of our humanity. These were ordinary people. I always listened attentively and felt such a deep compassion for them. After such a long confession, they needed a cleansing bath of love, needed to be soaked through with love, the love of our loving God. I knew it was God who was sending them to me. I felt so sorry for them. I wanted to reveal that source to them.

"How could I give from the gift of God to those who were in need? It was hard. I had to learn to give according to the conditions under which I lived without giving myself or others away. As soon as I started to share in people's lives, possibilities opened up for me. With case after case I learned when and where to take the first step and then the next and the next. I was sure that this was the essence of the charism I received with ordination. It was necessary for me to put aside my fear for myself and for my priesthood. Such an act of faith accompanies one forever. Once I

lay claim to my identity as a priest, I could not be separated from
it. Just like in motherhood, that connection is forever.

"There was a woman who refused to consider the Sacrament
of Reconciliation. She was one of those people who would never
think that this ministry should be given to women. She was just
not able to go to a priest. She knew she could not be open
with him, even if he were a saint. I understood her completely.
While the sacrament is a mystery, for it to be more accessible to
some requires a radical change in our understanding of things.
Such a complete revelation of one's inner being, particularly for a
woman, needs to proceed step by step in the context of a human
understanding. Some women can't share freely with a man some
problems of a personal nature, even with a man of God. This
often happens in cases where a woman's husband is a tyrant or
very patriarchal, so that the woman loses her ability to trust men
in general, thereby missing out on this opportunity for spiritual
transformation.

"Another woman came to me and told me her tragic story. She
said her husband had been sexually abusing her, how she could
not bear him anymore, how she could not go to the sacraments
anymore, because she felt like killing him. She said, 'I cannot go
to the sacraments, because there I again meet a man, and I am
not able to tell him these things. I am too afraid.' This woman
came to me many times. I would tell her how much God loves
her, that Christ is so concerned for her. She needed a woman to
minister to her. After several meetings, I prepared her to receive
the Sacrament of Reconciliation. She needed some help in understanding her inner self, which is sometimes difficult for a woman,
who will often have deep experiences but be unable to express
them adequately. She is afraid she will not be understood. She
has had her own experiences with men and finds she is unable to
meet Christ, who seems artificial to her and distant. She is fearful
of facing her own self, because to confront her guilt often means
to live through the devastation again.

"I cannot understand, when it is a matter of salvation or of helping souls in need, why the hierarchy of the church objects if a woman should enter into the process. Who is the priest? Someone to accompany people in their joy and in their suffering, who offers to go together with them, who is an experience of Christ to them, who works together with God."

For Ludmila, priesthood meant being there for others in need. "When God gives a gift, God also leads to you a person who has a need for that gift, one who will come and take from the gift and go away enriched. In those difficult moments when I was searching for ways to live out my priesthood, I said to God: 'I give myself to you totally. And God, if you agree with this, you send me people who need my help, because I have no other possibility.' And this is my testimony. I could not minister openly, not in totalitarian times, and I did not look for people. They just came to me. They would come to me in the art gallery where I worked as a kind of guard. Many strangers passed through there. We could not talk too much, but occasionally people would stop, and even a brief conversation would shift to a discussion about essence. Often we would continue talking somewhere outside the gallery. Many times someone would say at the end, 'It's a pity you aren't a priest, because we could finish with confession.' So in my heart I said, 'Let God forgive you, and may you see God's mercy.' I could not openly say, 'I absolve you.' I encouraged these persons to go to confession. I said, don't be afraid of the man. Go in all simplicity. The priest is there as a sign. At least you could rehearse with me what you have to say and how you might express it. Later at home I would reflect, 'This is the work of woman, the work that is not visible but is needed to be complete.' Priests may smile at this or dismiss it, but I have found that for many people, interpretation is the mechanism that influences them to change, that enables them to go forward to do what they could not have done before. I prepared people for confession when there was a need. The person needed to meet God, and God chose this way for them. I feel in my heart that when I have shared with another in this way, we have met within and encountered God there.

"When I was working in that gallery, crowds would come to view the collections, so I met a lot of people. Once certain people discovered that there was someone willing to spend time with them, they would come and share various things with me. They just wanted someone to listen to them, and in those moments of listening, I experienced a deep powerlessness. Because that feeling was so strong in certain instances, I had to turn all my inner being toward God and say: 'I accept this individual as someone you sent to me. I could only do this small thing. Now I give this person back to you. Do not abandon her. Or, be with him, Lord.' Some persons kept returning. Others came only once. When there were really many for whom I had a deep concern, I said: 'Lord, I cannot pray anymore. So then I take them all as one. I tie them together, put them in a bag, a big bag, and I give them to you as a parcel. Please, remember them.' At those times I cannot say that I felt I was doing something useful. Just the opposite. I felt useless, powerless. I was attentive, very attentive, so that the meeting would not become mechanical. I listened to them with care and concern, and then with all my heart, I gave them to God."

Ludmila was never certain what direction her newfound ministry would take. The driving force that had led Koinotes to consider ordaining women as priests, culminating in her ordination, had been concern for the sacramental needs of incarcerated women. "I thought, I will be in prison soon. There will be different types of women there, and they will not accept me. What reason will I find for ministering to them? I was simply getting ready, preparing myself for something different than what actually occurred." What happened was, in the course of events, she never got arrested. It was certainly better for Koinotes, for while she did not know everything, she certainly knew a lot. It would have been disastrous if the StB had somehow managed to extract information from her. Considering the scope of her contribution, one also wonders what Koinotes would have done had they been forced to go on without her.

"I wanted to serve women in prison. Every day I expected to be arrested, but I was not arrested. My post was vicar general in Koinotes. Then I started to learn what this ordination meant and whom I was to serve. On the day of ordination one does not become a priest; one accepts one's ministry. I accepted my ordination because I wanted to serve. The essence of priesthood is ministry, and I was the one to choose it. Although I was not imprisoned, I was in permanent danger." Life itself, lived in secret and attuned to danger, became the permanent context of Ludmila's ministry. "One accepts that ministry," she says, "and then one develops the charism, which is the special gift inherent in the call." As she practiced her ministerial skills of welcoming, listening, forgiving, encouraging, leading people to God, Ludmila linked all of these to the daily Eucharist. "I was aware that each Mass is an action that affects the whole universe." Day after day the blessings of the Mass and of her priestly calling came to that corner of the universe that was her pastoral charge. "What changed from the day of my ordination is this: I started every evening by blessing the whole world. And I was aware of the fact that it was the blessing of the priest."

In August of 1971 Leo Davidek, the brother of Felix, witness to Ludmila's ordination, died a tragic death during an archaeological expedition. It came as a shock to Felix. Ludmila mourned the loss with him.

For a time Ludmila had less work to do, as Koinotes struggled to adjust to a major structural change. In one sense it would never again have the same strength and dynamism it had before the group split apart. Some of the places where seminars used to meet had to be closed, because it was no longer safe to go there. The StB had started to harass them again. Josef Javora was used to this. "Our neighbor who lived in a different house with windows on the same level as ours was from the StB. In fact we had often seen his wife searching through the rubbish bin just outside the building, looking for envelopes with addresses."

Meanwhile, the breakaway branch was growing. They were ordaining priests and consecrating bishops and increasing in membership. Those that had split from Davidek over the issue of ordaining women because it was against canon law consecrated a married bishop, which was contrary not only to the canons of the Roman Catholic Church but also to the laws of the Greek Catholic Church. There would be other married bishops during the years that followed.

Sometime after Koinotes and the breakaway group had reestablished themselves and were functioning independently, Ludmila applied to the faculty of law in Brno for admission to the program. She received a telephone call from the woman in charge of the personnel department confirming her application. She remembered Ludmila from the time when she had worked at the institute. It was during the early years of "normalization" when the regime had begun to eradicate all vestiges of freedom following Prague Spring. She knew Ludmila liked law, and she recommended her for admission. Felix did not approve, although he encouraged everyone else to pursue further studies. He said to Ludmila, "Okay, I will not prevent you, but it will be impossible to combine both things. It is either law or Koinotes." There really was no choice. "When they told me I had been accepted and invited me to enroll for studies, I didn't go." There was another reason why Felix did not support Ludmila in her decision to study law. He was convinced that all of them would soon be deported to Siberia. Some years later she applied to a school in Slovakia to study economics. "My brother had studied in Slovakia. I felt I would be less visible there. Since we were not yet in Siberia, I thought I would finally go to school, but this time, they refused me."

Ludmila continued to accompany Bishop Davidek on his pastoral visitations of convents and monasteries. "He wanted those who were members of religious orders to initiate a program of renewal," she reports. "He was a strong advocate for a renewed life and kept in touch with the various orders." He also maintained close contact with those who had been ordained. Most Koinotes priests in Moravia were able to attend some of the society's meetings in Brno, where they could share their experience of ministering to a small circle of friends at home. Those who were unable to attend such meetings were visited when possible. Some of those visited were pastors, while others worked alone. Felix and Ludmila traveled to Slovakia countless times between 1972 and 1978. Felix also made a point of visiting priests in parishes that were part of the visible church and therefore beyond his jurisdiction. Those visits were not official. They were pastoral calls to encourage and support priests performing their duties in difficult times and in isolated places where the bishopric was vacant.

At that time bishops were interned at home and their diocese was placed under the leadership of a state-appointed vicar general, who carried out his duties under the supervision of a state secretary. Priests had no contact with their bishops. Davidek was careful to check beforehand where he could or could not go. The decision to visit was based on whether he would be accepted and whether he would be safe. Ludmila reports, "I was always with him on those pastoral visits. It was often difficult to decide whether or not to accompany him, especially when I could see other needs and other compelling ways to invest my energies. But in this I learned to abandon my ideas. Davidek wished me to accompany him, and he had a reason for it. He needed to know the terrain and to understand the situation. This called for a contrasting point of view, which was something I could give. Everything he did, and I learned to do, was for the benefit of pastoral projects. They were not always pleasant journeys for me. Felix did not tell those priests why I had come with him, and they were often uncivil to me. Some trips I will never forget.

"Once when we went to perform an ordination in the Czech region of the country, we had an accident with the car. We were carrying with us the *Pontificale Romanum* and a chalice, plus everything needed for the rite of ordination and the celebration of Mass. My sister and another bishop had come along with us. We had already gone some distance when the car hit a patch of ice, skidded out of control, and headed toward a brook. It crashed into a tree, which kept it from falling into the water, but the back had been badly smashed. There were no people around. Our coats, everything was in the trunk. Felix kept saying, 'We have to open the trunk. All our things are in there and the police cannot see them.' We clawed at the trunk with our bruised fingers and finally got it open. We dragged the big bag, Felix and I, over the fields and into the forest. We had no idea where we were going. Maria and the bishop remained with the car. We walked and walked and walked through the forest in the dark of night and then into some village. We took a train and then changed to another that took us to Brno. We arrived in the middle of the night, and I waited until noon the next day before returning home. I told my blind auntie who came to the door that she had to sneak me into the house so my parents wouldn't see I was injured. I had to wear pants for a month so people wouldn't ask about the bruises on my legs. The accident aggravated an old injury from a fall on the ice some years before. Spinal surgery had left my leg paralyzed for a time. Fortunately, once again, I recovered.

"One year after he ordained me, Bishop Davidek told me that I should not remain alone, that we had to begin to pray so that he might ordain at least one more woman." Within the next several years, Davidek ordained three other women so that Ludmila would not be the only one. Their ordinations were also secret. One of his reasons for doing this: so that "what becomes reality may never be erased again." A more fundamental reason: because there was a need. There were no contacts with Rome at the time and Davidek had been given the faculty to provide for the needs of the church. After he ordained these women, he did not ordain any more.

In August 1973 a second Council within Koinotes took place in Cerveny Dul with much less preparation and none of the intensity that accompanied the first. It was an attempt to define the role of women in ministry and was said to have been organized primarily by the women. Ludmila participated in its preparation. They designed the liturgy for a children's Mass, a liturgy for the ill and weak, and also a women's liturgy. Priests were sent this material and asked to comment on it. Except for a few individuals, they returned it without any notations. Ludmila says, "It was hard for me to understand this." She attended the Council for a very short time in order to read the piece she had prepared and then left because of illness. She reports: "I emphasized to Felix and to the woman in charge to record everything immediately; otherwise it would be impossible to organize a report afterward." Of course, that did not happen. "I do not have any material from this Council," she says, "only some small pieces of paper with Felix's scribbled notes. I tried to complete those materials for many years after the event, but after some time and the pressure to conceal anything of value, it was not possible any more."

The three other women ordained by Davidek eventually left the priesthood. There were many contributing factors that led to their decision. An overall feeling of apathy concerning women's ministries, lack of support and acceptance, an absence of pastoral opportunities, and an ever-present threat of danger made life extremely difficult for those who had been eager to serve. It was hard enough to be called to priesthood in a secret church, but to be a secret within the secret, as the women priests were forced to be, was a very large burden to bear. The intensity of negative reactions to the issue of women in ministry, pressure to conform to the expectations of church and society, and perhaps a growing uncertainty about the validity of their ordinations may have been too much for these pioneering women to sustain without the tangible affirmation of a supportive community.

Three more women were ordained to the priesthood in Slovakia, two by the Basilian Bishop Nikodem Krett from another
branch of the underground church and one by a Jesuit bishop,
who was a member of Koinotes. A total of seven women were ordained as priests in Czechoslovakia, as far as anyone knows. Only
Ludmila remained a priest. The other six did not, for reasons of
their own.

"My ministry consisted of individuals and hospitals, where the
priest was not able to go," Ludmila says. "It was easier for a woman
to get into the hospital when someone was sick." Her ministry was
carried out in simple and meaningful ways. "I visited an old woman
in a home for the blind. Although she herself could see, she had
accompanied her blind sister to the home to be her companion
there. I would bring them the Eucharist. When the woman lay
dying, I prepared her for the Sacrament of the Sick and for her
last confession. Then I went for the priest, who sighed as he approached her and said, 'I don't know what to say to her. With
these old, ill people, it is so difficult.' He did not know she was
facing death, so he gave her the sacrament and left. I remained
with her. Before she died this woman said: 'When I meet God
I will ask that women could also be priests.' I was very touched
by this. Here was an old woman in a home for the elderly saying such a thing. She said this during her final hours, when she
was already separating from this world and entering the next, so
I thought, she must be sensing something we here cannot know.
This encouraged me a lot. It was a validation of my priesthood,
and it was magnificent."

Why did Ludmila call the priest when she herself was a priest?
"In the beginning I had permission to administer the Sacrament
of Reconciliation only if I were imprisoned. Several years later
I received the faculty to administer the sacrament to those who
knew about my ordination and who came to me to receive it.
Several women and men received the sacrament from me. But
what would it have meant to others, especially people who were

approaching death, a new thing at such a sensitive time? One has to prepare them for something like this, for the ministry of a woman priest. When somebody is dying, you have to be very careful to give assurance and security. This is done best through familiar things with a basis in their past."

Ludmila was especially concerned about the dying. "I always brought my oils with me in case there would be some emergency somewhere, someone in danger of death." She was not allowed to minister in public, so she had to be discreet. To ensure the personal safety of all those involved in clandestine activities, the secret had to be carefully kept, not only from the communists, but also from those within the church. Individuals who knew about Ludmila continued to come to her for confession. Among those who did were many who refused to go into the confession box. They needed to be prepared for this.

The ordination of a woman was a decisive turning point in the development of the underground church and in the life of Davidek. "It seems to me almost from that point, from the day when he ordained me, that he had exhausted all his energies." From then on there was a distinct decline. It may have been imperceptible at times, but not to someone like Ludmila, who had worked with him so closely. "I could see that after the split he had lost some of his habitual dynamism, as if somehow he had achieved his goal." Sometime during 1974, he suffered a blood clot and nearly died. He stayed with Ludmila's parents until he was well again. The fact that Ludmila did not have outside employment during the years that followed proved to be a blessing. "It would have been impossible to do all the work that needed to be done if I also had a daytime job. For the first eight years we had worked day and night, and it took its toll on us. We still had to cope with the pressure and stress, but now I had time to do it. The work of Koinotes was very demanding. However, I always did what was needed, not what I would have liked to do."

Koinotes had its own internal structure. The term "parish" was not part of their vocabulary, except in a few cases involving the independent pastoral work of individual priests. Koinotes was simply a society of people, of friends. The pastoral project of the inner leadership circle was the coordination of all its expressions, which was difficult to realize. There was a group of clergymen who ministered to priests, to the wives of Greek Catholic clergymen, and to abandoned persons. Other persons were designated to take care of priests who had abandoned their ministry, and there was a pastoral ministry to those priests who were retiring, or were very old, or sick, or all alone.

There was also a specific category for the so-called "patriot priests," those who collaborated with the communists as members of an organization called Pacem in Terris, which had been introduced by the state. Whether to gain some advantage in their personal life or in their work as priests, or for reasons known only to the priests themselves, clergy connected with Pacem in Terris often cooperated with the StB or otherwise supported the regime. Davidek was severely criticized for reaching out and ministering to them, but he believed that this was essential. He said, "The priest has to be in those places where it seems that the Christ is losing." This project, even though it was precisely elaborated, was never fully developed.

Coordination of Koinotes and its multiple ministries was a time-consuming function that often meant driving long distances. Although they were not affiliated with Koinotes, there was a strong Czech faith community living in Romania, and when Felix heard they were there, he said: "We must go and see them. When their visitation was completed, Felix and Ludmila went looking for frescoes of the Byzantine Empress Irene, who in 787 had influenced the Second Council of Nicea, which was the seventh ecumenical council and the last one considered ecumenical by the Orthodox churches. Ludmila says, "We found those frescoes in a monastery in the mountains. It was on a treacherous road. A priest who accompanied us was supposed to take pictures of the frescoes, and he did, but on the way home he realized that he did not have film in the camera." Before leaving Romania, Felix and Ludmila visited a monument in the capital city of Bucharest and then went to an antiques shop, because Felix loved ancient art and antiquated things. Ludmila tells the story. "Felix asked the man to show him the most ancient and precious artifacts, and after a certain period of time, the man brought out a bracelet from Egypt, one with a lot of miniature bangles that make a noise when you move your hand. Felix looked at it and liked it a lot. He began bargaining for it. He really wanted the bracelet, but he would not agree to the final price offered by its owner. Suddenly the shopkeeper said, 'This bracelet is cursed. Do you really want it?' And Felix said, 'Yes.' So he bought it. I liked it very much. I said to Felix, 'I will wear it on my wrist, just for the journey home.' So I put it on, and along the way, I shook my wrist and listened. 'It makes such a beautiful sound,' I said, 'no evil spirit can be disturbed by this.' There were four of us in the car—the driver, Felix, the sister of my sister-in-law, and me.

"As we branched off onto the road that would take us out of Slovakia and into Moravia, we had an accident. Only one lane was open, because the other was being repaired, so two-way traffic had to squeeze into a much narrower space. A car ahead of us had just had an accident, demolishing the sign that said, slow down. Not seeing the sign, we drove full speed ahead, and before we realized what was happening, we had left the pavement and were flying through the air, then rolling, rolling, rolling over, until we came to a stop. It was a terrible crash. The car was split in two. The others had fallen out of the car, but the door on my side was so crumpled they could not open it. They thought I was dead. The driver and the sister of my sister-in-law were screaming. I sat there with blood coming out of my ears, and I said, "Keep quiet, I'm dying." I know that if someone is bleeding from the ears, then the cranial area is seriously injured, and so it may mean the end. But they would not keep quiet, because they were in shock. A tourist bus from Yugoslavia saw the accident and stopped. They came to me first to pull me out, because I was trapped in the car, but I didn't mind being there. I was calmly waiting for death. I had been to confession that afternoon and I was not afraid. I was experiencing a deep peace. Then suddenly I felt the ground. The Yugoslavians had set me down on the wet grass of the meadow, right beside the car. I did not recognize who they were, could not understand what they were saying. I kept asking myself, "Am I still alive? Am I still alive?" Then suddenly I knew where I was and was fully aware of what had happened.

"The driver and my sister-in-law's sister were taken to the hospital in the tourist bus. I went over to Felix who was sitting on a seat that had fallen from the car. 'What are we going to do now?' I asked. Felix would only say, 'They must not discover anything,' for we had with us in the car everything for Mass, and even some study materials. I dragged myself to the broken car, without shoes, without glasses, so I couldn't see anything clearly, and pulled out a piece of tarpaulin. I opened it up and laid it on the ground and then crawled on my hands and knees, searching for things that had fallen from the car. I crawled around the road. I crawled back and forth across the meadow adjacent to the car, and whatever I found I put into the tarp and then folded it all into a bundle. Felix asked me to find the nearest telephone and call the local parish house. 'Ask someone to come for us, so that we don't fall into the hands of the police.' And so I went . . . shoeless, bleeding, with all of my injuries, my hair sticking out all over the place . . . I went to look for a phone. I found one and called the parish house, and they said that the priest was not there. He had gone into the city. So I went back to Felix.

"When I reached him, the ambulance was there, but Felix refused to go to the hospital. He said he wanted only first aid. He repeated over and over, 'I am a medical doctor. Everything is in order. I am really okay. Take care of this woman.' But in fact he was not okay, as we would discover later. They put us in the ambulance and took us to Brno. I can't imagine what they thought of us, clinging to this bulky bundle when we were so badly bruised. As soon as the ambulance door was closed, I passed out and did not regain consciousness until I was in a bed in the emergency wing of the hospital. Felix, who had taken charge of the bundle, was delivered to the home of my brother Josef. A week later Felix was admitted to a different hospital. His spine had been fractured in three places. He was put into a full body cast and would be bedridden for almost a year. While I was still in the hospital, Marian Kabelka, one of our bishops, came to visit me. Afterward he went to see my brother Josef, with whom Felix had been living. He said, 'She will surely die. I had to give her the Last Rites.' He said I was blue, green, yellow, that there wasn't a place without a bruise, and there was blood all over me. My brother did not tell my parents. He did not want to frighten them. He said that I had some work to do and that I would be staying with him. I stayed at his place for some time after I was released from the hospital, but then we had to tell them the truth. It was impossible to conceal it any longer.

"When I was able to walk again, I went to see Felix in the hospital. He suggested that I ask someone to drive me to the site of the crash so that I could look around once more to make sure we hadn't left something behind. A wonderful man who had spent twelve years in prison and now had three children drove me back to that place. The moment I sat down in the car, fear came over me. I went rigid at every curve in the road. Then Lada said to me, 'Before every curve we'll sing.' He started singing and whistling, and as we approached a curve, we would both be singing and whistling, and then I relaxed. We didn't find anything in the field because it was a long time after and the grass had already been cut. I had hoped to find the bracelet. It made such a lovely sound."

Ludmila visited the distant circles of Koinotes on Davidek's behalf. Most often she was well received, but sometimes she was not. She had to travel far because Koinotes was widespread. She went by public transport. The connections were very bad. Sometimes she stayed in a hotel, especially in winter, but when there was a danger of being questioned by the StB, she would stay with someone she knew. Another set of travels related to her function as messenger. Often the message was a warning to watch out for the StB. The police knew there were ordained priests in the Koinotes network. They even knew who some of them were, and when someone was brought in for questioning, the police would name names, asking if we knew the persons.

The rule Davidek had established was: inform the individual through others if their name was mentioned in another's interrogation, because they could be certain they would be the next to be called. He would come from an interrogation and say, "Ludmila, go and inform these people that the police already know about their ordination. Tell them not to deny it. If they say openly, yes, I am ordained, the police will be satisfied for the moment and will not investigate further, but if they try to deny it, the police will think they are hiding something. They will persist in digging deeper, and this would be far more dangerous. The police will continue to patrol them anyway. They will have to reduce their pastoral activities for a time, but they do not have to hide the fact that they are celebrating Mass." She would deliver the message immediately to those intermediaries who had been specifically designated to go and warn the priests, so they would not be caught off-guard. Once, at a particularly tense time, Davidek sent a message to a group of priests telling them to let up on all activities for three or four months until things had settled down and the interrogations had subsided. They would not listen to him, because they had already affiliated with the other group. They accused him of saying yes to the police when asked if the men they had named were priests. Obviously, they did not understand Davidek. This was something he would never do.

In 1975 Libuse Hornanska, known locally as Liba, was ordained a deacon in the underground church. There were three, perhaps four female deacons within the Koinotes network. Here is Liba's story, which she tells in her own words.

"The desire arose in me around 1957, because I knew from the Scriptures that in the early church female deacons existed. It was very difficult here at that time. Priests had challenging assignments in places near the borders. A priest I knew was sent to one of those remote areas and I went along with him as a teacher of religious education. The parish was in the middle of nowhere, literally, and the priest was already ill with severe tuberculosis. He had to visit distant villages, so I took on some of his responsibilities, for example, at the school. The local people would tell me he was not even able to carry his bag up the hill to the parish house, because he was so ill. He had nobody else to assist him in the church. He needed someone to prepare the table and vessels for Mass. We had to have a special authorization to allow us to help him even in this very limited way. I realized then how useful it would be if a woman would be able to have this lower ordination as a deacon, so we would not always need permission for all these necessary things. That is how this desire arose in me, and it resonated with what I had found was already there in Scripture.

"Exactly ten years later, in 1967, I joined a group of women that had assembled around Professor Kratky. The group, similar to a religious order, was connected to Koinotes. Kratky had wanted to start a new congregation of religious women, and one year later, in 1968, he sent two of us to Rome to take our religious vows. We were received in a private audience by Pope Paul VI, who gave us permission to take our vows. He also gave us his blessing for our work in Czechoslovakia. I got to know then that Paul VI did not think negatively about the diaconate for women or even about the ordination of women. Not that he would allow it or publicly promote it, but he was sort of in favor of it, or so it seemed to me. I decided then that I wanted to be ordained a deacon. Before leaving Rome, we went to the church of Saint Mary Major and made our vows into the hands of our hidden bishop who was there in Rome with us. My religious name was Oblata Maria Tau.

"When I began to inquire about the possibility of ordination as a deacon, I discovered that Bishop Kratky, who at first had favored women deacons, had now changed his mind. He said to me, 'If you want to pursue this, go to Davidek.' He had lost interest in the group of women who had formed around him. He had been cooperating with Bishop Davidek for some time, but because of some divergence between them, they split, and he abandoned us. Not long after that, our group fell apart. People went elsewhere, especially to the lay movements that were already established here, or to some sort of religious order. Some joined spirituality groups, while others left and got married. So I went to Felix, we talked things through, and he agreed to my request. He said, 'Okay. You can begin preparing to be ordained a deacon. We will begin with tonsure.' Only a symbolic piece of my hair was cut in the brief ritual he performed.

"Two other sisters besides myself had come to Davidek, and he handed the three of us over to a bishop from Koinotes who prepared us for ordination. The other two women who were with me were much younger than I was. I am advanced in age, but I believe the Spirit is ageless.

"We studied during the totalitarian regime. I was very grateful for this opportunity. The Koinotes bishop who instructed us would send me to the old people's home where I prepared residents for the sacraments. He also allowed me to bring the Eucharist to them. When the bishop celebrated Mass, we three female deacons participated to the degree possible as deacons. For example, the bishop would ask me to preach the homily on occasion.

"Then on June 21, 1975, the bishop came up to me and said, 'Come to a meeting.' He didn't tell me anything else, but on the spot he announced, 'Now I will ordain you a deacon.' I was already fully prepared. I cannot say the name of the bishop who ordained me, because I do not have permission to reveal it, and he is now doing pastoral work in the official church. Although Bishop Davidek did not ordain any of us as deacons, I can say it was because of him that I was ordained. To be a deacon is my vocation. I believe that God has accepted it, and that it is valid. Sacrifice is important for me, because my name is Oblata, from *oblata caritatis*, which means 'given to love.' Oblata also means the unconsecrated host, which will become the body of Christ. It is for all humankind, so that all humankind will be transformed into Christ. My name is also Tau, from the Greek word for cross, because all of this process is connected with suffering, so transformation can take place."

There were other female deacons in the underground church in Czechoslovakia, but only two—Libuse Hornanska in Moravia and Dr. Magda Zahorska in Slovakia—have chosen to reveal their names.

FOURTEEN

O the depth of the riches and wisdom
and knowledge of God!
How unsearchable are God's judgments
and how inscrutable God's ways.

Romans 11:33

In 1976 the Vatican sent a representative, Monsignor John Bukovsky, to meet with Bishop Davidek. The papal messenger brought greetings from Pope Paul VI, asked about the work of Koinotes, and wanted to know if it was true that Davidek had ordained a woman. Felix was reluctant to respond affirmatively. He had always felt that this information had to be given directly to the pope. The issue of women priests was discussed. Ludmila was present for this meeting. She quotes from the minutes she recorded at the time. "When Monsignor Bukovsky asked Felix what his present activity was, he said, among other things, that from the point of dogma, he was working on dogma related to the ordination of women. Bukovsky responded: 'It is necessary to carry out some research.'" "This," says Ludmila, "confirms that the pope recognized Davidek's episcopacy." She adds some contextual information. "The meeting took place in the house of Felix's sister-in-law, which had been his family home. It was a very difficult setting. There was no space, no privacy, no peace and quiet, not what one would expect for a diplomatic mission. I had made a new white dress just for this occasion and wore a chain with a pendant in the shape of a big cross. This may have been the reason for the rumors that circulated later on, that I was a bishop."

Although that meeting was cordial and held no hint of censure, pressure to conform came later that year in the form of a prohibition from Rome. Davidek was informed that he should stop consecrating bishops and ordaining priests. The word was delivered orally through a Vatican representative in Czechoslovakia. Ludmila was not present at the time. She said: "Felix told me later, 'They want me to stop my activities.'" The ban came several times. However, Davidek felt these admonitions were based on insufficient information and should not be taken seriously. Vatican representatives tried to meet with him. They invited him to a hotel, but Davidek refused, once because of illness, at other times because he felt he would be walking into a trap. All hotels were equipped with concealed microphones to record such conversations, especially in the case of a conference with the Vatican. People who had no direct experience of communism would not understand this.

What more could he have told the Vatican emissaries? All activities were the result of special faculties given for a specific situation such as the repressive communist regime that was still going on. "This must not be understood as a refusal to negotiate or as disobedience," says Ludmila. "From his point of view it was a wise thing to do." Felix felt Rome did not understand the local situation. Cardinal Agostino Cassaroli openly criticized Bishop Davidek, and Felix wrote him a fiery letter in response. In fact, says Ludmila, "The letter was so fierce that I refused to sign it. I tried to get him to change it a bit, but he would not water it down." Unjust accusations against him began to appear in the press. As Ludmila says succinctly: "This was the last drop over the top of the chalice."

Davidek was not only angry. He also distrusted the intentions of Rome's representatives. There was a bit of history to justify his concerns. Following the Soviet invasion in 1968, Vatican policy shifted. Faced with the fact that communism was probably here to stay, deals were made with the government to allow the church to consecrate bishops for places with vacancies. Some were from Pacem in Terris. Davidek felt that the Vatican itself may have been infiltrated and that Cardinal Cassaroli might be collaborating with the StB.

In 1977 Ludmila moved out of her parents home and into a place of her own, a two-room apartment in a block of flats in Stara osada, a section of Brno. Felix came to live with her. This scandalized some people. Malicious rumors circulated, slandering Ludmila and her family by distorting the facts and the reasons why she was living with a man. For Felix it was just another move. He had slept in borrowed beds from the time of his release from prison. He never settled down in any one place, never had a permanent home. At first he lived for a short time in the house where he grew up, but because it was under construction and he had an allergic reaction to dust, he stayed with Ludmila's parents for a while and then moved in with her brother Josef and made that his residential address, which he registered with the police. One's permanent address had to be on record at the police station, so they would know where you lived. Although Josef lived in a two-room flat and was married and had two children, he gave a room to Felix. For years the seminars were held there and the space was filled with books. Felix stayed with Josef for more than four years and then occasionally with Majka, who was part of Koinotes. From time to time throughout the years he would return to Stepanov for an extended period of time. Now he was with Ludmila. He wanted to be in the city, where everything was near, where he did not have to depend on public transportation, and where he had anonymity. "His mail was sent to my brother's house, just as it had always been," she says, "because that was where he was registered for his permanent residence." He stayed for nearly five years. He was given the kitchen for a combination bedroom and study. Ludmila settled into the parlor.

The central site of Koinotes operations moved from Josef's house to Ludmila's apartment. All matters of importance that had to be communicated were written down on paper, which was torn up afterward and flushed away or burned. "Somebody was always on guard during conferences, watching the surroundings both inside and outside our massive apartment complex to make sure no one was watching us. Once, while we were teaching, one of the men in our group needed a cigarette, so he went outside the apartment to smoke and he surprised a man out there, someone we had never seen before. Startled at being discovered, the stranger pretended to be tying his shoelaces. When asked who he was looking for, he did not reply. He seemed very nervous and he quickly walked away. This was yet another indication that we were being watched."

Those who had been in prison would speak of the fear that arose whenever a certain envelope arrived. To be called for interrogation triggered a latent programmed response. An initial fear was followed by a string of buried memories releasing unresolved anger from out of the past. Felix, however, was different. "I never saw fear in Felix," says Ludmila, who was there at a time when Felix received a summons from the StB, "but he did have to struggle against it, and he did that by designing ways to take control of the situation. He was very good at that. His primary strategy, which I really didn't agree with, was not to react immediately. When an envelope from the StB had come in the past, he simply ignored it. They sent four notifications before he finally acted. He said it gained him time and sometimes more information about what it was they were after." Once again Felix received a summons to appear for interrogation, but four days later he became ill and could not go anywhere, so the StB came to him. This worked out well for Ludmila. "The interrogation took place in my apartment. This proved to be an advantage for me, because I could hear what they were asking and how he was responding.

"Then I was summoned for questioning, and I too did not respond. After a few days, the StB called me at my workplace. They went on the attack. They said that if I did not go there immediately, they would come and get me. In order to prevent that from happening, I went. Felix had prepared me in advance. He said, 'You direct the interrogation. Do not leave it to the StB. You have to take control.' This was very important advice because there are many interrogators there who are cross-examining you. Psychologically, the atmosphere is very tense. You can easily panic. Before I went I remembered stories I had heard from others interrogated and even imprisoned by the StB, how they woke them up in the middle of the night or came to them at meal time. My brother-in-law had said they would awaken him many times in the night with a bright light in his eyes and the interrogation would begin. Sometimes he stood with his arms outstretched for twenty-four hours out in the cold. He told how they prayed the rosary when he was in Jachymov. That prison is near a Marian shrine where people go for pilgrimage. From afar the prisoners would look for houses with their lights still on at night. Ten windows brightly lit would be a decade of the rosary.

"When it was my turn to be interrogated, I thought of some Scripture passages, especially the words, 'Don't worry.' I knew it wouldn't be easy, but I was determined to get through it. Of course, if they had started to beat me, that would be a different thing. Fortunately, they didn't. The first thing I experienced was fear—fear that I might betray someone, fear I would say something I shouldn't say. As they led me through the corridor, the fear began to subside. When they began to question me, I was helped by Davidek's advice. They pulled out a pile of papers and said, 'Look how much information we already have on you.' I said, 'You do have a lot of information.' But then they started telling me that I was in this place and that place meeting this and that person, and then I got a bit scared. They said, 'You want to belong to a religious order.' I thought, how could they know such a thing? But at that moment I heard Davidek's words and I remained composed. I thought, I am in control of this interrogation. I will not succumb to them. They tried to threaten me, to make me afraid by saying, we know this and we know that and if you don't respond to us, we will draw our own conclusions. I said to myself, this is only the beginning. If they start beating me, what will I do? Then I told my imagination to stop. Although I felt insecure and fearful at times, the instructions Felix gave me were sufficient for me to manage.

"My experience was nothing compared to those who had to endure torture. I cannot imagine what I would do if that had happened to me, if I were not allowed to sleep, if I were beaten or tortured. Just to picture myself in prison, not knowing if it is day or night, not knowing how long all this will take, having no contact with the outside world, being hungry and being accompanied by a dreadful spiritual dryness, because it was normal in prison to be spiritually bereft. Those who endured such things were martyrs. Felix would often say to the bishops and priests on the coordinating team at the core of Koinotes that they had to be prepared for persecution, even from the *curia romana,* who would render a persecution of a different kind. Whenever he returned from an interrogation he would say, 'God is going to build a major blossoming of the church out of all of this.' I believe it as well. These are the hidden sacrifices that fertilize the soil, so that fruit may come forth and flourish."

In September 1978 Bishop Felix Davidek ordained Frantisek Javora a priest in the Greek Catholic Rite. Ludmila, vicar general of Koinotes, witnessed the ordination. Frantisek was eighty years old. "It was Sunday. The sun was shining. It was a beautiful day. My father's longing had been fulfilled. The celebration was quite simple. It took place in the family home with my mother at his side. In his homily Davidek said: 'When someone is given the gift of marriage, it is a gift of the Holy Spirit. In marriage two dwell in one body. One affects the other. The one who has more at the moment of marriage can later lose or with patience gain. You gained this calling. You should thank your wife and ancestors, and even those we do not know who are praying for you.' Josef and Stanislav were also there. Some of his young grandchildren joined him later that night when he celebrated his First Mass. I know that my father then said to my mother, who already had problems walking: 'So you see, now you will not have to wait for somebody to take you to church.'

"My mother had known of my father's desire and supported it completely. She used to say to him jokingly when he did something wrong: 'You should have been a priest, not a father.' Or, '*Tatinek, Tatinek,* you should have been a priest. You must have been standing in that line when Saint Peter was distributing the skills.'" Her brother Josef knew all along that Ludmila was a priest, but her father never knew it. Ludmila could not tell him. Even though he would have understood and fully supported her priesthood, she just did not want to risk causing scandal to her mother, who was much more traditional and had a deep respect for priests, all of whom, of course, were men. Her father used to encourage Ludmila when she was still in her teens, "Look around and don't be afraid to do even those things other people are afraid to do." Yes, he would have understood and Ludmila longed to tell him, but she refrained from doing so.

Ludmila's mother had no problem with Josef, her son the married priest, who often returned to the family home to celebrate Mass. For his children, Josef, Marcel, and Michal, this was just a normal part of growing up. "When I was a child," says Michal the youngest, now married and living in Brno, "we always participated in the Mass. In the kitchen. In the living room. Anywhere. When we were somewhere on holiday, sometimes in a tent, we had Mass there or out in the open. I think every child at times doesn't like going to church very often, so sometimes it was a burden for me, being there every day at Mass. My parents never forced me to go. I just went. I went because I couldn't imagine being someplace else when right next door there is Mass."

Old age for Ludmila's parents was a beautiful time. They prayed together and read in the evenings. There was a joyful spirit there and a spirit of deep trust. They shared intimately in the Eucharist, reaping the fullness of the harvest from all the seeds they had sown in this life and in the life of the spirit. "My mother once asked the parish priest when he would be coming to visit, because she had some questions for him. He looked at my father and said, 'Here you have your priest.' He did not know my father really was a priest." Her mother just smiled. Frantisek had often said to his children when they were growing up: "I left my homeland, just like Abraham, so that you might receive greater riches of spirit." Now the riches were returning to him and to his bride a hundredfold.

Toward the end of 1979, when Davidek suggested he would consecrate two more bishops, Ludmila refused to witness them. "I personally held the opinion," says Ludmila, "that he should submit to the prohibition until there was clarity, but Davidek held an opposite opinion. I had a greater trust in the providence of God." Ludmila also felt there were too many questionable things. "I knew the candidates. I even helped them to organize and prepare what was needed for those consecrations, but I refused to participate in either of them. One took place that year, the other in 1987."

Sometime after 1980, Ludmila tried one more time to enter a religious order. The pull toward the kind of total commitment religious life offered had continued unabated. Now that the activities of Koinotes were somewhat less demanding, she decided to answer the call. "I met with the mother superior. I said nothing to her about being a priest. I only spoke about my cooperation with Bishop Davidek. I created a kind of model for how I would continue working within Koinotes even if I entered the order. Since convents were closed and we lived at home, my proposal would have been possible. I had to continue with the underground church, because at that time I really thought that communism would last forever, but I planned to reduce the amount of my work.

"I knew some of the sisters who were secretly attending lectures and seminars as part of the underground church, but I shocked the mother superior, even frightened her with my frankness. Her manner was somewhat sophisticated, and I was so full of energy and non-traditional ideas. She said she would get back to me regarding my request for admission to the order, but she did not do so within a given length of time. The reason was that she sent her letter through a Koinotes clergyman who went there to hear confessions. He put it in his pocket and forgot to give it to me. I waited and waited to hear from her, but word never came. I hung in a vacuum, my future on hold, and continued to work with Koinotes, calling on God to help me in this time of uncertainty. Then as the weeks and months went by, my thoughts turned to other things. One day the priest reached into his pocket and found the letter there. He handed it to me, saying: 'I found this letter in my coat pocket. I didn't know it was for you. I've had it for a very long time.'" And indeed he had. He gave it to Ludmila two years after the mother superior had given it to him. It turned out to be a letter of rejection. "When I read it," she said, "I couldn't even remember what it was about. It had been such a long time ago. So I had a good laugh and went on with my life. I knew God's hand had been in this. It was God's way of guiding me."

Ludmila bore no hard feelings toward the messenger. Quite the contrary. "Vladimir was such a good man and I really liked him. He worked as the driver of a tram. He used to say that he would pass by a church on his way home from work at night. He always stood by the wall of the church and did an act of adoration at two o'clock in the morning, and he would bless the people. One night when he was kneeling by the church, a policeman came up to him and wanted to lock him up. He asked him what he was doing there and he said, 'I am praying.' The policeman didn't know what to do. He said, 'So, now, just go on home.' Once when he had entered his tram and before settling into the driver's seat, he made the sign of the cross. A woman on the tram began knocking on the glass partition separating him from the passengers. She had seen him do it and it had frightened her. She said: 'Oh my God, driver, are you planning to have an accident?' Vladimir was startled. He did not know what she meant by this. 'You made a cross,' she said to him. He replied, 'No, no. God comes with us.' It was so commonplace, so natural for him to act the way he did.

"How important it is that priests work among people, mingle with people, because it can have such deep meaning. It would not be bad at all if priests would have two or three hours of normal work each day. When priests are there in a regular job, they are more accessible, and people feel more comfortable with them and are able to be more open. A priest who lives his life with God brings this to wherever he is. People need something visible, something tangible, and together with that comes the spirit, the spirit of the priest, the spirit of God, and that spirit is revealed in very ordinary ways."

Ludmila was always acutely aware that the many demands of ministry had an effect on the life of prayer. "Our celebration of Mass used to be short. Breviary prayers were often replaced with the rosary, because it was possible to pray the rosary even as we traveled. Our trips were interlaced with prayers. An increasing amount of work, exhaustion, study, and travel took something from my prayer. It is impossible to live this way for long. The soul weakens in its ability to sense God's manifestations. Only a living relationship creates the bond with which God forms the soul. This does not happen within a year, but only after many years. One always has to start anew. Only later did I understand how my mother helped me with this problem, without ever knowing she had done so. What I learned from her became the pillar of my pastoral ministry among individual women. She taught me that we can pray anywhere, during any kind of work that is being done attentively and well and to the best of our ability. In such a work God is present. We only have to know this and try to give it our heart. Many people wish to have spiritual development without obstacles or even effort, and so they will never understand God's love or the poverty of our humanity."

There were times when Ludmila saw into the depths of her own human weakness, and by embracing that insight was able to catch a glimpse of God's unfailing love. "One day a letter arrived from a Salesian priest with whom I had worked closely in the days before Koinotes. We had written to each other through the years, usually at Christmas. Now he was an old man and wanted to meet with me. He suggested as our meeting site a village near Olomouc in the middle of Moravia. I was very ill at the time, but nevertheless I went. He invited me to join him and begin some kind of ministry to older women. He had wanted to do the work himself, but he no longer had the energy that had been present when he was younger, so he had thought of me. I was tempted by his invitation, but I felt myself incapable then of taking on anything else, because I had so little strength. I even thought I would soon die, but I did not say that to him. I simply refused his offer. This was not easy for me to do. I was never able to say no to someone who needed me. He was disappointed in my refusal. It had taken him by surprise.

"In the course of our conversation I missed my bus to Olomouc, where I would have connected with one to Brno. He accompanied me to the railway station. It was five kilometers away, or at least it seemed that far to me as we walked and talked in the hot sun. After he had put me on the train, he said he was sorry I refused him. He had been sure I would accept.

"The train took me into Olomouc, but I had missed my connection to Brno, so I stayed there overnight at the home of one of my friends. She left for work in the morning, and as I was preparing to leave for the bus, I suddenly felt so sick that I was unable to stand. I do not remember ever feeling so sick before. Water began to pour out of my nose. I did not know what was happening. I just knew that I could not leave. I lay down on the bed fully clothed. My room was at the back of the apartment. When my friend returned from work at four o'clock in the afternoon, she found me there in a stupor. Frightened, she asked me what was wrong and then phoned a doctor whom she knew, for she worked in a hospital. After she had described my symptoms, he explained what he thought it was. He told her not to take me to the hospital or I would die there. This was a complicated illness and they would not know what to do because they would not know exactly what it was. I needed first aid immediately.

"Now this doctor said to my friend that he had a daughter who had gone through a near-death experience, and once she had recovered, she converted to Christianity. His daughter had a circle of friends who shared a similar experience, and one of them had a gift. She could diagnose what I had. He promised to send the woman to me. She arrived around 6:00 p.m. I heard her say from a distance, although I could not see her: 'She is almost out of her body.' She asked my friend my baptismal name and then called out to me: 'Ludmila, do you want to leave? You cannot leave yet.' And you know what? After all the difficulties and my fatigue and my overwhelming tiredness, I really wanted to die. I was not afraid of death. I tried to respond to her, but she was praying the rosary, and she was kneeling at my feet. Now it was around midnight, and throughout the rosary she told my friend to prepare a tea for me and to give it to me to drink. Before she had even brought me the tea, I caught the scent of it three rooms away and felt like vomiting. So the woman began another rosary, and then I fell asleep.

"The first thing they gave me when I awoke was a tea made from nettles. Then the woman repeated her question, asking me whether I wanted to live. She said my response was very important, and I answered, 'yes.' Then she said that she thought things would proceed better now and that she would be going home, but she would return if needed. Before she left she said to me: 'You will live for a much longer time, because you are needed. At your head . . . near your head . . . Christ is standing there. He is protecting you. You cannot leave yet, but remember everything that you dream.' And she left. Three days later this woman returned. She came in the evening, and by then I was able to see. I will never forget her face. I could see the anger in it. She scolded me severely saying that I was a very egotistical person, and it was all because of my selfishness that I was in the state I was in. I felt the need to defend myself, but she wouldn't let me do it. She had said those things in a very negative and condescending way, as if she were scolding a little child. Then she turned around and left.

"You cannot imagine what this did to me. I had tried to give myself totally. My life was full of sacrifices. I had given my time, my flat, my person. I had given my all. I had almost no place to lay my head. Often I felt hounded. I realized later that it was as if someone had sent the woman to do this. And can you imagine the great grace I received, that in that moment I was able to say to God: 'If I am like this, I accept it. Now it is up to you what you will do with me, because I do not see myself this way.' The experience of accepting myself, of accepting even this in myself was deep and liberating. We cannot know ourselves by ourselves. Sometimes we need a big shaking up to see our human wound-edness, for all of us are selfish and we cannot see it. It is only when all these rough layers fall away from us that the real essence of being is revealed, and that is a very, very slow process. Even though in that moment I felt such pain that I thought I would die of it, I started to feel also the strength in me and the desire to endure.

"The next day I was still very weak, but I decided to go into the city, because I wanted to repair my mother's dress and I needed some materials. I would do that in the morning, and in the evening I would leave. As soon as I entered the shop, something happened to me, and I don't know what it was. I stumbled, in a way, but it was as if someone else had caused it. Then I felt such a terrible pain, my hair felt like it was standing on end. Suddenly my leg was useless, and I dragged myself back to the house. It seemed like nothing was wrong with my leg, but the sharp pain contin-ued. I stayed for two more days, until I had been a whole week in Olomouc. Then they drove me home in a car, because I couldn't use my leg." The sharp pain continued off and on for more than a year. Two things of significance resulted from that journey. Ludmila began the trip with one brave decision, not to accept an invitation that she knew she could not handle, and then ended it with another.

"When I returned from Olomouc, I made a decision to do one thing. I would ask Davidek to move out of my flat. I don't even know how I came to this conclusion, but I insisted on it. It was very difficult for me. Emotion and reason surfaced in turn, one after the other, but I just had to do it. I changed my life dramatically by proceeding in this way. It was even more difficult for Felix, and I was aware of that, but this would not influence my decision. Afterward I would return to this choice time and time again, when he was mired in difficult situations, but for now it was enough to know that I needed that space for myself. Felix had a free room at his sister's place, and my idea was simple. He would move back there, because the political atmosphere was no longer so difficult. I should have realized that one cannot simply go home again without significant adjustments, especially in the state he was in, for his health had begun to fail. Even psychologically, it would be very hard for him, for his sister's family had its own daily rhythm. However, my situation wasn't easy. My parents were old, they needed me. I had to have time for them."

But most important of all, Ludmila needed time and space for herself. "I felt deeply this hunger for time and space and especially for stillness. Oh, how I needed this! Now there was a flat near my apartment that a woman had bequeathed to Felix before she died. That seemed the perfect solution, but Felix had to leave it soon after moving in, despite the fact that it now belonged to him. The communist regime had its own laws, and according to their procedures, they could give it to whomever they wanted. They may have denied it to Felix because they had no one there to monitor him. So he went to live with his sister in Chrlice, but only after spending some time in Stepanov.

"Collaboration was more difficult now because I had to travel

back and forth between Davidek's place and mine, which for a
time meant commuting between Stepanov and Brno. But I was
returning to quietness, to silence, and to my privacy. I was returning to my own space, a place I could call home. This, the quiet,
the silence were treasures to me. I cannot live without silence. I
had to have it. I had to. And I needed to be alone. I experienced
the strength that the soul acquires through silence. Even if I had
only one hour a day, it was enough for me. I could go wherever I
had to go, and silence went with me.

"Once, near the end of the year, I went to the Sacrament
of Reconciliation. The priest started asking me some unpleasant
questions that had nothing to do with what I was confessing. This
priest, who knew Davidek, even though he did not belong to us,
addressed me as somebody who was ordained. He did not say it
nicely when he asked if I was a priest. Had I known him to be a
problem priest or someone I should suspect, he could have asked
me a thousand questions concerning my ordination and I would
not have answered him, but because this was Davidek's acquain-
tance and he was questioning me as if he were fully informed, I
responded openly. I was accustomed to being transparent in the
context of the sacrament. Davidek at the time had told some
people about my ordination without informing me, and that had
upset me a lot. Because this priest was his friend, I assumed he
too had been told. He asked me directly, 'Are you a priest?' and I
told him, 'Yes, I am.' He began to chastise me. He was very angry.
I knelt there silent and rigid, as if I had turned to stone. Had
a sinner come to me, one who was filthy from head to toe with
every kind of sin imaginable, I would never have been able to say
to that person what this priest was saying to me. Later I would
learn what was behind it, the layers of misinformation, but then I
was simply in shock. I left the confession box without absolution.
It was unbearably cruel."

It had been the worst of times for Ludmila. The last thing her
bruised and battered spirit had needed was abuse. Physically, she

was exhausted, for she had been ill for quite some time. She was experiencing spiritually the dark night of the soul. "This was a difficult period for me of spiritual emptiness so deep and large I could not talk about it to anybody. There were moments when I really needed this sacrament as a means of spiritual help, and I was trying to find a place where I could explore its possibility for myself.

"I was in such an agonized state after leaving the church that evening that I walked through the narrow, deserted streets groaning out loud. The sounds came from deep within with a piercing intensity. I had been so serious about my spiritual life. I had done everything conscientiously. At that moment my spirit recoiled. I was filled with desolation." It was yet another breach of trust for one who was so trusting. Ludmila's profound anguish had come at a difficult point in her life. "My father was hovering between life and death. I could not go home, even though I knew they were waiting there for me. I continued to walk the streets, for I needed time to get used to the new and shocking situation. Finally I said, 'I don't know what else I will have to face or how long this will last, but I want to accept it.' That made me a little calmer. Not completely, of course, for it would take much longer to ease my mind and soothe an open and painful wound. I am convinced God always helps me at precisely the right moment. I am willing to accept everything, and not simply accept it, but to integrate all that happens into my life, because there is no other way." Ludmila returned to the same priest for confession the following week. She felt she could not leave the situation unresolved. After some discussion, he did give her absolution, but it did not eradicate the pain she had suffered in the interim.

"I did not tell anybody about this troubling incident then, not even Felix, who at the time was living in Stepanov with his former parishioners. I did not think it would be wise. Later, when I urged Felix to tell me who it was he had told about my ordination, he would not do so, and I no longer remember why. For ten years, only a very small circle knew I was a priest. I asked Felix, my bishop, to take away the burden of silence from me, and he gave me permission to reveal it more broadly within the framework of Koinotes. I went to visit a priest who used to collaborate with us. I opened a part of my heart to him, including all the good and bad things of the present time. He listened to me in silence. I am not sure whether he understood why I had come to him. I missed spiritual discussions, those times when I was able to confront my experiences and reflect on the things I enjoyed. I needed this talk so much in order not to become my own prisoner in my priesthood.

"When I finished, he was silent. He had nothing to say about the core of my problem. From our exchange I realized that he had missed the point completely. Perhaps I was asking the impossible in turning to him for help. From the depths of my heart I thank all those who somehow helped me bear those moments. I had to undertake that journey. It belonged to my spiritual development and my inner growth as a priest. I was unable to overcome the incident that had triggered such a response, but maybe I have managed to cope with it—well, I have managed to cope with it—but whenever I return to it, I relive it all again."

Ludmila's spiritual search continued. "Sundays I would go to services in a church. Not all the time, but once in a while. Even though I was celebrating Mass myself, I would go to a public Mass, not at the very beginning, but then afterward, yes. I always felt the Mass to be a communion, a shared celebration. The priest, when once he saw me in the church, changed the theme of his preaching right in the middle of his sermon. He started yelling through the whole church: 'This sort of woman may think she is God-knows-what that she would want to become a priest. Let her look at Mother Teresa, such an honorable woman, who is taking the children from the street and doing the worst sort of work.' Mentally, I took him on. 'What do you know about it? If I could see children on the street around me, I would also take them in, all of them.'

"And then I thought, how different our ministry is. For the one, the girl or the woman who is respected by society, for her it is difficult, but she still can feel that inner drive that comes from knowing the values that she is bringing to others. But I'm standing here in a service that has to remain a secret. And I know it is a service. I know it is a ministry. His words were a deep offense to me. I stopped going there for Mass on Sunday after he did this to me several times again. You cannot imagine what it feels like when everyone seems to stand against you, when you think they are pointing a finger at you as if you were a heretic, saying to you, 'How dare you!' My priesthood was being held against me, false things were being said about me, everybody was rejecting me, or so it seemed to me at the time. But from that feeling of isolation maturity also comes by being faithful to the call." In the absence of physical and spiritual support, one learns to lean on God.

"During this very painful period I started to ask myself how my priestly charism could be developed in such a situation. I realized that by receiving the priesthood, nothing really happened, that it was only the first step. I was aware of this even before, but now it was like some culminating point. I felt I had to stop everything, to distance myself from everything, so that I might discern what sort of situation I was in. And so for a certain period of time I did not celebrate Mass. It was not a long time. I had told this to my bishop, but he didn't respond to me. I was not too enthusiastic that Felix remained silent. I expected that he would take some time to talk about this with me. Then he was gone, for he had moved out of my apartment, so I followed him to Stepanov to discuss the burden on my heart, but he would not say a word. On the way home I sat thinking things through, and I was upset with him and hurt by his silence, but I am not upset anymore. He may have been troubled by what I was going through, but what could he have told me? He knew for sure I would turn to God and fight my battle there. But I was not up for battle. My 'attack' on God stayed fairly calm. In a quiet way I kept saying: 'Will this last long,

O God? It is so long already. Isn't the situation I am in simply a mistake? Will it ever end?' "

Davidek did take seriously Ludmila's struggle as a priest. "It was his conviction that a woman has to make a way for herself and not be guided by male opinion or copy a male priesthood. He always said, 'Don't worry, I will give a seminar on that topic soon,' but he never did. Perhaps he did not have the strength to do it anymore. I view the fact that he said nothing as God's guiding me." With no one else to turn to, Ludmila was led in spirit by the Spirit on a priestly path of the heart.

The lack of verbal support, however, was beginning to take its toll. The two who were closest to her and knew about her priesthood, Felix and her brother Josef, were extremely supportive in their own quiet way. She adds: "I believe that two other bishops tried to help as much as they could by the way they acted toward me, but we never talked about it." Ludmila needed more than implicit support, no matter how affirming. She needed someone to talk to openly about her priesthood, someone who would be able to discuss it with her so she could clarify her options, make some decisions about what to do, gain a perspective on how or if her priesthood was accepted. She reveals: "I am a communicative type of person. I am able to open myself and share, but when I feel that the listener is not interested, I stop talking and do not continue. My brother Josef is a quiet man. He is a literary type and does not talk much. We are very different. My way of thinking and expressing myself, and his way of doing so, sometimes do not walk together. He would always hear me, but I could not expect him to comment on or analyze what he had heard in the way that I would have needed. He was the one I used to turn to back then, because he is a very attentive listener. I could also talk to Davidek, but the work of Koinotes kept us so busy that we seldom had time to sit down and talk. Later, when he was already ill, I did not want to trouble him. He suffered so much for ordaining me. It was a completely new thing, uncommon, without precedent. He referred to this during the Council. I do not resent anything he has done with regard to my ordination, for there was no other way he could have gone about it. He is my intercessor now, and not only mine, but intercessor for all women who have the priestly charism."

At the core of Ludmila's spirituality was the celebration of Mass. "I used to say to God, 'If I should discover, even when I am fifty, that you wish me to stop doing this, I will, but please, let me really know it.' I thought that if later I saw that this service is not in accord with God's will, I would stop. I never doubted the sacrament, but there came a time when I did not know what to do, when all around me I heard threats of invalidity and other condemnations. Gradually all the moments started to fit together as a mosaic and I understood that everything is done by Christ. It was Christ who served from this gift, through me, who brought those people to me, who cooperated with me during the Sacrament of Reconciliation, from whom I received everything that belongs to the essence of priestly ministry.

"Sometimes I concelebrated with other members of Koinotes who knew about my priesthood and supported me. I have never understood why not one of them ever invited me to preside. When I was alone I celebrated at home. I had to find the time when no one would disturb me, and that was very difficult when living in our family home, because the house was full of people. I usually waited until late at night, and I would ask my guardian angels to protect me during that time. I can't remember ever having to stop and start again. I always made it through to the end, which was also a sign to me that this was in harmony with God's wishes. For me personally and for my life as a priest, relationship with God is priority. Love of other people flowing from the love of God is the measure of everything. Priesthood is reflected in the whole of life and in all its activities. The Eucharist, which is the celebration of God who unites us, extends throughout the day."

Because so few people knew she was a priest, most of the

time she celebrated Eucharist on her own. This led Ludmila to a deeper understanding of its communal aspects. As a result, her introverted nature was rewarded with a theological basis for her natural preference. "Although I preferred to be alone rather than with a group, I knew Mass should be celebrated in community and I didn't have a community, so I created one. I invited the mother of Jesus and other saints to come to the Mass, my guardian angel, the saint of the day, the women who were celebrating their name day, the great female teachers of the church, like Teresa of Avila." With celestial hosts filling her celebration space, Ludmila never lost sight of the cosmic implications of the Eucharist, the Mass.

"Sometimes the gift became a sacrifice, for example, in public settings, at the time of the homily, during funerals or baptisms, and on various other occasions. I had the words in my mind, words to nourish the spirit, words that people were hungry to hear, words that were easy to understand and much more closely connected to life, but I was not allowed to express them. Sometimes I just wanted to scream." Her ordination was to have been a sign of God's inclusive new creation present here and now, but the sign remained invisible, which is not the nature of a sign. "I never celebrated Mass in public. I had to ask myself if what I was doing was right. At times I hesitated. But I believe it was right. Looking back, I know I was led." There is a time for everything. Living according to those wise words is in itself a sign. "People in need would come to me, among them were even priests, and they would unknowingly partake of this gift. For me, this was another sign." Totalitarianism was not the acceptable time for this sign's full revelation. Perhaps the hardest of all the demands related to her code of silence was hiding the fact from those she loved and who loved her most of all. "I never celebrated with my family. Even when my father was seriously ill and Josef and I had prepared everything for him so that he could preside at Mass, I did not concelebrate with him. My brother Josef did. I repeated everything with them, but I said it silently. My father never knew that I too was a priest." Father, daughter, son—priests of God in the hidden church, visible yet invisible—not to have shared that with her father, not to have been able to tell her mother, was truly to feel the cross.

"With the words of consecration, I always realize this closeness to God and I know that I am only a means, that God works through me. It is Christ who makes the changes, and Christ does this in cooperation with me.

"How beautiful the prayer before communion: 'Let this be healing for my body and for my soul.'

"Every sacrament changes us, but we are the ones who have to make this change, with the help of God. If you ask me how I live my priesthood, here are the answers. It is nothing special. It is something that is taking place in anything I do."

There was very little time for Ludmila to be in that silent space she cherished. Life beyond her dwelling place made its own demands. "I was aware that my father was dying. The man who meant so much to me had been in a kind of clinical death for approximately a month. He had come out of it, but we knew this was the beginning of a journey from which he would not return. I loved him dearly, so I said to myself, 'You have to go home. You have to be with him.' I was going through the most severe crisis of my life and I felt so weak. My father did not know what was happening inside me, but he saw the changes in me. Once in the evening, when I was watching him, he suddenly woke up and said to me: 'Ludmila, I feel a bad spirit's presence.' It was shortly after the incident during the Sacrament of Reconciliation. I said to him, 'It is quite possible.' He had this perception. He knew me very well. People who have a serious sickness, especially those who are at the point of death, are very perceptive. I had said nothing about what was worrying me, but I knew he felt my suffering. I'm speaking here about the priesthood. Even though I never told him, somehow I think he knew.

"While he could still communicate with us, my father spoke

of the salvation of souls in a way that transcended the limits of our family. Just before he died, he said: 'If anyone comes to my grave to pray, let them pray for the salvation of all and not only for me.'" Frantisek Javora died in April 1982 at the age of eighty-four. He left a void no one else could fill in the hearts of those who loved him. He took with him part of Ludmila. "Each death takes from the family something no one can replace. After a time, either shorter or longer, what left us returns in a different form and our communication is also restored, but this time it is through Christ."

Ludmila began to spend more time with her mother and her sister. Maria's life had been irrevocably altered when tragedy struck unexpectedly before her father died. At the age of thirty-eight she suffered a stroke that left her partially paralyzed. Her thinking and speech were not affected, but her motor skills were gone. The vivacious, inquisitive woman who loved to study philosophy was told she would never walk again, but her brother Vojtech said, "Don't believe it. Exercise and you will do well." That is what he told her, and that is what she did. She was utterly determined to prove her doctors wrong. She taught herself to walk again, but in those early years, she needed extensive personal care. She lived at home with her mother as she courageously rebuilt her future, one small step at a time.

The pain of loss and misunderstanding had paved the path on which Ludmila walked her sacred journey. While she might have hoped for another way, she accepted everything as part of her life in God. Her desire for holiness had been with her since she was a child. Sanctity "has to be always connected with suffering, and later abandonment. Those who bring the Gospel words should be aware of this. Suffering does not come only with illness. Pain is also present when we have to leave our ideas." Ludmila lived each day receptive to whatever that day would bring. She recalls one very special grace in the midst of a difficult time. "I went to another church for confession, and a young priest was there. Afterward he

took me to the sacristy and he gave me a bouquet of field flowers
that were in full bloom. Such a human gesture from a priest . . . this
is something unheard of and something very precious. He had no
idea who I was. I was so happy about what he had done. I carried
those flowers back home as if they were a treasure, like it was
when I was a little child and would go to church with my father
and we would play along the way. We would open our arms wide
and stretch them out over the fields, and my father would say: 'It
is beautiful, isn't it?' As I was carrying my lovely flowers, it was
as if I heard bells ringing. Those flowers in the fields were called
little bells, for they were filled with bright little bells, and there
were quite a few in my bouquet. As I went from that church and
from that young priest, I felt as if God were returning me back to
those moments when I was a child, back to uninhibited freedom."

There were other signs of reassurance that God was there in the
shadows, leading her to the light. "It happened, for instance, that
I went to a church and was sitting quietly there. A priest came up
to me and asked if I would help him prepare a woman for baptism,
and I said yes." Simple services performed with love were core to
her priestly ministry during this time when inwardly there seemed
to be nothing there. "There was so much evil around me. I saw
myself as if lying on a floor, surrounded by people with dirty shoes.
Whenever I took a breath, I would breathe in the dust. When I
would lift up my eyes and want to look up, I would see only those
dirty shoes and those people walking around me. In this state I
lived for a long, long time, maybe ten years. I stopped asking God,
'How long?' I would say, 'As you will. I will remain like this as long
as you want. I want to believe and to trust you unconditionally.'"

Another time she was sitting in a church quietly reflecting. "It
was evening and I was just sitting there as I like to do, not thinking
about anything, when suddenly I heard a voice. The voice was
like an echo. It said: 'I don't want you like this anymore.' I was
astonished. It was as if someone you love wanted to get rid of you,
was pushing you away. I said, 'What shall I do?' I don't know if

it was the same voice, but in my soul I heard the answer: 'You are mine. You're not alone.' And from that moment on, my life changed tremendously. I don't know how to express it, but an inner calm, a security, permeated me. I returned to my spiritual core and made a list of questions I would ask myself, which I would respond to leisurely. I was accustomed to examining my conscience each day, but I was doing it in a very complicated way with questions Felix had proposed to us, such as: How am I organizing my time? Are my values in the right proportions for studies, for prayer, for service? What is my main fault? What is my desire for holiness like? Questions of this nature. I knew I would not return to this again. Instead I started to ask myself questions concerning the presence of God. 'Where did I meet You today? Where have I seen You today? Where have I heard You today?' A very simple, beautiful life began opening before me. A new language developed in me. It was a language I as a woman had long desired to know."

The questions Ludmila had used for years as guidelines for accountability and for growing in sanctity were part of a Koinotes spirituality that helped to bring her to that place where she could let them go. "Those psychologically constructed schemes," she says, "were graded from I through IV, from beginners to well advanced. I consider them very important, because patience teaches us values and responsibility for entrusted gifts, for the world, for humankind, and for the church. All in all they direct us to a concrete spiritual program, one that is not separated from the reality of life, where the spiritual life and this life do not stand against each other but are integrated in all their fullness, leading us to human wholeness. Even though I later abandoned the questions and replaced them with different ones, what is essential is the fact that one has some questions that one turns to for deepening values and embracing sacrifices.

"The time when I turned to those questions and held them up as a mirror to my soul became a fixed point for ending the day. They were with me habitually as a natural part of my day. None of the questions was directed at any particular sin. They were meant for spiritual self-reflection. For example: What is my love for God? for others? for myself? Am I longing to become an apostle of the Parousia? Have I concern for the world? Do I long for sanctity? Am I willing to bear the burden of the day? What is my appreciation of the Mystical Body of Christ? What is my appreciation for humanity and for the church as an open community? What is my joy in the spiritual life? What have I managed to die for today? Am I able to handle myself? How? Am I able to handle others, not by directing them, but through my personal sanctity? And there were many others.

"Thanks to this spirituality, I literally 'fell in love with salvation.' For me salvation is not a term focused only on the future or something we only learn about. It is something I live daily, something that I form and that forms me, something through which I give myself to the One who gifted me and entrusted me with life, who invited me into this process, and who complements my incompetence. I am happy I can knowingly share this with others. I do not exaggerate when I say that I am fascinated again and again during the process of growing spiritually. It inspires me to be its apostle and to keep on moving forward."

Ludmila went back to work again outside of Koinotes, even though her health was still problematic. "Not an occupation, just part-time jobs, to help here, to help there. I did it to have some contact with the outer world. I felt that need deeply, and it was good." Even with these new demands added to her administrative work and ministerial functions, Ludmila never lost her thirst for learning. She would read books and attend lectures whenever she had a chance, which was a bit more often now that she was living on her own. One day she acquired a secret tape featuring a well-known theologian in one of the other branches of the underground church and wanted to go and hear him. "He spoke in general terms about the ordination of women, and I was so delighted. I tried to get into his seminars—Felix could not continue ours anymore—but it was very difficult. He and his circle knew that the police were suspicious of them, so every new member had to be recommended by somebody trustworthy. One of his closest co-workers spoke in favor of me, and when I arrived my sponsor said, 'Do not tell him who you are.' And he knew why.

"This seminar had a very different atmosphere. In Koinotes we could address openly all difficult questions, even pastoral ones. Felix would always say that people grow and mature through a process such as this, but in this other group, it was different. Certain topics were open to priests, others to laity, and the information was not shared. Someone in the audience asked if there were some married priests anywhere in the country, and the seminar leader said no, there were no such cases here. I jumped up and said that in a nearby parish there was a Greek Catholic priest with a bi-ritual faculty who had been there for many years, so why not speak of it? I was careful not to mention those who were secretly ordained. He started to reproach me. He said that this cannot be mentioned in public. I did not agree with him. Otherwise, I would have to say that their system of studies was precise.

"He spoke once about the ordination of women. I was interested in hearing more about it, but he pointed out to me, in a humiliating way, that I should not continue this topic. A woman, a medical doctor who was his close co-worker, said, 'But you didn't understand this woman.' He responded: 'I will not continue with this topic.' I was so upset by this. I felt there was more behind his words for him to have behaved so rudely. I went home and tears ran down my face. I was certain he knew something about me that had caused his behavior to change. About six months later I met him in a tram while on my way home from work. A major Catholic poet lives next door to me, and I knew that's where he was going. I invited him to come and visit me also, but from the manner of his response, it was clear this was out of the question. I quit his seminars."

The issue of women's ordination, its theory and its practice, was foremost in Ludmila's mind. So was her concern about how they were going to finally resolve reporting her ordination to Rome.

"Before I agreed to be ordained, I asked my bishop how he was going to inform Rome about my ordination. Felix said that as bishop, it was his responsibility and that he would notify the pope, but it had to be in person. He promised to work on it. Occasionally I would ask him when he was going to inform the pope and what he was doing about it. He kept promising me he would talk to the pope personally, that this could not be written, that it had to be orally explained. I know he really meant it. He was making every effort to find a way to get to Rome." A number of things prevented Davidek from fulfilling his word. Being isolated from the rest of the world because of communism meant communication could not proceed through ordinary channels.

He tried to set up an appointment with the pope through Cardinal Stefan Wyszynski of Poland. Messages from the Vatican had indicated it would be possible within a half year or so, but it never happened. He would have had to receive government authorization to leave the country. Had he wanted, he might have been able to get permission to go as a tourist. Ludmila had hoped he would. "Because I really needed to have this thing sorted out, I asked him about going to Rome as a tourist. Perhaps, once there, he would find some way to make contact with the Vatican. He refused to consider it. He said, 'This is a thing that has to be dealt with officially, not something that can be done by a tourist on a trip.' He insisted on a diplomatic invitation. He did not like to step down from that level, and I could not blame him for this. Of course, myself, I would have solved the problem in a completely different way." Eventually, she did.

When Davidek's health began to fail, Ludmila grew concerned. "Even before Davidek became ill, I knew that his journey to the Vatican would never take place. When over the course of time I saw all the obstacles preventing him—his illness, his inability to

travel, his lack of success in making contact with Rome—I decided to take action. I informed the pope in a very simple way, in
just a single sentence, without any diplomatic finesse. 'Holy Father, I have received priestly ordination under these circumstances
_____, and now I am announcing it to you.' Then I went to
Felix and said to him, 'Felix, I know that you will not be going to
Rome anymore, so I have decided to write to the pope myself.' I
do not know what he thought about it. He never said no, don't do
it, and he did not comment on it. I took the letter personally to
Cardinal Frantisek Tomasek in Prague, and said, '*Solo papa.*' That
means straight to the hands of Pope John Paul II. He said, 'Okay.
I will give this letter to the pope.' Then he added, 'Anyway, it is
invalid.' He did not ask me anything about it, and so I did not
comment on it, but I did admit I was ordained. Then he said,
'When I come back from Rome, I will call you and tell you what
happened.' But he never called me back. So then I concluded, the
pope knows about it and he didn't send any message, so it means
it is all right. Today I smile at this straightforward simplicity."

Did Cardinal Tomasek really give Ludmila's letter to the pope?
"Absolutely," says Ludmila. She is adamant in her response. "He
promised to give it to the pope." She insists he kept his promise.
They had met several times before, so she was no stranger to
him, and at the time she had given him the letter, he had asked
her to do some work for him, and she had gladly done it. He
was a trustworthy man, and no matter what he thought about
Ludmila's ordination, he would have honored her right to inform
the pope, and he would have kept his word. Ludmila cannot reveal
the details, but she says, "I know the pope received it. He was
showing the letter to someone else. I heard this from a priest who
was present. I cannot say his name, but I know he speaks the
truth."

Ludmila continues to wrestle with several troubling questions.
Why did Cardinal Tomasek not say anything more to her about
what had transpired with the pope? This is a very important

question. An issue of such magnitude surely called for a direct response. When word of her ordination had been published without
her consent, Ludmila was told that the pope had been so broad-
minded as to rescind her excommunication. That was the first
she had heard anything regarding excommunication. "I wonder,"
says Ludmila, "whether I was excommunicated only after the news
was published or had it already happened at the moment when
the pope read my letter to him? Was this why Cardinal Tomasek
did not speak with me? Because he did not want to tell me? Or
was it because no action had been taken against me and he did
not want me to know this, for fear I might interpret that to mean
validation?"

While Ludmila was in the process of resolving the issue of informing the pope, her sister Maria, through heroic effort and sheer
determination, was learning to be independent. Sometime after
their father died, Ludmila helped her sister move into her own
apartment on the outer edge of the city. It was in a district surrounded by trees and songbirds and beds of flowers, which were
Maria's source of joy. There were signs that *maminka* would soon
be unable to do all the things she had been accustomed to doing,
and both daughters wanted to ease the way for her.

Ludmila was a lot like her mother. She had the same vitality
and organizational ability, a deep spirituality, an unwavering faith
in God. Even in terms of looks she seems to have taken after
her, but there the similarity ended. "I had major conflicts with my
mother because she disagreed with my cooperation with Bishop
Davidek. One of her sons had been incarcerated and now here
was her daughter, with one foot already in prison, putting herself
in danger. This was hard for her to accept." Ludmila knew that in
certain things there would always be disagreement, for their lives
were very different, but where it really mattered, they were of one
accord. As the end of their time together drew near, Ludmila was
even more aware of how much her mother had suffered in her
personal life and through the suffering of her children. How hard

it had been to raise them during five decades of war and foreign supremacy. Yet she also realized that every child was accepted as a gift from God and loved individually.

"When she was in the hospital and we her adult children were standing around her bed, my mother said: 'Do sing for me my favorite song.' I said, 'Which one is your favorite?' I named all of them. She said, 'No, no, that's not the right one.' We were at a loss, because we did not know which one it was, so she started to sing it herself. She sang, 'I want to be a child of the Virgin Mary. I want to commit myself for this, stand under her protection. That's my whole desire.' The song ended with, 'When I will be close to heaven's gate among your chosen children, you Mother, kiss me.' We said, '*Maminka,* we do not know the song.' She said, 'My God, I did not know you did not know this song.' My brothers and my sister and I just stood there astonished. We had always heard our mother singing, but we never heard her sing that song."

Before she died their mother confessed her love for her family home. Some might say it was a place of unrelenting hardship, of one calamity after another with the care and feeding of a family of twelve, with one son dead before the age of twenty-one, another paralyzed for life, and a daughter left with broken dreams inside a broken body. To her it was otherwise. "My dear little house, how I loved you. How much happiness there was inside of you." Her children knew she meant it.

"As my mother lay dying, I had the feeling she was saying good-bye to every detail in that house, that the house itself was losing something that was irreversible. As she was taking her last breaths, I felt the whole house breathing, I felt her spirit very strongly present everywhere I went. She turned to me and asked, 'What will become of Maria when I am not here? Do not leave her alone.' When I reassured her, it seemed to me from that moment on she let go of her life here with us and began living in the future. She was no longer interested in anything but God. She simply put everything else aside and was completely absorbed in herself and in her transition. It was three days before her death. I told her that evening that I was a priest, but she was already dying and she did not respond. Yet I felt that her soul had responded, because it seemed like we suddenly understood each other in a very different way. I like to think that somewhere, somehow our souls met and in that space she knew and did understand.

"From the moment my mother had characteristically placed all her worries in God's hands, she did not return to them again. She seemed to me as a bride anticipating that union with her heart's true love, and in those final moments, I understood her in a way that I never had before. Usually we see a bride as one who is at the culminating point of her life, but the bride has no experience. She is open toward the future and ready to give herself totally to another. I had a deep sense at the deathbed of my mother that I was not next to a dying woman who was finishing her life but next to a bride who had her whole life before her.

"My mother had an understanding of men and was able to express it. She taught some of that to me. On the day we buried her I watched her sons, who were already grandfathers, carry her body toward eternal rest, and they were again the children whose mother was leaving them." Ludmila Javorova died in November of 1986 at the age of eighty-eight. Her daughter knew that the spirit of the one who was both mother and bride would continue to live on in her. "When she was dying she called out to me. Those were her final words." The elder Ludmila's favorite flower was the forget-me-not. Her eldest daughter is one of many who will always remember her. She says, "I often turn to her. I dream about her all the time.

"My parents had been together for fifty-seven years this side of paradise. With each of their deaths I became aware of a summary of my own life and of my own vocation."

After leaving Ludmila's apartment, Davidek moved back to Stepanov, where he had lived as a parish priest following his ordination and where his work with seminarians officially began.

The site was strategically chosen for reasons of security, even though it was some distance from Brno. Koinotes members traveled there to participate in his seminars or whenever they needed to meet with him. Eventually Felix returned to Chrlice to live in his family home with his sister Debora and her three children. Debora's teenage daughter began cooperating with him in matters concerning Koinotes, and Ludmila went there daily to deal with necessary issues. The travel between her place and his was very time-consuming, not like it was when they lived in rooms adjacent to one another. Sometime in 1983 Felix made a brief trip to Japan with one of his bishops, Dusan Spinar. He had been asked to substitute for someone who at the last minute was unable to go. On his return Felix fell ill, and from then on he and Koinotes experienced a gradual tapering off of activity and strength.

This second wave of diminishment followed a period of growth and expansion that culminated at the beginning of the 1980s. Then almost every diocese had its own Koinotes circle, and the pastoral work had escalated. Priests were busy all the time. It was exhausting to do secret pastoral ministry after working hard at a job all day, but they did it, even on weekends. When Felix became ill, the frequency of their meetings rapidly decreased. This had begun even earlier, because interrogations had resumed in Slovakia and some members of Koinotes had emigrated as a result. Some existing activities were maintained, but nothing new was started. Everybody was tired. Ludmila had to take care of her parents, her sick sister, and Felix. At that time she had a strong intuition that she should begin looking for similar groups in order to carry on the work she and Felix had started together, because she wanted to continue with theology and she could no longer count on him.

One reason why Davidek had to reduce the amount of work he did was because of a personal attack initiated by another branch of the underground church and unjustified criticism from the official church. False accusations bordering on slander had been picked up by the Voice of America and by an underground magazine and disseminated in the press. Allegations began to circulate that Davidek's consecrations were not valid. He was accused of having consecrated Fridolin Zahradnik, who was married, but that had been done by one of the bishops who had left Koinotes after the 1970 Council and not by Davidek. Those who knew nothing of the background or the circumstances of various events had simply lifted things out of context. All of this caused uneasiness among some of Davidek's priests and collaborators, which in the end led to his seclusion. "He suffered a lot from this," Ludmila explains. "Through it all he never complained. Only his closest friends understood how difficult this was for him. We knew he had done everything 'for the church.' We had heard him say many times, 'I will sacrifice everything for the church and for the world.'"

Sometime after 1983 Felix suffered a massive head injury in a fall from a staircase and underwent surgery at home, because he refused to go to a hospital. To him that was less frightening than falling again into the hands of the dreaded StB, which had its contacts absolutely everywhere. The same attention to details of security and safety that had kept him out of jail since the day of his release from Mirov twenty years earlier would continue to the very end. He was bedridden following surgery. Ludmila describes the sanctuary of the recuperating scholar priest. "Felix's room looked like a labyrinth made of books. There was a path to the bed between all the books that were literally everywhere. Davidek was busy reading and writing, and he needed to have his resources right there within his reach." He slept on a very small part of the bed and the rest was covered with books.

About a year later Felix suffered another near fatal accident while he was lying in bed. Ludmila had bought a hot plate for him and placed it within reach beside his bed so he could heat some water for coffee or tea. She doesn't know how it happened, because Felix never told her, but when she entered his room one day she found him seriously burned. Somehow his shirt had caught fire, perhaps from touching the electrical heating unit on the portable hot plate, or maybe from a cigarette, for he was a heavy smoker. The result was massive burns over his back, side, and leg. Again he diagnosed himself and refused to call a doctor. He decided on a course of treatment. Ludmila was asked to accept the role of nurse, together with her brother Josef. They asked Bishops Jiri Krpalek and Ivan Klement to help them from time to time.

"This was the worst illness I had ever treated," Ludmila recalls. "Following Felix's instructions, in the beginning I came to see him twice a day. He told me exactly what to do and what I had to buy. I had to sterilize everything without any technical equipment. All the completely burned skin had to be painstakingly removed again and again and the sensitive areas lubricated. Whenever I would touch him, he would break out in a sweat because of the excruciating pain, and the pus would run down his legs. He lay on his side for six months. Our friend Majka got us some medication and eventually his burns healed. The treatment he prescribed for himself took about a year, but he never really recovered and remained bedridden until his death in 1988. During the years of his confinement, I would celebrate Mass with him. He would always wait for me to arrive, and we would celebrate together."

It was an indescribable period for Felix's loyal and generous friend. Ludmila was almost always exhausted. "I would come twice a day, sometimes more often, if necessary." Traveling between Stara osada and Chrlice took a lot of time. Daily she cleaned and dressed his wounds, changed his bed sheets, emptied the bucket used for a latrine, cooked his meals on occasion, sat and listened to him, and brought her world to him. It troubled her that this man who was bishop, mentor, and friend to so many had little or no personal contact with those whom he had served. This was partly due to a practical reason—he did not have his own entrance to the house in which he lived—and partly because of safety. He had very few regular visitors. Besides Ludmila and her brother Josef, he could count on bishops Krpalek, Klement, and Blaha, whom Ludmila had asked to come, and Bishop Josef Hinterhölzl, who never failed to cheer him up. Together they would dive into theological depths, and Felix would emerge refreshed.

Davidek was so grateful to any visitor who inspired him to theological thoughts. He was not interested in official visitors, because he did not want to explain to anybody the nature of his condition and why he was in such a place. "For me it was hard to understand the lack of visitors, because I expected people to be more faithful and more devoted to him," says Ludmila. "All of us had been united by one person, and that was Felix Davidek. Some priests would come to talk, but only now and then. His sister would stop in once a day, but otherwise he was alone. When I would come late in the evening, and my last connection home was at 11:45 p.m., he would often tell me shortly before, 'Do not leave yet.' It nearly killed me to say to him that I really had to go. Sometimes I would turn around and come back because I understood the burden of being bedridden and alone. He would tell me, 'I will not keep you here. Go. I will sacrifice it for the sake of the church and the world and the souls in purgatory.' Then I left.

"Twice during his last two years I found him covered in blood. His blood was on the floor and in his bed. When I asked him what was happening, he would say: 'Oh, it is nothing to worry about. I had something similar in prison. I was also bleeding. I will diagnose it in a few days.' I thought it must have been a cancer, but he said no, it wasn't. For a time he would not move in his bed. He would not eat. He would only drink lots of fluids until the situation stabilized. We had an agreement between us. He promised that when he was critically ill, he would let me know and would allow me to take him to the hospital."

Ludmila and her brother Josef are really the only ones who can speak about Davidek's final days. Except for two nights, when they took a brief break, they were there through it all from the beginning to the end. "I had this intuition one day, before I went for my usual daily visit with Felix. I felt a strange uneasiness, so I went to one of the priests, and I asked him to come with me and help me change Felix's sheets and attend to some other things, because it was really difficult for me to do it on my own. The priest said he did not have the time, so I called Ivan [Bishop Klement], who lived near my place, because I felt I would need his help, and, as it turned out, I did. When we entered the room, we saw that Felix had fallen out of bed. We picked him up and put him back. Before we could even do that, Ivan had to climb on the bed and remove all the books, because there was no room for Felix. I washed him and we changed his bedclothes and made him comfortable. He said he did not remember how long he had been lying there. He may have leaned over to vomit and was unable to get back into bed. He started to hiccup, and his whole body trembled. Then he began to vomit continuously, and that was the beginning of the end."

Several days later, with Davidek's permission, Ludmila took him to the hospital. Her brother Josef and Bishop Ivan, who had helped her in nursing Davidek, assisted her in this. "We arrived at the hospital around 10:00 p.m.," she says. "After examining him, the doctors reported that the situation was serious. Insufficient activity of the heart had caused a vein in the abdominal area to break, something that was not uncommon and could be surgically corrected. Even though Felix was extremely exhausted, they decided that surgery was necessary and scheduled it for the following day. I did not want to bring him to the hospital, because I knew that he was dying. When I told Felix exactly what I thought, he said: 'I have always understood myself, but now I don't know what is happening with me.' I told him to keep calm and not think about it, to give it all to God, that maybe he would meet Jesus soon. When I said this, he closed his eyes and fell asleep, but whenever I started to pray the prayers for the dying, he would always wake up.

"I considered surgery a drastic step and was not in favor of putting Felix through suffering on top of suffering. He was already in his final moments." Ludmila and the others who were there with her—Josef, Ivan, and Jan Blaha—had to leave because of hospital regulations. The next day they went ahead with the operation, and he died shortly after. It was August 16, 1988, fifteen hours after he had been admitted. He did not live to see the liberation of Czechoslovakia and the end of the totalitarian regime.

The hospital notified Ludmila. On her way back to the hospital, she stopped at Bishop Blaha's place to tell him Felix had died. She invited him to accompany her. She wanted to know the cause of death. A nurse at the hospital told her it was an intestinal aneurysm that was inoperable because of his condition. His intestines looked like those of an eighty-year-old man. Felix was sixty-two. The years in a maximum security prison had left their mark on him. Ludmila picks up the narration.

"As I came out of the hospital, I saw a hearse in the yard. I knew this was for transporting the dead, so I said, I will not leave because they must be coming for Felix. I stood behind the hearse, and in a little while I saw them carrying Felix's body up from the basement of the building. I was horrified. There was such a lack of respect. A disgusting sheet made of rough, black gummed material that had been used for a very long time, as far as I could see, had been thrown haphazardly over his naked body. And he had been always so aware of what was appropriate in every situation! All of a sudden Felix's arm fell out from under the covering and his hand nearly touched the ground. I shouted, 'Felix!' The attendant began to yell at me. 'You, madame, go away, or I will take him back.' I said to myself, 'I am not leaving.' I hid behind the hearse, so he wouldn't be able to see me. They carried him to the hearse, and when they were putting him into the back, I went up to him and said, 'Felix, thank you for everything, and God be with you.' Then they closed the door.

"Bishop Blaha was also nearby. He was standing inside the

building, hidden behind the door. We watched as the hearse drove
slowly away. Suddenly it stopped and waited in back of the hospital while a little boy came running to me. The driver had given
him a message. 'Lady, if you want to say goodbye to your dead, go
to the fields between the old Brno and the hospital. The driver will
wait there for you.' Imagine, this was during Totality, when everything was so strict. He didn't know me. He didn't know Felix. He
was a stranger to us. So I shouted to Blaha, 'Come! Come here!
We have to run to the fields.' There is a field road behind the
hospital and a hill running down to old Brno. It was 4:00 p.m. in
August and the sun was merciless as we ran down that hill. This
man was not afraid. When we arrived he was waiting for us. He
opened the back door, took Felix out, uncovered his face, and left.
He said, 'Take as long as you want.' So we prayed for Felix and we
thanked him and we both said our goodbyes. Then I thanked the
man and asked him, 'Where are you taking him?' He said, 'To the
children's hospital.' Again, can you imagine? That was the place
where Davidek used to work.

"The next day I went to the pathology department at the children's hospital. The guard asked me what I wanted. I don't know
what I told him, just that I had come to prepare a very important
person for burial and that I wanted to dress him myself. Now Felix
never, ever was seen dressed as a bishop, at least not locally. He
wore the robes just once, when he was in Poland at a priest's First
Mass. He was dressed as a bishop then and I wanted to dress him
as a bishop now. The guard said, 'Lady, I am not letting you inside
this room. You would be scared of all the dead bodies.' I said, 'I
am not afraid of dead bodies.' He wanted to frighten me, so he
said, 'They are lying there on a pile, one on top of the other.' But
then he said to me, 'Okay. If there is no talking you out of it, just
come and bring your things. I will take him out for you, and you
can dress him.'

"However, as it turned out, he did not let me into the room.
He took the clothes I had there with me and dressed Felix on his

own. Then he brought him out and into a hall so that I could freshen him up. So we were able to dress him as a bishop. That was unbelievable at that time and it had such significance. For me this meant the final uncovering of all the layers concealing his person over a long, long time. I thought that these things, uncovered at last, were now resolved in their own way."

Bishop Felix Maria Davidek, dressed in his bishop's robes, without the miter because he had never worn one, was given a public burial in Turany from the church of the Virgin Mary in Thorns, where he had been baptized. His funeral was conducted by Ludvik Horky, the vicar capitular of Brno, an ex-Pacem in Terris priest. The church was packed with people. "I put many orchids in his coffin," Ludmila says, "because Felix really loved them." After the funeral Koinotes members criticized Ludmila for dressing him as a bishop. They wanted to see him that last time as he was in their memory of him. Ludmila replied firmly: "The dress belongs to him. During his entire life he couldn't be a bishop in public. He crossed over into eternal life as a bishop, so he should be there as a bishop." He was buried in the village cemetery adjacent to the church.

Testimonies to Davidek's life and spirit were prevalent following his death and continue today. "I consider him a genius," says his friend Majka. "I admired most his generosity. There were problems around his personality, but I do not consider this essential."

Maria Javorova says, "He was a very compassionate priest. It's a problem for me that I got to know him when I was young, because I will forever compare everybody to him, and I cannot find anyone else that has been like he was for me. However, I often blamed him for putting such enormous burdens on people, for instance, with my sister, who was fully available to him late into the night, even when she had to go to work in the morning. My parents and I would tell him we did not think it would be so intensive, and then he would apologize. He would change for a day or two. The third day it was the same."

Josef Javorova: "He bound himself to the Holy Spirit. This was Davidek, and this is also us. To abandon ourselves to Spirit, to abandon ourselves to the work of God is to say the same thing. There were many things that were over his head. When we asked him what would be happening next, he really didn't know. He put his trust in the Spirit."

Jan Blaha: "Davidek was a man gifted with a high level of intelligence. We could not believe his knowledge, his ability to organize and manage. He was especially charismatic. His vast wisdom was a gift from God. His inner being, deeply connected to God, went out to others from the fullness of his human spirituality. I was closely connected to him and collaborated with him. He was mentor for me. He brought light to my various problems and was able to find solutions. His work yielded very rich fruit and was both a blessing from God and a sign from God. I am convinced that this kind of gifted individual is born only as an exception. I am also convinced that he was sent to do something important for the church of the future. He was an exceptional man, a great man of spirit. It is not possible to find somebody similar to him."

Ludmila Javorova: "Felix came from a very aristocratic environment where they didn't show their emotions or feelings. I didn't like going there to his family when I was a child. Everything was very beautiful, but I didn't understand their relationships. His father would sit and smoke his pipe and not say a single word. Felix was so different from his early environment. He was a smart and graceful man of highly refined manners. He was able to talk to everyone with the same love and interest. He would talk to an old woman the same way as to a president, and he would deal with a president as if he were an equal, because for him we were all brothers and sisters. If he was authoritative, then his behavior was based on the fact that the other person must be willing to accept it. He did not open his heart much to others. I could understand that. He had the responsibility and the situation was often complicated. It was a double-edged sword. He was a man of superior intelligence with a broad educational background, a theologian, physician, anthropologist, lawyer, I could even say an administrator, and he had a highly developed sense for aesthetic and cultural values. He loved music and literature and so many things that I cannot name them all.

"As a human being, Felix always tried to stand on the same level as the person in front of him, but on the other hand, he could also be indiscriminate, even ruthless, especially when he was tired, which means he was sometimes controversial, but he was able to admit it. Unfortunately, there were not enough people who were able to talk about this with him. He longed for human good will so much, and I believe this was because of his upbringing and his imprisonment. He could foresee the needs of the church, and he was able to act immediately without unnecessary delays, even before his internment. He persisted in this until his death. His ability to distinguish spirits came from the essence of his charismatic gifts. As a bishop he did not demonstrate his hierarchic power, as we are used to seeing. Service to him was a true service to all God's people, and it really mattered to him that the people of God would see him this way. When he arrived from prison, I had the feeling that this person was still starving for something, I don't know what, maybe love, but he seemed to be driven by this. He even expressed it in one of his poems, that he was leaning into the well and he was still thirsty. Once he even said he was sorry he had never found anybody who really shared his vision, but despite that, he had to continue.

"Felix always said he had to assess what the Holy Spirit was saying to the church through the mouths of ordinary people. He felt a responsibility as bishop to fully identify with the whole of the church, not only a particular locality. He lived this conviction. He would say, we live it as the whole church. He did not consider Koinotes as something set apart or as something different. He would say, well, we have to do something here, but it is for the whole church. It would be repeated to us as if it were one of the ten commandments. We belong to the whole church. We knew this as something totally self-evident.

"He and I did not always agree. For example, I would have asked the bishops to work much more independently, and this was where we clashed. It was sort of a friction between us. And I have to say that at one time I even wanted to leave because I felt that his need to be in control did not leave any space for God. By this I mean that such a way of proceeding does not take into account the fact that things could develop in a different way, that it is up to us to find those ways when we are in relationship with God, trusting all along that God will add what we are unable to do. His way was different, and I didn't want to carry on along this line. I asked Felix to put in writing that he was taking this vicar general function away from me. He gave it to me in writing, but then we continued working together. Later on I realized that I would never leave this work. Occasional human failings were not sufficient reason for leaving. Besides, he was already ill and he would have been completely alone."

FIFTEEN

Sing, O heavens, for God has done this.
Shout, O depths of the earth,
break forth into singing.

Isaiah 44:23

Approximately fourteen thousand pilgrims traveled from Czechoslovakia to Rome for the canonization of Saint Agnes of Bohemia
on November 12, 1989. Five days later on November 17, a student rally in Prague turned into a demonstration that marked
the beginning of a six-week period known as the "Velvet Revolution." Inspired by liberating events elsewhere, in particular the
demise of the Berlin Wall in neighboring East Germany, massive public demonstrations took place throughout the country.
Peaceful initiatives included the emergence of two political or-
ganizations, "Civic Forum" in the Czech region, led by Vaclav
Havel, and "Public Against Violence" in Slovakia. These coordinated protests resulted in a bloodless victory over communist
forces to end four decades of totalitarian rule. A democratic
government took control on December 10 and elected Alexander Dubcek speaker of the Federal Assembly. Vaclav Havel was
elected president of Czechoslovakia on December 29. Three years
later, on December 31, 1992, Czechoslovakia ceased to exist as
a national entity. The Czech Republic and the Slovak Republic
were declared separate nations in 1993.

The fall of the communist regime at the end of 1989 meant
the Catholic Church could now function fully and freely without
external coercion. Pope John Paul II made a brief visit to Czechoslovakia in April of 1990, and in 1992, for the first time in forty

years, all the bishops went to Rome for their *ad limina* visit with
the pope. By that time Miloslav Vlk was archbishop of Prague.

The underground church in Czechoslovakia had been an or-
ganic, multifaceted movement with no central coordination in
which hundreds of priests and a number of bishops had functioned
in separately organized groups. The largest of these, it has been
said, was the network known as Koinotes established by Davidek.
Because there was now no longer need for its continuation, clandestine clergy of the underground church began to shed their
cloak of anonymity, fully expecting unconditional acceptance by
Rome. That did not happen.

The so-called "first line" clergy of the visible church, those
who had been licensed by the government to minister openly and
were therefore products of the communist-controlled seminary or
repentant Pacem in Terris priests, were quickly reconciled. They
continued their active service, often doing what they had been
doing before. Among these were a number of clergy who had
collaborated with the regime. Clergy of the "second line," who
chose to be active underground in order to keep the integrity of
the Catholic faith alive, were treated differently. Their ministry
had been invisible and their ordination secret. They had made
this choice precisely because a Vatican directive prohibited cooperation with communists who had taken control of the church,
yet Rome's response after 1990 was to withhold official recogni-
tion until the validity of their priestly ordinations and episcopal
consecrations could be corroborated. This prerequisite proved extremely difficult to accomplish, for the very survival of the hidden
church and its individual clergy depended on a strict code of secrecy with no written documentation. Suddenly, in Rome's eyes,
what had been considered legitimate under the forces of communism was now perceived as a parallel priesthood and a problem to
be solved.

In 1992 the Vatican issued a pastoral letter ordering all underground priests who were still unidentified to report to their

bishops, saying: "It is time to put an end to this extraordinary state of affairs. It is no longer possible to have twin priesthoods, twin Masses, twin administering of the sacraments, and twin spreaders of the Gospels." The same letter was published again in 1995. On February 14, 2000, Cardinal Joseph Ratzinger, as prefect of the Congregation for the Doctrine of the Faith, issued an Instruction explaining Rome's decision to require ordination *"sub conditione"* for priests whose ordinations were considered to be of doubtful validity. The text states:

> Being ordained *"sub conditione"* means that if their previous ordination was valid, the second ordination ("subject to condition") would not have any effect, given that they were already priests; if, on the other hand, the secretly received ordinations were not valid, they, being newly ordained, would be certain in conscience that they were really priests.

Ordination *sub conditione* is the Vatican solution to two distinctly different situations. The first concerns celibate priests; the second concerns priests who married. The priests themselves have never doubted the validity of their ordination. It is a problem only with Rome.

Approximately fifty celibate priests who had been secretly ordained reluctantly submitted to Rome's insistence on reordination and have since been reinstated into parish ministry by their respective diocesan bishops. Married priests were also asked to submit to conditional reordination within the tradition of the Eastern church. The Vatican created a special diocese—oparchate—in the Czech Republic's Greek Catholic Church, which is affiliated with Rome and allows married priests. Twenty-two married priests were ordained *sub conditione* within the Greek Catholic rite but were denied bi-ritual faculties, although such a practice had a lengthy tradition in Czechoslovakia prior to Totality. Those who were consecrated bishops in the underground church present another challenge to the institutional church. They have had to promise not to practice episcopal ministry.

There are still a number of priests, both celibate and married, who have refused to accept *sub conditione* ordination. Their status remains unresolved. They believe their ordination was valid and that their priesthood is legitimate. They resent the implication that their years of priestly ministry under difficult and dangerous conditions and their own personal integrity are now being called into question. Hans Jorissen, retired professor of theology in Bonn, Germany, touches the heart of the issue when he says: "Reordination is permitted under canon law only if there are justified doubts, but not if there are unjustified allegations."*

At the center of the controversy concerning valid ordinations and consecrations was and still is Bishop Felix Maria Davidek. Ludmila points out: "The truth was that Davidek never told anybody who consecrated him, so that was a major cause of the tensions back then. He was able to be as silent as a grave. He did not want to endanger his consecration. He could validate the details, but he is not here anymore."

This is how Ludmila remembers the sequence of events. "Davidek, a former political prisoner, was always being watched by the StB, so he could not leave the country to seek episcopal consecration. Jan Blaha, a seminarian, was free to travel. He left Czechoslovakia to be ordained and came back with a mandate from Pope Paul VI that led to his own consecration as a bishop and the subsequent consecration of Davidek by him. This was done with the permission of the Vatican." Jan Blaha's credentials are considered above reproach. Rome accepts the validity of his episcopacy, although he is now a parish priest and does not function as a bishop. Rome also accepts the validity of Davidek's episcopacy, but questions the legitimacy of some of his ordina-

---

The Guardian (London), November 2, 1996.

tions and episcopal consecrations. Were those whom he ordained to the priesthood properly prepared? Were their ordinations valid? Where is the evidence supporting their claims? These are some of Rome's concerns.

Ludmila adds this piece to the story. "Jan Blaha also brought with him an oral message from Pope Paul VI. The pope said that the men studying for the priesthood should not be given tasks that were too demanding, because they also had to go to work. They should be given only the most necessary assignments in preparation for ministry. They could then continue their education and complete it over a period of time. This bit of advice was helpful. Later on the pope would send his personal messenger to Bishop Davidek to acknowledge him. As I have already pointed out, I was present when that messenger came."

Davidek made it clear that as bishop he had the right to make decisions for the good of the local church, and in this he acted according to the authority invested in him as bishop of Koinotes. Those outside his jurisdiction could not fully comprehend why certain things had to be done. Rumors had begun to spread about his psychological state. After all, he had ordained a woman, or so it had been said. When he suffered a head injury in a fall, there was speculation he might be mentally unbalanced, even schizophrenic. The allegation that he was schizophrenic has again come to the fore, even though there is no diagnostic evidence to corroborate such an assertion, even though many who had worked with him insist that this is absurd, even though there are witnesses to testify he was mentally sound and making vital contributions right up to the time of his death. This false rumor stems from a statement made by a psychiatrist who had not examined Felix, says Ludmila, and also from his detractors. "We sent two detailed statements to Rome, one from a doctor who had operated on Felix when he was physically ill and had subsequently cured him, and the other from a psychologist." She wonders what has become of this evidence refuting the spurious allegations of schizophrenia. No doubt certain individuals in Rome simply came to the conclusion that was most convenient for them.

Among other things, Davidek has been falsely accused of consecrating many married bishops and ordaining female deacons. Neither of these accusations is true. However, he did consecrate one married man whose wife was seriously ill, but first he asked for and received from the man a written statement testifying to his promise to live celibately. This happened about a year before Davidek's death, when he was already ill and unable to walk. He was ambivalent about this consecration, but Koinotes members in Prague had been pressuring him for a bishop of their own. Ludmila says, "He told me what he intended to do, and I did not agree with it. When he heard my negative response, he said to me, 'I won't do it,' but then eventually, he did. I was not present for the consecration."

In the rush to discredit Davidek, some core characteristics of his episcopal ministry have been overlooked. He believed in a sacramental priesthood with apostolic succession. Therefore, he was careful to ensure that the ordinations he undertook followed the Roman Pontifical and that all procedures were correct. He was completely dedicated to the church, respected its traditions, and he believed that whatever he did locally was on behalf of the church as a whole. He never thought he was anything but an integral part of the official church. Ludmila says, "His relationship to the church was so genuine, even though his relationship to the curia was sharp." Koinotes was only one aspect of the underground church in Czechoslovakia. However, it is generally agreed that the network that functioned under Davidek was the most influential. It may also have been the largest numerically, and geographically the most widespread. Many priests and bishops trace their ordinations and their consecrations, either directly or indirectly, back to Bishop Davidek, which is why Rome cannot simply close the book on him.

Ludmila's life changed dramatically after the death of Felix and the end of the communist era. The intense pressure of attending to needs so demanding, so all-consuming was suddenly no longer there. Gone, too, was the context of her dedicated life—priestly ministry in a stark and repressive society as a member of Koinotes. The paradigm shift in society was reflected in her experience of church. Before, when all was hidden, Ludmila could exercise her priestly ministry in meaningful ways. "After the revolution," she says, "when everything began to focus on secretly ordained priests, and very few knew I was a priest as well, I began to bring to a close my priestly activities, because we were entering a new situation that could be unbearable for penitents. I suspected that my ordination would not be accepted. Some who were part of my ministry did not understand, but I insisted on their returning to the fully restored church."

Immediately after the fall of communism, before the break-away group surfaced with its own perspective on the evolution of Koinotes, Ludmila began gathering the facts to be communicated to Rome, because the scope of her information was so extensive. "I tried to get in touch with everybody, either directly or indirectly, tried to reintegrate those who had been silent, either recently or in the past. I gave Bishop Blaha a list of as many priests as I could remember. I wanted him to take me with him during negotiations with the church. It had been a principle since the very beginning of our cooperation with Davidek that no one was to act on their own with regard to important issues, because we did not all share the same information. I was not invited to any negotiation. None of those who were core to Koinotes leadership were invited to participate. Blaha went ahead on his own. After his first few meetings with church officials, I was no longer informed about what transpired in subsequent transactions.

"When we who had been part of Koinotes came together after the Velvet Revolution in order to meet one another, it was clear that I was unacceptable to some. No one told me to leave the meetings, but neither did anyone introduce me in a proper way.

Consequently, it happened sometimes that after I had made a comment, someone would say: 'Why does that lady meddle in it?' My protest was insufficient. I was never able to find out why not one of those men had been able to say that I had been vicar general for years, that during the time of my tenure I had the authority to act on certain things, which meant that I have the right and the responsibility to comment on those things now. Everyone at the meetings seemed focused on their own problems. In the end it was expressed that I should not speak out, that I should not identify myself and my role within the community, that I should remain in the background. I had a different opinion, but once that view had been stated, it took on a life of its own. But that would open up another chapter, and the story would never end."

Certain developments troubled Ludmila, for instance, the attack on Davidek, and the fact that she had not been consulted when the validity of certain clerical ordinations had to be verified. In her role as vicar general, she had witnessed a number of clergy ordinations and episcopal consecrations. Some might be quick to answer that Rome would certainly not rely on the testimony of a woman. Ludmila says the exclusion did not come only from Rome. "When things began to open up, those priests who knew I was ordained began to distance themselves from me. Having to deal with their own insecurity, they realized I could be a hindrance to their acceptance by the church." To appear supportive of women's ordination in theory or in practice would place another obstacle on the path to their validation. "I felt so much my powerlessness over against their fear." When Ludmila wanted to speak out, she was told, "You can't take a public stand on that." They may have had good reasons, she says, but their refusal to acknowledge her role and her reality was tantamount to rejection. She had no illusions that the Vatican would have recognized her priesthood, but she wanted to be counted, to have it go on record that she too had been ordained. Nobody from the hierarchy spoke to Ludmila about her ordination. She says, "They knew about it, but they didn't think it was valid, so they just let it go."

Ludmila knows one of the women priests in Slovakia and is very impressed with her sincerity and dedication. "I cannot speak about her," she says, "because she would be identified and she doesn't want to be. She is afraid of Rome. This is really a very good woman. I appreciate her very much. I admire her. I respect her. Of course, I am not surprised that she does not want to go public. The social pressure is terrible, unbearable, and it is even more difficult in Slovakia than it is here. It exhausts all one's energies just to remain in the struggle. The only way we can make it is to depend completely on God."

Certain church representatives tried to persuade Ludmila that she had to have a bad conscience about having been ordained. "They knew I was a priest. I said I doubt that someone would be able to discover this fact, that I had a bad conscience, by putting only two or three questions to me. And these were not even questions; they were accusations. If my conscience had been so bad, if I had been so guilty, how could it be that God had not sent me any messenger long before this, because I speak with God daily. I have spoken about this, about my ordination, and every day I ask God to guide me in my understanding of priesthood. I have never felt within me that I would have done something that God did not wish."

Because she could no longer carry out certain activities, Ludmila's priestly ministry took the form of teaching children. She was able to do this freely and openly, not like during Totality, when she had to instruct them in secret. In 1990, Ludmila received approval from the bishop's office to fulfill the role of catechist. Since then she has taught religion, an optional subject in state schools, to children between the ages of seven and fourteen and prepares the children in her parish to receive their First Communion. "I have one principle," she says. "From the first grade, children should be taught how to listen." She teaches listening, very effectively, in creative ways. Her catechetical ministry in the Church of Saints Cyril and Methodius, her parish, no longer in-cludes adults. During those early years following the revolution, her pastor permitted her to prepare people for baptism and also for marriage. "At first the priest used to come and listen to what I was telling couples. He would say, 'How interesting,' but then he would let me be. Once after he had begun the wedding Mass, he called out to me in the church and said, 'Since you have prepared this couple for marriage, come up and talk to them.' The priest did not know of my ordination, so I took it as a sign from God affirming my ministry." At another time a priest invited her to give a series of homilies during the month of May. "It was after the revolution and it was quite a distance from where I lived. No one, not even the priest who invited me, knew that I was a priest. Here was another sign. To me it was not important how many signs I received. It was sufficient simply to see certain incidents as signs, and there were enough of them. As for the homilies, the experience of standing in front of people cannot be compared to standing at the table by yourself."

From time to time Ludmila would try to initiate a conversation about issues she felt were important to women. "Once I asked some women the question: 'When you pray alone, do you pray in the language of women or in the language of men?' " In the Czech language the male or female gender shows in every verb, noun, and adjective. Liturgical prayers are ordinarily in the male gender, which is considered neutral. "For most people this is unimportant, but for me it has major meaning, to speak in the language of women, because then my self-reflection before God really goes into depth. The experience of my own being is quite different when I express myself out of my own essence. Some people would laugh at this. They would see it as extreme, but I'm far from extremes. I see myself as a woman, and I am more and more grateful for it, deeply grateful for it, and I would say it in my prayer too. There are some women who don't mind at all that they pray in a man's language. I mind it. I have the Breviary all crossed out. When somebody inherits it someday, he's probably going to get scared. He will ask, how did she pray? When I'm with women, when we're at meetings or catechism class, once in a while I try to lead the conversation this way, and then there's a very cold silence. They do not feel the need. Even those who have studied theology do not feel as I do inside."

Ludmila continued to keep the fact of her ordination to herself, yet once the hidden church was exposed, there were persistent rumors of the existence of women priests. Already in 1990 the Austrian periodical *Kirche Intern* with offices in Vienna had uncovered the name of Ludmila and had sought her out. They got bits of information, but not what they were looking for: her definitive admission that she was a priest. Again and again they returned to the question, "Were you or were you not ordained?" Ludmila danced around it, refusing to admit it, yet reluctant to lie. Sensing there was something more to the story, they returned to Brno the following year, and the next, and the next, and sometimes twice a year.

"In 1995 they called again to tell me that several of them were coming to visit me. I received them in my apartment. One of them was a Franciscan and we had an interesting discussion. I asked him if it was difficult to keep a secret in their profession and he said no, it was not. We started talking about the underground church, as we had done several times before. Suddenly, I said to myself, enough of this circling around, of searching for the right words to avoid telling a lie. I said that I would not tell him anything more, only that there is a woman who is ordained, and that he had to keep this information confidential." He was told he must not tell anyone about what she had entrusted to him, and that he should not continue to look for anything more on this subject, because that was all she would say. "That is why I revealed it, so he would stop coming to me, but I spoke with the understanding that it would not be published. He promised it would not be." The delegation returned to Vienna. Later that day the chief editor telephoned Ludmila. They would publish the news in their magazine, he said. He would not, could not keep it secret. She heard from him again after that, the day he sent her flowers.

The November issue of *Kirche Intern* arrived at Ludmila's place in Brno. She says, "I thought I would collapse right there between the doors of my apartment." On the cover was Ludmila's animated face and beneath it the screaming headline: '*Ich bin katholische Priesterin*'—'I am a Catholic priest.'" Shock. Panic. What to do now? What she always did when she had to gain control of herself in an out-of-control situation. "I closed myself in a room, and I knelt before the cross with my head in my hands as I used to do in difficult times. I said: 'I cannot change the reality. I will go forward, and with every step I take, I will hold on tight. I will not deal with anything but this. I will do everything calmly, accept everything calmly, and then I will speak and act. I will not look to the right or to the left. I will just go forward. At first I told myself, 'No, no, no! Oh my God, that's terrible.' Then I told myself, 'Why not? Take it all as it comes.' And that's exactly what I did."

For ten days following the publication of her admission, all Ludmila could do was sit by the phone and answer the many calls, unless the doorbell rang, and then she would go to the door. "The newspaper men were like flies around me. I didn't want to be tough, but in one case, I had to be. I even closed the door on them. They were reporters from Germany, and I said, 'Sirs, I have not invited anyone. I do not want to publish anything.' After I had closed the door, I really felt sorry for them, because they had traveled so far, but what was I to do? You cannot believe how many people came from around the world. Some thought that I was a bishop. They wanted to be secretly ordained, people who called themselves Christian. I lived through those moments as if in a dream."

Ludmila spent a lot of time doing damage control. "I had to go to my relatives and explain everything to them. Then I went to see my pastor. I expected I would be forbidden to teach. That's how bad it was. He was an elderly man who had been a priest in the underground church and was ordained within Koinotes. I went to his office and said: 'Father, I'm so sorry. I am about to cause you a lot of trouble.' I asked him if he would come with me to some quiet place, and then I told him that I was ordained. I told him how the news had come out, and that they would surely be coming to talk to him as well. He said, 'They already came to me and I told them it wasn't true.' He had received a call from some agency that morning but had no idea what it was about. He was very understanding. He just said to me, 'It happened.' Finally, I wrote to my diocesan bishop. He had known about me unofficially, but now he heard it directly from me. I told him my priesthood had been made public against my will, that I hadn't told anyone publicly that I was ordained, and that I would not speak about it anymore. I also told him that I had never publicly celebrated Mass, and that I was available to respond to any questions."

Ludmila had written to the pope sometime around 1983 and heard nothing in response. But once everything was out in the open, thanks to an Austrian magazine, then the Vatican reacted. In 1996 she was summoned to the bishop's office and notified that she was formally prohibited from exercising her priesthood, which was considered invalid. She was told not to reveal the details of the prohibition, and therefore she will not. Prior to this, informal statements attributed to the Vatican had circulated in the press and elsewhere, stating that if women had been ordained, their ordinations were not valid. This formal ban on priestly activity was given privately to Ludmila and was not made public. "I was given the prohibition, and I accepted it, because what could I do?"

Ludmila appreciated the way she had been treated by the bishop of Brno. "My bishop was very tolerant, very human, very tactful. He did not want to hurt me in any way, but of course he was in charge, he had to solve certain things, and he didn't have the authority to do it the way he might have wanted, because the prohibition came from Rome. My case was very difficult to solve, because I had done nothing against the church and I hadn't acted publicly. I was sorry, however, that nobody asked me how it happened that I came to be ordained, or why I accepted ordination and under what circumstances, and how I had worked with it. A prohibition was issued, and no consideration was given to what would happen next. There was no concern for the person. To take away something I have identified with for twenty-five years, something that I worked with and wanted to develop, for me this was very hard, because I could not discuss it with anybody. Whether it is even possible to take away something that I view as God's gift, now that's another matter. I was even asked by certain people whether I had considered affiliating with another church where I would be allowed to celebrate the sacraments, but I would consider this a betrayal. There are so many empty parishes, so many empty churches. I could go there to lead the Service of the Word, but I am not allowed even this. I suggested this to my bishop. I promised I would not overstep my bounds, that I would go no further than what is now permitted, but he said that, despite my promise, it was impossible."

Fallout from the disclosure caught up with Ludmila in some strong negative reactions expressed within her parish. She continued to prepare people for the sacraments, but once they learned from the media who she really was, everything changed. Although the priest never told anyone, inevitably word got out. Questions appeared in the parish newsletter. Questions were also put directly to Ludmila. "How do you imagine your future activity in the church?" "Isn't this a case of seizing power and seeking personal fame?" The parish became a divided camp with Ludmila in the middle.

At this time a newly appointed curate arrived to assist the elderly pastor. He had been studying in Rome when the news broke about Ludmila. His superior telephoned him and said, "In your country you have a woman ordained a priest." He was inflexible in his response. "As I am alive, nothing like this has happened in my country." As fate would have it, he returned to Czechoslovakia, was appointed to a parish, and the woman whose existence he had denied was right there in his parish. "He really persecuted me," she says. "You cannot imagine how much. For instance I used to do a special liturgy with children of the parish at the beginning of the school year. It was organized in such a way that the children would do it all themselves and their parents would attend it. I do something similar before Christmas, because I want the children to experience the sacraments as celebration. We had prepared the Gospel, some intercessions, and some questions to think about and were in the middle of it when the door flew open and the priest came in. I saw him enter but I continued on. He stood before the children and their parents and said to me furiously: 'I do not want you to do such things.' He said a lot more than that. I thanked him and continued."

Afterward Ludmila went to him and told him not to do that again, that if he had any concerns he should come to her ahead of time so that they could discuss them. He said, "I will not discuss anything with you. With you I will not negotiate." As he said this he was marching around the room. "He couldn't even look at me." Ludmila had been helping the children acquire an ease with going to confession. "The confessions take place at little tables where there is a candle and Scripture open there. The children would tell their parents at home that they gladly go to confession when it is at the little table, but not in those confessional boxes where you kneel and look through the bars."

During Advent Ludmila had the girls bring candles from the sacristy to light the Advent wreath. The old parish priest was always happy that she did this with the children, but he was in the hospital, so the curate was in charge. "I entered the sacristy with the children to help them light their candles, and the priest shouted at me in front of the children: 'Nothing like this will happen here. Now go away, quickly, because I have to celebrate the Mass, and I do not want to get angry.' He was on the verge of exploding. I responded from an inner calm. I said, 'Father, let's not make one another angry, because all of us go to celebrate Mass, not only you. Now lighting the Advent wreath is the custom in this parish, and I do not want to cancel this custom, because it is very meaningful to the children.' He said with increasing anger: 'I have to leave.' He just did not know how to behave, and he could not work with a woman. Because our pastor was sick, he spent two years here in the parish."

While certain people were against Ludmila and the whole idea of women priests, there were others who were for her. "Not a lot of them," she admits, "and there was not much support in public, but there were people who came up to me and said 'thank you' after church on Sunday. Affirmation came not only from women. There were several men who had no problem accepting women as priests." Her sister Maria remains one of her staunchest supporters. "Mary said to Jesus in Cana, 'They have no wine.' Maybe nobody would notice it, and maybe Jesus wouldn't even have done this miracle, but then he did, because of a woman. This seems to me to be the best thing I can say about my sister's ordination."

Word of women priests in Czechoslovakia crossed the Atlantic early on. The *National Catholic Reporter* broke the story in the United States in an article by Tim McCarthy in September 1990. "Informants said Davidek did eventually ordain at least one woman, but they did not know who or where she was, and their story could not be confirmed." The following year, on December 8, an article appeared in the *New York Times* under the headline, "Women Ordained in Roman Catholic Church." It confirmed that there were "at least three women ordained as priests . . . all in the town of Brno."

Ruth McDonough Fitzpatrick, the national coordinator of the Women's Ordination Conference (WOC) in Washington, D.C., read the *New York Times* report and decided she would go to Czechoslovakia to find the women who had been ordained. Others expressed an interest in joining her in the search. She gathered information, put together a small delegation, and raised the money for the trip. Shortly before leaving, she discovered Frank Mikes, a former Koinotes priest who had left Czechoslovakia and was living in the United States. He knew one of the women personally. By the time they were ready to embark on their quest, Ruth had obtained the name and the telephone number of Ludmila Javorova in Brno.

In May 1992 Martha Ann Kirk, C.C.V.I., assistant professor of theology, Carolyn Moynihan, a family therapist, and Dolly Pomerleau, co-director of the Quixote Center in Hyattsville, Maryland, traveled to Czechoslovakia with Ruth. They had a map and a lot of determination. Ruth never doubted that they would find Ludmila, even though none of them spoke the language and they did not know where she lived. "Our goal was simple," says Dolly, "to go to Czechoslovakia, meet the women priests and the married priests, and seek to build solidarity."

It took a while before the group finally made contact with Ludmila. A priest in Prague, their first stop, told them their trip had been in vain. He said his bishop had told him that the women who were ordained had died. In Brno a group of eighteen people interested in hearing about the church in the United States invited the women to meet with them. During their time together, the U.S. delegation learned a lot about the underground church. After several hours of intense scrutiny, they were deemed trustworthy and introduced to Ludmila later that evening. The women urged Ludmila to go public with her story, but she said it was not the time.

A second delegation returned to Brno in 1996. Andrea Johnson, executive director of WOC, together with Maureen Fiedler, S.L., and Dolly Pomerleau, both co-directors of the Quixote Center, invited Ludmila to the United States to meet with other

women and men who support women's ordination. In the after-
math of her untimely exposure to the public against her will, she
decided it was time. She had to set the record straight. What had
been said about her and nearly all the direct quotes attributed
to her were not a valid testament. It was time to step out of the
shadows, to speak out of the depths of her conviction the truth
of her priestly call.

On October 27, 1997, Ludmila flew to the United States accompanied by her friend Magda Zahorska, an ordained deacon
from Slovakia, Magda's sister, Elena Backorova, a lay associate,
and their interpreter, Jana Shropshire. The private two-week visit
was a whirlwind of meetings, formal and informal, in Cleveland, Baltimore, Washington, D.C., and somewhere in New Jersey.
The itinerary included a session with three U.S. bishops who listened to Ludmila's story with interest and respect. Bishop Frank
Murphy, now deceased, said to her: "You must write." Andrea
Johnson pushed the idea further and spoke of the need for
a book.

Ludmila held her audience captive everywhere she went. She
said to those assembled: "Yes, I celebrated Mass. I know that the
church does not want this, yet I think it is necessary to talk about
it, to work for it and to pray about it, so that people will eventually accept it." She listened to the stories of American women
who also feel called to priesthood and offered a word of caution.
"The role of the church is to unite, so if the question of women's
ordination would not unite people in the end, it wouldn't be any
good. So we have to work at that." Amazed at the statistics that
indicate a majority of Catholics in the United States are in favor
of women priests, she said: "If such a high percentage is for the
ordination of women, then you must knock at the door of heaven
with persistent prayer. It is necessary for the church to pray together for a solution to the problem of too few priests and not
simply say no to women. How then can it know what the Spirit is
saying to the church? Shared intercession shapes attitudes, and at-

titudes give strength, but it takes time to see whether the charism has been given or not. Our time and God's time are two different stories."

She told the gatherings of women and men what they already knew. "The church does not recognize my ordination." She also made this statement. "I want one thing to be clear. If the bishop doesn't authorize me to function as a priest, I know that I cannot do it, and I will not." In response to those who would ask why she doesn't just leave the church, she replied: "I cannot leave the church. I belong to it, I form it, and I have to build on it."

Ludmila's sacramental priesthood and the wisdom of her experience have much to teach us all. "It was so unexpected. I did not anticipate being ordained. I accepted it as God's gift. God gives gifts for no reason at all, so I will never find an answer to the question, 'Why me?' although I have asked many times. I want to be responsible for the gift I have been given and follow it through to the end, to develop its possibilities in the circumstances I am in. I received a great, great deal through the church. I cannot be taken away from the church, not now, not ever, so I subject myself to what they want, but I cannot return the gift. How can a human being who is so small and so limited give a gift back to God? We have to work on it, but we also have to wait. I know I am walking on very thin ice, but God will do whatever God wishes whenever God wants to do it, and it will be when we least expect it."

She found a great love for the Eucharist among the women and men she met as she shared her own thoughts on the sacrament. "Communism made us strong," she said. "For example, in how we understood communion and applied it in different ways as a spiritual generator, because that is what it is. I'm still doing it." The limits imposed by a totalitarian regime caused her to reflect more deeply. For this reason she feels "the experience of Eucharist is much more intensive." The limits imposed by the Vatican, she believes, have not yet been fully explored. "We all celebrate together, but I don't preside." However, she is quick to remind everyone: "While I do not have a public ministry, it doesn't mean I am losing my priesthood."

Her generous perspective regarding the injustice of prohibition reflects the deep integration of her life with the life of God. "Our story of salvation continues, and it has happened many times in the history of salvation that mistakes have been made. God uses them, builds on them, and in this way God's greatness can be seen. To open your privacy to the public in this way is not easy, but every human person has their own dignity before God, and this is the root of my security. Many times I thought about these things, especially during those times I could see nothing open to me, nothing that I was allowed to do. Christ also gave up everything to cancel differences between people."

Always Ludmila's message instilled and inspired hope. "I evaluated everything from the perspective of my priesthood. This has become second nature for me. Even if I could not speak openly about it, even when the prohibition came that prevented me from doing anything connected to my ordination, so in fact I have to say that God is not as humans are. God opens new possibilities." The new possibilities are often contingent on letting go of the old. "I simply want to say that I respect the things I promised to respect. What I have promised, I do. What I promised not to do, I don't do."

It was an exhausting tour. "After several days I knelt down in the evening and I found I could not pray. So I just stretched out my hands and said, 'I know you are leading me and I want to go with you.' This was such a deep experience. It cannot be expressed in words." Although it had not been easy for one accustomed to seclusion to stand there in the public forum, Ludmila found it had been worth the effort. "My time in the United States helped me to develop further some of my perspective on priesthood, what it is about, so I am very grateful for those meetings. And I gladly return to those memories." Her final farewell gift came during her journey home.

"When I was coming to America, on the plane up there in space like a bird, I had a sense, a vision of freedom in everything, everywhere. The experience was completed when I flew back home. I went to the lavatory, and when I was away from my seat, all the signs went on saying that we should put on our seatbelts. But I didn't do it. Now my seat was not near the window, and as I was returning to my place, I saw one window seat that was free. So I said, 'I want to look out the window. I will go and look down.' I could see from the windows on both sides of the plane that half the world was in darkness and in the other half there was a beautiful clear morning. I was running from one window to the other and no one was saying anything to me about fastening my seatbelt, nothing.

"It was such a beautiful moment. I imagined such beauty will live forever. I love space, and there was space to the right and to the left of me. It was an unforgettable experience, impossible to express in words. Magda kept calling me to come back to my seat, but I wouldn't do it. I prayed: 'Dear God, you have prepared this for me to say goodbye from the United States. How beautiful you are.' That moment I was not interested in anything else. I was like a little child who wanted to hold on to something and wouldn't give it up. It was so beautiful. What a coincidence it was—but I think that there are no coincidences—because in the moment there was everywhere the sign, 'Fasten your seatbelt...Fasten your seatbelt,' I was in a place where I did not see the sign, so that I could see what I saw through the window. Such are the gracious gifts of God."

Ludmila returned to Brno and settled back into a routine that had quite a bit of variety but was nowhere near the intensity of what she had just been through. She was glad to leave the frantic pace of America to the Americans. She was also grateful to God that the web of global interconnectedness clearly included her. She now knew experientially that she was not alone. "From what we lived through," she says, "we consider everything valuable and necessary, even if it is not so. We are strongly persuaded that such an extensive work that requires significant change in human thinking is not in human hands and has to be entrusted to the Holy Spirit. What has been started, others should continue. I cannot recall who said these words, that 'it is not a human virtue to take more than one step.' One step has been taken. It is now in the hands of the Holy Spirit. In this lies our hope."

Sixteen

For I am convinced that neither death, nor life,
nor angels, nor rulers, nor things present, nor things to come,
nor powers, nor height, nor depth,
nor anything else in all creation,
will be able to separate us from the love of God in Christ Jesus.

Romans 8:38–39

Ludmila shared many things in the telling of her story. Only a sampling has been included between the covers of this book. The following bits and pieces of her narrative show her penchant for reflecting on experience and hint of a spirituality that is very deeply rooted and passionately embraced. "Very deep experiences have no words," she has said from time to time. More often than not, this is true. The following may be the exception.

✛

"I can see how God has been at work in my life from the very beginning. I see God's hand in everything. Through times of crisis and intense suffering, through all those times of abundant joy and deep, satisfying nurture, I have been led to be fully aware of my complete dependence on God."

✛

"Trusting in God is not just a theory, but a reality. When unlimited trust in God is present, there is also present unlimited trust in people. And it cannot be cancelled in any way. When it is there from childhood, it cannot be cancelled. I am not able not to trust."

✛

"My home was the work of my parents who lived an exemplary life. Their common life was framed with Christian ideals and profound faith. The reality of life was so difficult, that even after so many years, tears appear in my eyes. Each difficulty was a bore into the well of faith, and from this stream I was breastfed."

✛

"When I fell in love with God midway through my teens, it was as a young girl who for the first time experiences love in her heart. I was filled with this love and I felt so enriched by it. Among the gifts it gave me was the ability to forgive. It taught me to accept bitterness and disappointment, to not be afraid of entering places where I knew I would not be accepted. Ordinary days, all their difficulties, all their happy moments were impregnated with this love. It lit a fire inside me that nothing can extinguish. I did my work with precision, did my very best in everything because I wanted to be more like the one I loved."

✛

"When Totality was already well established and the troubles came, only then did I start to search. Faced with the reality that surrounded me, I began to talk to God in my own personal way."

✛

"When Davidek was speaking about 'micro-moments' in the use of our time, I knew exactly what he was talking about, because I had this within me for a long time, ever since my childhood. Spiritual talk, a song, were for me micro-moments. My relationship to Christ was made up of many micro-moments. These played an important role under the pressures of time and other tensions. The peace I enjoyed in the years beforehand when I had time for spiritual things, for prayer, meditation, spiritual reading had been preparation for this. So the peace, the calm, the serenity were already there within me when it came to the more difficult times."

✛

"When there were difficult moments in my life, I was not content with myself. I would always return to those moments within and I would think them through again. I would ask myself: 'How could I have lived them in a better way so that I could be at peace with myself, so that this might not have happened?' The idea of reliving those situations in order to overcome them became part of my spiritual practice. I began asking myself personal questions within my inner being, and I would talk to God about all those moments and about people whom I had met. Tell me, O God, how did you imagine that I might overcome this moment? Of course, sometimes nothing would come. When my inner state was empty, I had to remind myself to remain open toward that situation and not to close it off, because God responds differently than we do and we may have to wait for awhile. God would always answer me, even if after many years. What was important was to stay attuned to God's voice, so that when God spoke I would know that now God is responding to me and to that situation. To be able to do this is a gift."

✛

"Spiritual experience is a gift that I cannot give myself."

✛

"Once I accepted the fact that I was stuck in my spiritual development, the moment came when I knew I had to get out of the situation that was causing me to be this way. After such a realization, the first step is so heavy. I believe that for this first step, only God can do it in partnership with the person. I believe that God goes with you there to the place where you are stuck, and with love pulls you out of it. Otherwise you would be unable to do it. That's how it was for me, but in order to realize this, we often need another person."

✛

"I was tempted many times to leave Koinotes to enter a contemplative religious order. Even though I had this desire and I searched for ways to fulfill it, it was always clear from the circumstances that this was not the way, because I could see the needs and I had to respond to them. We don't do what we want to do but we do what is needed. That was our spirituality."

✛

"One significant experience happened while I was participating in a meditation exercise. I was very tired, and when one is tired, one only does what is really necessary. I had never spoken before about major disputes or contradictions that had occurred. My belief was very simple and my faith was very deep. I had already spent many years in spiritual darkness and human emptiness. That also belongs to life, but if that condition lasts too long, the one involved develops unusual sensitivity and perception. So it was with me. When I came to this meditation exercise, I heard the lecturer speak about God's love and I experienced all of it as though it concerned only me. The words that were said touched me deeply and that experience remained through several hours of silence, tears, inner calm, and peace. It is hard to speak about it, because it was so personal. When you have such an experience as I had, you feel a great relief and you realize that everything is related, and you are able to accept everything. Just before my mother died, she put everything aside and was completely absorbed in herself and in her transition. It is not in our power to effect this. So too it seems that all those external things affecting me are now becoming less. It can be a kind of poverty, but it exists, and so I accept it."

✛

"A mother's life is rich and profound, but if a woman is totally absorbed by her family, by her children, if she has no time to balance her giving with fulfilling her personal needs, there is a danger of losing her personality. A mother can give to the extent that nothing at all remains of her individuality. Then one day, after her children are gone and aging brings feelings of emptiness, she feels worthless within, and even before others. With too many women today there is suffering without self-reflection. Too often priests encourage women in this stereotypical pattern of total self-giving without taking into account their individuality or allowing for their human and spiritual growth."

✛

"God uses us as instruments. Felix would repeat that an instrument can be used to the point of such abrasion that it becomes useless and has to be replaced. 'Jesus, thank you for all the difficulties and for all the losses that you are leading us through. Do not set us aside as your instruments, but help us to trust and to cooperate with you.'"

✛

"Without God nothing good will happen. Even if everything we have done seems somehow to be dissolving into thin air, we have to believe we are an instrument of something we will appreciate or discover fully only in the future. Life itself goes on and God's work is not finished yet."

✛

"In the litanies, we call Mary a 'spiritual vessel.' A vessel is filled so that its contents can be distributed. To be vessels of the Spirit—it is to this that we are called."

✛

"What we learn from the Holy Spirit is one uncertainty after another. With the Spirit there is uncertainty, but there is no fear. When there is fear, the Holy Spirit cannot do anything."

✛

"The work of the Holy Spirit means you are left with something you have to do and you know that you have to do it. It begins to develop right in front of you and you become part of the process and so you have to continue this way, not looking to the right or to the left. But it is necessary to be really focused. Like a mother watching over her children, it's not that she thinks of them consciously all the time, but they are in her awareness always. They are her second self."

✛

"My deep need is to create something connecting with everything, something that will be a life wider than what we have now. In essence that means to live guided by wisdom. Koinotes was not oriented to making little kingdoms, but was like an organism that connected everything to everything, and it was alive."

✛

"I am dying to yesterday. I am entering today and then tomorrow. That's how the new tradition gets born. What happens in our spiritual life is also true of our everyday life, the fact that life can change. I leave certain things behind, and I start something new that is needed. So while we stick to tradition, at the same time there has to be a new tradition being formed as well. In the church there should be at least some little signs that these new things are in process now in preparation for the future, so that people can get used to it gradually. When people understand what the new thing is about, they lose their inhibitions. And when they prepare themselves for new things, they go to meet them joyfully. Not everyone, of course, because that is not possible, but individuals, yes, and that is enough."

✦

"To want to become a priest was quite normal for me. I had newspaper clippings and information from the Voice of America that spoke about the needs of women, about the struggle for basic rights, although among the people around me there was not a single woman who was as intensely interested in these things. I gathered information, but I still have no idea how the desire grew within me in such a concrete way or how it came to be there. Many questions have been raised concerning how it happened. I simply stand in awe before this mystery. I can only say there was a need and that need was of the same urgency as, for example, the need for food. I acknowledged the need, was sensitive to it, so that when the call came, I was ready to respond. When I look back, I think that this gift, this call to priesthood must have come at a time when a significant loss of freedom had stifled many people. This tension between activity and its suppression is directly proportionate to the needs that a woman perceives."

✦

"I didn't aspire to power, I didn't do it to compete, I just wanted to serve. I wanted only to make the life of others lighter. I believe that the essence of the Gospel is to make the yoke lighter for people and I wanted to help. It was also a matter of my desire for holiness, for sanctity, which was always in me. I wanted to instill in others this fire I felt burning within me, but in a natural way, in a way that belongs to Christianity and coheres with salvation."

✦

"My priesthood at the beginning was full of freedom and open to opportunities. After awhile it became a means of finding a new way to God. The many feelings I had as a newly ordained priest gradually grew silent, and in that silence, mystery appeared. I began to give up my own images and ideas, and out of the depths of this emptiness, new dimensions of faith emerged. I came to understand myself in a very different way and to understand others differently as well. I started to learn how to live in the present. My priesthood deepened when I discovered that the soul cannot mature without silence and a certain emptying of ourselves."

✛

"I can see an important contribution to the church in the fact that we have done it, we have ordained a woman as priest, because I see how my thinking has been changed by it and stabilized by this sacrament. I was aware of the responsibility that comes with this ordination. It wasn't, like, now there is something here that wasn't here before. It wasn't, now I have it, but rather, that I have to give from it and devote myself to it completely. This realization became my greatest suffering, because the way suddenly was closed to me. What was I to do? I began to ask questions of myself. Should I leave it all? Or should I continue? If I continue, then how?"

✛

"My priesthood as a woman has been different than the priesthood of men. At first I wanted to push myself into a role that was not mine. I was tempted to fulfill all the traditional expectations of the male priesthood, but that was not possible to do. Because I had no clear guidelines for expressing my priestly ministry and I didn't want to give it up, I had to ask God what to do. I had to search and pray. I started to look at how this charism was being developed within me in what I was already doing."

✛

"I began to notice things I wouldn't have noticed otherwise. I would translate everything automatically into pastoral terms. To use a familiar comparison, just as a mother sees the immediate needs of her children and at the same time is always looking ahead to the future, so too in pastoral situations. While I was busy attending to pastoral needs, I was seeking to discern ways I might lead others to human wholeness according to Gospel values. The crux of the priestly attitude lies in not losing one's sensitivity, in embracing sacrifices, in being faithful to prayer. At times when I was exhausted and people continued to come, I suddenly discovered I still had something left to give. Tired or not, these people are here, and I can and will do something. Sometimes, after the person left, I would feel drained of energy. Five minutes later another would come and it was the same all over again. When there is a need, I am given the strength."

✦

"It was a lot of work. I had no time, but what I put my emphasis on was doing this ministry sincerely. I was able to get really excited, and at that moment I gave everything. I didn't lose any of my sense of duty that I previously had, but exercising my priesthood became a priority for me. It happened on its own."

✦

"I was a disembodied person in my ideals until I was twenty-five, because I went in a straight line in pursuit of my goal. Then the reality of life began to form me as a human being. The priesthood brought a unity, a harmony, to my humanity."

✦

"We cannot avoid the question of integrity or wholeness to which all of us proceed. We cannot exclude anyone from the process of becoming fully human, neither a woman nor a man. Personal experience is essential. God gives us the ability to experience ourselves and to assume relationships. The art of developing this is something we have to learn. As we learn to overcome the tensions and the difficulties in life and those times when there is a

lack of love, we are given hope. We experience hope. The great
thing about all this is the hope, and the realization that it is within
reach of our hands."

✛

"The sacramental element plays a dynamic role in this process.
There is a major difference between speaking with someone con-
versationally or in dialogue and speaking with that person on the
basis of a sacrament. Sacraments are instruments God uses to influence us. However, both participants have to be aware that the
essence of the sacrament is that it does not go in one direction
only. It affects both priest and penitent, but this requires our cooperation, our participation. Service to the suffering cannot be
done in a way that says, 'I have something that I am going to give
to you,' but reciprocally, so that both sides are enriched. What
separates our self from the sacrament is the fact that the development of this two-way process has been blocked. We remain at
some former level of sacramental understanding when we should
have gone beyond it into greater depth. I know this developmen-
tal understanding is not linear and that these changes cannot just
happen. Still, in today's society the possibilities are different than
they were before. We need to open our eyes and our spirit, so
our sacramental sensibility can undergo a change, so that in the
Sacrament of Reconciliation penitent and priest both gain."

✛

"Where do I consciously meet Christ? How do I hear and perceive
Christ? Through books, people, life itself, like any other Christian.
In this the priest is nothing special. As a priest I am simply a ser-
vant, and I serve as I am able. However, when it comes to meeting
Christ, there is a difference between knowing and actually perceiv-
ing that Christ is within all these situations. The difference is in
discovering the beauty of life and entering into the depths of life.
It is essential that we make an effort not to lose this knowledge,

for example, by taking it for granted. As Christians we are called to be the salt of life, to be responsible. Because we are responsible, we try to do everything well, try to do our best, and make every effort not to fail."

✛

"Everything I do—teaching children, reaching out to others—is an expression of my priesthood."

✛

"From my experience as a priest I know that priests have to remain in touch with the living God, and we must do this every day. If we are not personally in touch with God, we cannot withstand, we cannot continue. With God's help we live out our call, but only by persistence. That meeting between priest and God is not only as celebrant of the sacrament, but must also include meeting God in a contemplative way. Priests need to be aware of the importance of togetherness and of knowing human needs, even when people are unable to express them. God gives the grace for this, if we cooperate. When we do there is a chance that we will form a deeper relationship with God. This 'contemplative dimension of the sacraments,' a teaching of Felix Davidek, becomes a way of life. So too the priest as teacher cannot be only a teacher of morality but has to be a teacher of human integrity, and that calls for contemplation."

✛

"I can see much deeper into the sacraments now, but sacraments that are lived out, for sacraments are not only something we receive; they are something that we live. This then is the contemplative dimension of the true meeting of God. It seems to me that this perspective will be liberating for people, even if it is one of the more difficult changes to accomplish, because it is not easy to get out from under our stereotypes."

✦

"Only in moments of contemplation is one alone before God."

✦

"People would come to participate in the Sacrament of Reconciliation, and then they would leave. They did not use it fully. There
is so much more to it. For example, just to have taken a moment
to be united with God through our poverty is such an enriching
thing. One leaves the experience strengthened. It may be that a
woman has a closer relationship to such moments, that it's easier
for her to interpret them, because she has such a strong desire to
hand herself over. If we are really seeking the things of God, then
I don't think it is important whether it is a man or a woman doing
the self-giving or presenting the sacrament. What is important is
to move beyond the external manifestation to its inner reality.
The Sacrament of Reconciliation goes much further than just doing it. An awareness that salvation is a shared responsibility must
become internalized. It must be something that we own."

✦

"Love is very simple, but there are so many layers, like so much
dust, covering over the concept of love. God loves in a different
manner than we do, and in this we have to change our thinking.
God is offering everybody the opportunity to learn this."

✦

"We keep hearing that we have to change our thinking. Basically
I think we need to see things differently, that the better thing to
do is to change our way of seeing, to see things not as the world
sees, but as the Gospel sees them."

✦

"When I saw how the men who were priests were living more or less according to a stereotypical pattern, each having his own little parish or group while I had to give up one thing after another, I felt that someone should at least appreciate something I was doing. I was having health problems and financial problems along with many other things. Some years were especially difficult. Only much later I realized that I had to leave even this idea, that someone would appreciate something I do. Only then was I free. I believe that God sent me this discovery, that the way to fulfillment is through loss."

✛

"As I look back on my ordination, I cannot say that Davidek made a mistake. Why do I think he did the right thing, that it was a good thing to do? I know that if I were not practicing my ministry, I would never have been able to understand it the way I understand it now. I would not have gone to the heart of it, because to judge something from the outside is to see it in a completely different way than to know it from within as something you have lived. Here is the point of mystery. It is not easy to be open and to communicate what this means. It is similar to a relationship whose very intimate details simply can't be shared."

✛

"The only problem I had was, how was I to give testimony to my priesthood? How could I witness to the fact that the priesthood of a woman is possible, if my ministry was anonymous? I could not expect that those to whom I ministered would admit it publicly, nor did I even want that. I had to accept that this is really God's concern from A to Z."

✛

"Whenever I stood at the altar—I don't know how it is for a man—but as a woman I was not able to forget or to put aside those things that are part of my very being. I would always feel this deep cooperation with Jesus and knew that it is Christ who transforms. This is the point of the most intimate cooperation of human and divine. The purpose of Eucharist is the unification that follows, which flows into all aspects of pastoral ministry. What a pity that God's people are so seldom shown this aspect of Eucharist, for it is from such an awareness that responsibility is born. It was natural for me as a woman and a priest to join all these things together."

✛

"I subordinated many things to my priesthood. In fact, I subordinated everything to it. We women know how difficult it is to give up our imagination. I accepted my priesthood as it was, without imagining how it should be or even how it could be. Nevertheless, the impulse to imagine myself in various situations remained inside me and images kept emerging. Time after time I had to put them aside and again step into nothingness. It sounds simple and unambiguous, but it was not. It was a gradual process and is essentially the work of a lifetime."

✛

"Should we just leave the future of women's ordination to one half of humankind? Should we leave the decision to men? Then I think it will never happen. These two halves, men and women, have to meet somewhere on this. Only by coming together, by understanding each other, can we take the next step forward. Through unity and partnership winds the path of salvation."

✛

"There is no heaviness here in the realization that I am a priest, but rather a setting free, because now I know the meaning of my life and how to make sense of it. I know that every little thing is directly targeted. I experience in a much deeper way the beauty of creation. I feel more one with creation in the sense of respect and admiration. I even enter into my prayer of praise in a much deeper way. Life in its essence is more and more enchanting for me. I think this is the result of my priesthood."

✦

"I go through life with a sense of direction, but it was somebody else who put me on the way and who is leading me still. To every young person I say, 'Get to know your predecessors, because the good done by those who have gone before is the good God is giving to you, fundamental human good.' Our predecessors built something for us. I find I am a part of this process, but I must also influence it. This I feel very strongly."

✦

"We should be grateful to our ancestors. They prepared our future, which is now our present. Their prayers, those simple rosaries said during the long winter evenings bore fruit for future generations."

✦

"As to the mystery of Christ being shared with others, many people have told me that if there were a shortage of priests here, perhaps then it would be possible to ordain women. I see it another way. There is always Christ standing behind the change that occurs in the sacraments, and Christ made no distinction between women and men. If a woman is able to communicate or to bring these moments closer to people, why should she be prevented from doing so? That is one consideration. The second is that priesthood plays a role in living into the depth of our human existence as women. This has been my experience, and I can testify that it is so."

✦

Ludmila's brother Josef is a man of few words, but he usually makes them count. When asked what he thought about his sister's

ordination, he said he had written a poem that said all he had
to say.

> We both know very well
> Your ordination is valid
> In the order of Being you are a priest
> in the order of Law you are not
>
> But it is impossible for Yes and No
> to be valid at the same time
> Order of law is changeable
> Order of Being is not
>
> The changeable
> is subordinate to the unchangeable
> Submit to the Law then
>
> Being is with you
> as with Jeanne d'Arc
> the Stake burns up
> but the Heart does not burn out

—J.J.

Epilogue

Ludmila's flat is located in a large housing complex consisting of several twelve-story structures the length of a city block in the Stara osada section of Brno. The exterior is stark, especially on a cloudy day or when there is a summer storm and the stone walls weep in the rain. There is a double entry to reach her first floor unit. I push the button, identify myself, and am buzzed into a small public foyer that leads me to her door. She is warm and welcoming. I feel like I've just dropped in on a friend, forgetting there was once an iron curtain that came between her and me, making a moment such as this unimaginable. I leave my shoes just inside the door, because that is the custom. With me is Martina, who will translate and interpret for us.

The narrow hall in front of me is the length of my living room at home. I've already had the tour, the first time I came to visit. There are four rooms, all on the right: a tiny toilet, a small washroom, the kitchen, and a combination bedroom/living room. The two main rooms are utterly charming. The kitchen, with its large windows, white filmy curtains, African violets, pottery, and an oasis of green, growing things, is flooded with light. The kettle is on for coffee. Recorded music fills the room, not with Moravian folksong, but the familiar sound of my choir and me singing "Mother and God." I explain to Ludmila that the song is about God as *Maminka*. Without a pause, she replies: "You know, through all of our conversations, it seems like we are missing the most important thing, that God is both male and female. This consciousness is a great richness." I couldn't agree more.

We take our coffee to the living room. One whole wall holds shelves of books. There are photos of her family. On the walls are depictions of Christ and Mary the mother of Jesus, along with some lovely paintings that are part of her heritage. Divider shelving separates the sleeping area from the common room, a bed and a tiny table on one side, chairs and a coffee table on the other, and green plants everywhere. In between are curios from around the world and other cherished mementos. The room is filled with memories. I can feel it in the air. A large portrait of Felix Davidek on the wall above the sofa makes certain he will not be ignored. I want to hear more about Felix the poet. "Do you have any of Davidek's poems?" She says she has them all. I ask to hear one of them. She pulls out a book from the bookcase, *Tropical Asia: Country and Life,* and turns to the title page where Davidek had written a poem in 1973 to commemorate her birthday. It is not exactly a poem, she says, and then proceeds to read it.

> By this nature the Journey started
> in the Nature of Your mature Personality,
> which I would never have understood,
> if I hadn't started right from here—
> > The sea is deepest
> > right there, where You are
> > and Stars are highest
> > over Your head—

———

"I was very angry when he wrote this." I couldn't imagine why. "I asked him why he wrote such things." Because he was a poet. "These things shouldn't be written." Why? Was it too romantic? "No, too unrealistic. It was about this mature personality." I couldn't resist saying to her: "No wonder men have such a hard time. They do something nice and we yell at them." We both dissolve into laughter. She says: "The trouble is that one always realizes too late." She reaches for another poem that captures the depth of feeling of both the mystic and the man.

A poem is perfect
ONLY
in its deep desire to be SILENT
         before the LISTENER.
Through SILENCE
to take out one's sword and one's cry,
and one's song of love:
Only the song of love for the NEW
not yet in act,
nor in words...
What has not been for so long a time
and for a long time we will not see,
what is not gone from nor in memory:
what is only after it has been SAID TO BE...
And then it comes
only as tender intuition
hot flowering tears
anticipating silent STIRRING:
that gentle occurring
of still NEW WORLDS. . . . .

                    June 5, 1978 / 10:37–10:48

Davidek recorded the date—and the time it took to write the piece—on the poetry he wrote. That was an eleven-minute poem.

Ludmila notices a letter in the papers she is perusing. "Here is something I sent to the priest who was shouting at me from the pulpit." She explained: "For a while I didn't attend that church, but then I returned because I thought, what if his conscience is reproaching him for his outburst in the church and his disrespect for me. I felt I should take the first step." So after some time she went to see him and there was some reconciliation.

At one point I pressed Ludmila to tell me something more about her celebration of the Eucharist. She went to the bookcase, got up on a chair, took a small box from an upper shelf and brought it

to the table. Inside were her sacred vessels and other things used
for celebrating Mass. She took them out, one by one: a stole small
enough to be hidden in a pocket; a tiny brass chalice and paten; a
purificator; a very small glass for water; a spoon; a small container
for hosts; a crucifix from her mother's sister in the convent of the
English Virgins; a relic of Saint Ursula; and a silver depiction of a
popular Czech image of Mary, mother and protector of her people.
"It is so small, all of this, so that these things could be hidden,
so we could put them in a basket in order to transport them. We
used these Mass items a lot in our travels."

"You said you celebrated the Eucharist by yourself with the
community of the saints."

"Until it was forbidden by the bishop, yes, I did do that. However, the church declared my ordination invalid, and so everything
that God gave me through Bishop Davidek was taken away
from me."

"Do you really believe that? Do you believe your priesthood
was taken away from you?"

"No, I do not believe that. The ordination as such cannot be
erased. It cannot be taken away. I have been a priest for thirty
years and nobody can erase that. They cannot say it did not exist."

"But they are saying it did not exist. The Vatican has said that
your priesthood did not exist, that your ordination was not valid."

"We are talking about two different things. I cannot say I do
not accept the prohibition I have been given, because I do accept
it. After my priesthood was made public, the church declared it
invalid. They were speaking legally, on the basis of church law. I
have not been given the right to continue, and I have promised
I will not publicly do this. But the sacrament also has a sacral
aspect, not only a legal one. When we speak from this perspective,
nobody can tell me that my priesthood does not exist, even if they
say that these two aspects, the legal and the sacral, cannot exist
apart from each other but only in harmony. What happened to me
occurred during an exceptional time in history and in a particular

place. In the history of salvation, God accepts things at certain times that are not permitted at other times. God permitted my ordination."

She makes a convincing case. Our conversation shifts to her time in the United States. I ask her to share some reflections about why she went and what she experienced.

"When you invited me to cross the ocean, I did not know if I would be able to manage such an experience. But I had to meet the women, because I did not have anybody here who would fight for their independence. Just as the stomach gets empty, in the same way, the soul can get empty. It digests everything and then it's empty. I had this feeling that the next priestly energy, so to speak, needs another inspiration for the future that is ahead of me here. That's why I decided to go."

And what about the people she met? "I have to say I felt God's love and God's leading so deeply there in America."

A group of women who aspire to priesthood gifted her with a stole made by the Carmelite Sisters. She said: "When I die, please allow me to wear this stole." She began to reflect on her death. "I'm looking forward to that. And I say this from my heart, I'm looking forward to that moment. I'm not afraid of it. The music will play and everything will be very beautiful. I just want people to feel joy that I am at my destination. It can be early, it can be later—nobody knows. But the most important thing is to remember that it's the goal. My security is based on the knowledge that Jesus Christ is here with us. This is a great security, and I walk toward him."

I talk with her about a sacramental consciousness she brings to all of life through her understanding of her priesthood. I say: "Your gift as priest of God, Ludmila, has been to raise awareness to the sacredness of life that is unfolding all around us. Perception is so important. Nothing is different yet everything is different when we perceive the power of God in the ordinary things of life. You bring to the daily an awareness of its sacramentality, helping all to see that it is here the priesthood of all believers can always choose to preside."

We share some final thoughts about women and the priesthood. She says: "There are those here who are ready to discuss the ordination of women, but they are not able now to support it and to fight for it." This is not only true of the Czech Republic. It's the situation everywhere. We have pretty much covered the topic, I tell her, for I have her many reflections on tape. I recall her sister's comment concerning the necessity of women priests. "The priesthood of women is very important because of the presence of a woman among the priests, a woman who is equal to them, in partnership with them. It is true that priests are surrounded by women, but that's a different story. You have to be on the same level with them. This perspective is very important." We agree that partnership between women and men in both religion and society is vital to moving forward into true mutuality.

When Ludmila sees the sketch of a young girl by Czech artist Alfons Mucha chosen for the cover of the book, it reminds her of a dream she had. "I went into the church," she says, "but instead of seeing a community there, I saw men's black umbrellas. They were everywhere, not only in the pews, but all over the place. No people. Just umbrellas. I was taken aback by that, so I went into the sacristy. There were no umbrellas there. Then I went back into the church. Suddenly, out of the sacristy came priests vested for Mass. They lined up around the altar and motioned to me to go away. I was not happy about this. I wanted to speak up for myself, but I did not know how. Then I looked up at the sacristy window, which opened into the sanctuary of the church, and there was the pope looking at me. The pope motioned to the priests that they should let me be. I had the feeling that I should not stay, but then I found myself saying, 'The pope decided to stand up for me.' I sensed that he had said, 'Let her be.' That was the end of the dream."

We talk for a while about the symbolism of men's umbrellas and the pope. Then Ludmila points to a painting of the Madonna and the Christ Child by a Slovak artist that hangs above her door. She says that her life was deeply impacted by that image of Madonna and Child. "I was very ill, near death, in a semi-conscious state. Vojtech, a priest who has been one of the most ardent supporters of my priesthood from the very beginning, was at the door of my apartment. My mother went to let him in. I was in my room in the back, yet I heard my mother say to him, 'She is very ill.' When I heard his voice, I opened my eyes, and my glance fell on that picture. Suddenly, I was fully conscious and mesmerized by the image. In no time at all I was well again. It was then that I understood what pictures can mean. They return you to reality. They restore your spirit."

I ask Ludmila to say something about the significance of her name. She had been given her mother's name, which is also the name of a ninth-century Bohemian saint. Born in 860, Saint Ludmila, who was the grandmother of the good Saint Wenceslaus, and her husband, Prince Borivoj, were baptized by Saint Methodius, the apostle to the Slavs. They built the first Christian church in Bohemia in the vicinity of Prague and zealously promoted Christianity. Saint Ludmila, who was deeply religious, was martyred for her faith. "Was she a role model for you?" I ask. "No," she is quick to answer. "My father was the one who chose this name, and I will tell you why he did it. It consists of two Czech words, *lidu* and *mila*, and it means to be friendly to people: from *lid*, "the people," and *mila*, which means "friendly, pleasant, agreeable." Having come to know Ludmila, I can say that the name she was given is certainly appropriate.

Conversation turns to the book. Both of us find it hard to believe that what had seemed so elusive a short time ago would soon be reality. She says, "It is a miracle that someone from another part of the world would find me here—this little person, in this little flat." A miracle, indeed. We laugh recalling the circumstances that brought me here to her.

I had flown to Cleveland to hear her speak when she was in the United States, and then I returned to Hartford. I never expected to see her again, but within a week, there she was, sitting across the aisle from me on a crowded Connecticut train, heading to New York. Several days later, in the middle of the night, I awoke out of a deep sleep and knew I would write this book, although the thought had never entered my mind. Once fully awake, the cold hard facts were no deterrent. I did not know a word of Czech. I had to look up Brno's coordinates on a map. Yet I knew that the Spirit who had made the call would see things through to completion. This deep trust in the Spirit, something Ludmila and I shared, was what had brought us together and what would bring this book to birth.

"If it had not happened the way it did, I would have been brought to you," she says. "I feel protected, like the child who comes to her mother and hears her say, 'Don't be afraid.'" I am grateful for her trust and for the strength of her affirmation. Ludmila gives her reasons for going public with her story. "I feel things are passing through me, that it is not me in the center, that it is God who is in charge. I cannot prove anything to the church. I don't have anything in my hands, no documents for verification. I can just speak the truth about the things I have lived. I don't have the intention to push anything forward. I just want to testify. It is not a new testimony but a confirming once again of everything we already know from our cooperation with God and the cooperation of God's people. In a way it is my duty to leave something behind, to write my memories. I attend to one thing only, so that what has been here for thirty years doesn't get lost, doesn't get erased. I feel responsible for this. And I really, really pray that God will bless this work."

She had made a comment earlier, during my first trip to Brno. "Because you are awakening memories, I am thinking of many things I have not spoken of before." She repeated this thought again. "I have spoken about some sufferings, some troubles in my life. In fact, I have never spoken in this way with anyone, only with Felix in the very beginning." She adds: "And I am saying genuinely that I do not see anything extraordinary in my story. Suffering is part of the normal process when one seeks the truth in life. But when we look back to draw energy and hope, we see how God intervened in our lives, so there is no reason for us to be sad."

I tell her how I feel about knowing there is so much more to her story that will have to be left unsaid. "The recording of any life is always incomplete," I say to her. "There will be more that you will remember, more you may want to tell. A book is only a beginning. In the end, Ludmila, you will be the only one who really knows your story, that piece of the larger story, which is God's story in the world."

"If it was only about me, and I didn't see the future, I would just close the door and that would be it. I am aware of this, but I am also aware of your difficulties in writing this book."

"And I am aware of your courage. It will be difficult for you when this book comes out."

"That will be the next hard chapter of my life." I am painfully aware of that fact. I remember something she said to me earlier about one of her daily prayers. It echoes a prayer of my own. She said: "God, lead me. Lead me to the end."

I know Ludmila will continue to teach, because she loves the children and relishes her ministry. I ask her, "What else do you like to do? What nourishes your spirit?"

"I am very happy to be alone, to get absorbed in thinking, in contemplation, or to go to the woods where it smells beautiful. I like being tired after a walk in the woods, not like when I come home from school feeling utterly exhausted.

"I love my trip to church in the morning, when the sun shines and everything is clear, when the city is waking up and the birds are singing and the bells are chiming, especially the chiming. I love the sound of the bells. I prefer walking to taking either the bus or the tram. I love summer evenings when it's warm, and the flowers, and the seeds.

"I like to prepare children for First Communion, and I like their First Communion day. I like rivers, and birds, and looking forward to reading without being disturbed."

"I don't like fog or rain, or walking when it's very windy. But especially, I would not like to be engulfed by the ordinary. I would not like to live an empty life."

Out of the depths
I cry to You,
O Holy One of Blessing.
I am here.
Hear my voice.
Out of the depths
of doubt
and desire
and dogged determination,
deep
calls unto deep
trusting
Spirit
to speak and act
always
in ways
too deep for words.
Out of the depths
of persecuted faith,
out of the depths
of bottomless hope,
out of the depths
of consecrated love
from catacomb
and
martyrdom
and deep underground
witnesses come.
Out of the depths
of hidden need
buried treasure
dormant seed
the future is arising
a future so surprising.
It is here
I hear
Your voice.

Koinotes Bishops

Koinotes Bishops as of 1967:

Jan Blaha
Felix Maria Davidek

Bishop Davidek consecrated seventeen bishops between 1967 and 1987:

BEFORE THE END OF 1970:

Stanislav Kratky*
Eugen Kocis
Ivan Ljavinec
Jiri Pojer*
Josef Dvorak*
Dobroslav Marian Kabelka
Martin Hrbca
Josef Blahnik

FROM 1971 THROUGH 1979:

Jindrich Pesek
Oskar Formanek
Marian Potas
Jiri Krpalek
Ivan Siard Klement
Vaclav Razik
Dusan Spiner

FROM 1980 THROUGH 1987:

Josef Hinterhölzl
Karel Chytil

Eugen Kocis consecrated Bedrich Provaznik* before the end of 1970.

Bishop Davidek ordained approximately sixty-eight priests.

---

*The bishops who left Koinotes in 1971.

Significant Dates

1898	September 19	Birth of Ludmila Vrlova, Ludmila Javorova's mother
	November 18	Birth of Frantisek Javora, Ludmila Javorova's father
1918	October 28	Czechoslovakia becomes an independent republic
1921	January 12	Birth of Felix Maria Davidek
1924	May 26	Wedding day of Frantisek Javora and Ludmila Vrlova
1932	January 31	Birth of Ludmila Javorova
1939	March 15	German occupation of Czechoslovakia
	September 1	Beginning of World War II
1945	May 7	Germany's unconditional surrender to Allied Forces
	May 8	European celebration of the end of World War II
	July 29	Felix Maria Davidek is ordained a priest
1948	February 25	Communist takeover of Czechoslovakia
1950	April 22	Davidek arrested by StB
1964	February	Davidek released from prison
1967	Summer	The first Koinotes seminarians are ordained priests
	July 12	Jan Blaha is ordained a priest
	October 28	Jan Blaha is consecrated bishop
	October 29	Davidek is consecrated bishop
1968	August 21	Invasion of Soviet army; end of "Prague Spring"
1969	February 26	Josef Javora, Ludmila's brother, is ordained a priest
1970	December 25–26	Koinotes Council delegates meet
	December 28	Ludmila Javorova is ordained a priest
1973	August	Koinotes convenes a second Council
1975	June 21	Libuse Hornanska is ordained a deacon
1978	September	Ludmila's father is ordained a priest
1982	April 7	Death of Ludmila's father
1986	November 30	Death of Ludmila's mother
1988	August 16	Death of Bishop Felix Maria Davidek
1989	December 29	Fall of communism; end of the "Velvet Revolution"
1993	January 1	Czech and Slovak Republics become separate nations

ACKNOWLEDGMENTS

THE FOLLOWING have contributed significantly toward the realization of this book:

- the Women's Ordination Conference and the Quixote Center, especially Ruth McDonough Fitzpatrick, who led Martha Ann Kirk, C.C.V.I., Carolyn Moynihan, and Dolly Pomerleau on a trip to Brno in 1992 and found Ludmila; Andrea Johnson, who, with Maureen Fiedler, S.L., and Dolly Pomerleau, visited Brno in 1996 and then brought Ludmila to the United States and convinced her to publish her story;

- the Crossroad Publishing Company, especially Michael Leach, now executive director of Orbis Books, who took the first steps toward publication; president Gwendolin Herder, who wholeheartedly supported the endeavor and saw it through to completion; Paul McMahon, John Tintera, and Matthew Laughlin, who made sure it happened; and copy editor John Eagleson, without whom I cannot imagine sending a book to press;

- Hermann Herder of Freiburg, Germany, whose gracious hospitality made my trips through Vienna to Brno moments to remember;

- Christine Schenk, executive director of FutureChurch, who was instrumental in my meeting Ludmila in 1997;

- Carolyn Sperl in the library at Hartford Seminary, whose help in assembling resources was indispensable; her husband, Gottlieb, who speaks Czech and was there when I needed him; and Marie Rovero; Donna Manocchio, for finding the cover illustration, and much more;

— those who so generously supported my research and writing in the United States and Brno; and the countless individuals and groups—students, acquaintances, and friends—who have kept this project in their prayers, especially my mom, who died before the book was completed.

I remain indebted to my translators and interpreters in the Czech Republic:

— Klara Lukavska and Katerina Lachmanova from Prague, who facilitated the initial phase of data gathering; Michal Javora, Ludmila's nephew; John Thomas; Zuzana Synakova, Czech language specialist;

— and especially Martina Hoggardova and Magdalena Karelova in Brno for translating and interpreting cross-culturally our many conversations, e-mails, and manuscript drafts with such dedication and precision: there would be no book without you.

Ludmila, I have been deeply affected by the witness of your life and your spirituality. Thank you for the privilege of accompanying you in the telling of your story and, for one brief moment in time, becoming a part of that story. In the realm of the Spirit, where our spirits dwell, such a moment lives forever.

MIRIAM THERESE WINTER

March 2001

OUR RESPONSIBILITY for the history of salvation, church communities, and personal experience with God's manifestations led me to share my deepest inner self with you, the reader. Before you put this book aside, join me in praising God.

This book does not record the complete development of the silenced local church Koinotes, nor does it even begin to address the contributions so many have made to the process. God willing, church historians will continue to deal with this. The book outlines the fact that the charism of priesthood for women does exist. It also introduces the question of whether the Spirit of God in ministerial service is being systematically extinguished through juridical decision-making.

I give thanks to all who, through their silent participation and life sacrifices, contributed to this work: to sister Miriam Therese Winter for the strenuous task of putting this book together; to my sister Maria, my closest family, my friends, women from the Women's Ordination Conference; to Andrea Johnson, who, together with the already departed Bishop Francis Murphy, was the first to insist I publish my story; and to the translators and interpreters, in particular Martina Hoggardova and Magdalena Karelova.

LUDMILA JAVOROVA
February 2, 2001

253

RESOURCES

The primary source for this true story has been a series of face-to-face interviews with Ludmila Javorova. Secondary sources are listed below.

History, Politics, Culture, Religion, Catholic Church, Underground Church

1973

June: J. K. Zeman. "The Rise of Religious Liberty in the Czech Reformation." *Central European History* 6. The Roman Catholic Church in Czechoslovakia.

1983

Vaclav Mali. "On the Situation of the Church in the CSSR." In *Martyrdom Today.* Ed. Johannes B. Metz and Edward Schillebeeckx. Concilium. Religion in the Eighties. New York: Seabury Press; T. & T. Clark, Edinburgh.

1988

August: *Prague Winter: Restrictions on Religious Freedom in Czechoslovakia Twenty Years after the Soviet Invasion.* Washington, D.C.: Puebla Institute.

1989

February 22: Pedro Ramet. "Catholics under Communism: The Case of Czechoslovakia." *Christian Century.*
Summer: Jan Carnogursky. "The Secret Church and Pilgrimages in Slovakia." *Religion in Communist Dominated Areas.*
Summer: "Catholic Proposals for a Solution to the Problems of the Church." *Religion in Communist Lands* 17.
Norman Stone and Eduard Strouhal, eds. *Czechoslovakia: Crossroads and Crises, 1918–88.* New York: St. Martin's Press.

1990

Summer: "Catholic Church and Political Change: Czechoslovakia." *Religion in Communist Lands.*
November 7: "Tomasek to Retire." *Christian Century.*

Milan J. Reban. "The Catholic Church in Czechoslovakia." In *Catholicism and Politics in Communist Societies*. Ed. Pedro Ramet. Durham, N.C.: Duke University Press.

1991

July 1991: Jan Korec. "Secret Bishop." *Catholic Digest.*
Summer: Otto Madr. "The Struggle of the Czech Church: What We Can Learn from a Theological Analysis." *Religion in Communist Lands.*
December: Sabrina Petra Ramet. "The Catholic Church in Czechoslovakia: 1948–1991." *Studies in Comparative Communism.*
Patrick Michel. *Politics and Religion in Eastern Europe.* Cambridge, U.K.: Polity Press.

1992

March 14: "Secret Priests and Bishops Called to Order." *The Tablet* (London).
March 28: "The Complaint of an Underground Bishop." *The Tablet* (London).
May 2: "Underground Priests Step Forward." *The Tablet* (London).
May 8: Eugene Kennedy. "Moves to 'Control' Czechoslovak Priests Are Certain to Extinguish Spiritual Flame." *National Catholic Reporter.*
May 9: "The Faith of the Underground Church." *The Tablet* (London).
May 16: Michael J. Lavelle. "The Cost of Freedom: Conversations in Czechoslovakia." *America.*
June 26: John Paul II. "Updating Pastoral Priorities." Audience of Pope John Paul II to the bishops of the Czech and Slovak Federative Republic at the close of their *ad limina* visit. *The Pope Speaks.*
June 27: "A Warning to the Catholic Church." *The Tablet* (London).
July 26: Felix Corley. "Married Priests Trouble Church in Czechoslovakia." *Our Sunday Visitor.*
August 22: Gail Lumet Buckley and Jean Kennedy Smith. "Prague Spring, 1992: An Interview with Father Vaclav Maly." *America.*
August 22: "Underground Clergy Still Not Reconciled." *The Tablet* (London).
August 23: "A Light Now Extinguished." *National Catholic Register.*
August 23: Desmond O'Grady. "A 'Solid Oak' of the Church in Eastern Europe Dies." *Our Sunday Visitor.*

1993

Felix Corley. "The Secret Clergy in Czechoslovakia." *Religion, State, and Society.*

1994

November 12: "Solution in Sight for Married Priests of Underground Church." *The Tablet* (London).

Petr Fiala and Jiri Hanus. *Koinotes. Felix M. Davidek a Skryta Cirkev.* Kniznice Revue Proglas.

1995

April: Marci Sulak. "An Analysis of Relations among the Vatican, the Catholic Church, and the State in the Czech Republic." *Religion in Eastern Europe.*

1997

Fall: Daniel DiDomizio. "The Czech Catholic Church: Restoration or Renewal." *Religion in Eastern Europe.*

Edward Joseph Valla. "The Catholic Church and the Re-Emergence of Civil Society in Czechoslovakia: 1985–1990." Ph.D. diss., University of Connecticut.

1998

Jan Pavlet, S.J. *On the Way to Jesus: Czech Jesuits during the Communist Oppression.* Rome: Refugium Velehrad.

1999

Petr Fiala and Jiri Hanus. *Skryta Cirkev. Felix M. Davidek a spolecenstvi Koinotes.* Centrum pro Studium Demokracie a Kultury.

December 17: Jonathan Luxmoore. "Cardinal's Life Shaped by Slovakia's Troubles." *National Catholic Reporter.*

2000

February 11: Congregation for the Doctrine of the Faith. "On Bishops and Priests Ordained Secretly in the Czech Republic: Declaration of the Congregation for the Doctrine of the Faith."

2001

February 9: Margot Patterson. "Priest, Professor—Now President?" *National Catholic Reporter.*

March 16: Jan Blaha. "False Witnesses" [Letter]. *National Catholic Reporter.*

"Brno—The Metropolis of Southern Moravia." *www.ipm.cz/EN/BRNO/brno .html.*

Radio Prague's *History Online. www.radio.cz/history/history09.html.*

Ludmila Javorova / Women Priests in Czechoslovakia

1990

September 21: Tim McCarthy. "Married Priests among Slovak Church's Woes." *National Catholic Reporter.*

1991

October 2: "Czech Priests in Limbo" [married men ordained during communist persecution]. *Christian Century.*

December 8: "Women Ordained in Roman Catholic Church." *New York Times.*

December 20: "Czech Church Admits Women Were Ordained." *National Catholic Reporter.*

Franz Gansrigler. *Jeder war ein Papst: Geheimkirchen im Osteuropa.* Salzburg: O. Müller.

1992

May 13: "Czech Priests Defrocked" [review of clandestine ordinations]. *Christian Century.*

Dolly Pomerleau. "Journey of Hope: A Prophetic Encounter in Czechoslovakia." Hyattsville, Md.: Quixote Center.

1993

April 10/17: "The Vicar-General Was a Woman." *The Tablet* (London).

September 10: Peter Hebblethwaite. "Secret Ordinations Kept Czech Church Alive." *National Catholic Reporter.*

1995

October/November: Ingrid H. Shafer. "Reading the Signs of the Times. Reflections on the Global Church." *http://astro.ocis.temple.edu/~arcc/IHS1195.htm.*

November: Von Werner Ertel und Georg Motylewicz. "Ja, ich bin katholische Priesterin!" *Kirche Intern* (Austria).

November 10: Andrew Brown. "Bishop Ordained Woman as Catholic Priest." *The Independent* (London).

November 10: Richard Spencer and Sean O'Neill. "Woman Claims She Was Ordained as Catholic Priest." *The Daily Telegraph* (London).

November 11: Andrew Brown. "A Priest Must Be a Baptized Man." *The Independent* (London).

November 11: Andrew Brown. "Woman Claims She Was Ordained to Priesthood by Catholic Bishop." *Irish Times.*

November 11: Frances D'Emilio. "Vatican Says Ordination of Woman Would Be Invalid." Associated Press.

November 11: "Woman Confirms She Was Ordained Priest." *The Tablet* (London).

November 11: Ian Traynor. "Czech Woman Priest Emerges from the Shadows." *The Guardian* (London).

November 13: VCM. "Javorova's Ordination Was and Is Illegitimate — Spokesman." CTK National News Wire: Czech News Agency (CTK).

November 14: VCM. "Javorova Says She Never Gave Interview on Her Ordination." CTK National News Wire: Czech News Agency (CTK).

November 18: Christa Pongratz-Lipitt. "Journey Out of Silence." *The Tablet* (London).

November 22: M. Lawson and J. Stojaspal. "Illegally Ordained Female Priest Finds Life in Spotlight Too Bright." *Prague Post.*

November 24: "Czech Woman's 'Underground' Ordination Uncertain—Bishops." CTK National News Wire: Czech News Agency (CTK).

1996

January 28: Jadwiga Zurowska. "The Church's Underground Foundation—Czech Republic." *Warsaw News* (Prague).

April 4: *Christus Rex* Information Service. *"Lösung fur verheiratete Priester"* (Austria).

April: Steve Kettle, "Women Priests and the 'Church of Silence.'" *Transition 5.*

April: Josef Pumberger. "Viel Gegenwind: Die Kirche in der Tschechischen Republik." *Herder Correspondence.*

June 8: "Cardinal Confirms Catholic Woman's Secret Ordination." *The Tablet* (London).

November 2: "Acts of Faith." *The Guardian Weekend Page* (London).

1997

Edward Joseph Valla. "The Catholic Church and the Re-Emergence of Civil Society in Czechoslovakia: 1985–1990." Ph.D. diss., University of Connecticut.

December: Dolly Pomerleau. "Ludmila Visit." Hyattsville, Md.: Quixote Center.

Winter 1997–98: Andrea Johnson. "Czech Woman Priest Pays Private Visit to U.S." *New Women, New Church.* Newsletter of the Women's Ordination Conference. Washington, D.C.

1998

May 6: Radio National Transcripts. *The Religion Report.* "Catholicism and Buddha's Birthday." *www.abc.net.au/rn/talks/8.30/relrpt/trr9819.htm.*

May 15: Maureen Fiedler, S.L. "Dear Friend. . . ." *Catholics Speak Out.* Hyattsville, Md.: Quixote Center. See *www.quixote.org/cso.*

September 5: Licia Rando. "Czech Woman Priest Visits." *www.inclusivechurch.org.*

September 20: "Thought for the Week." Sacred Heart Parish, Waterlooville, U.K. *www.hullp.demon.co.uk/SacredHeart/thought/sep20th98irish.htm.*

B.A.S.I.C. Brothers and Sisters in Christ. Praying and Working for the Ordination of Women in the United States. "Czech Woman Priest Pays Private Visit to U.S." Posting of article from WOC newsletter, Winter 1997–98. *www.iol.ie/~duacon/javorova.htm.*

1999

Petr Fiala and Jiri Hanus. *Skryta Cirkev. Felix M. Davidek a spolecenstvi Koinotes.* Centrum pro Studium Demokracie a Kultury.

Petr Fiala and Jiri Hanus. "Dossier: The Practice of Ordaining Women in the Present Church. Theological Preparation and Establishment of the Ordination of Women in the Clandestine Church in Czechoslovakia." In *The Non-Ordination of Women and the Politics of Power.* Ed. Elisabeth Schüssler Fiorenza and Hermann Haring. *Concilium* 1999/3. London: SCM Press, and Maryknoll, N.Y.: Orbis Books.

October 1: John L. Allen, Jr. "After Cold War, Cold Peace." *National Catholic Reporter.*

2000

February 25: Jonathan Luxmoore. "Re-Ordination an Option for Secret Czech Priests. No Mention of Women Ordained in Underground." *National Catholic Reporter.*

Jan Blaha declined an invitation to contribute his perspective to the telling of this story. Except for his testimony regarding Bishop Davidek on page 196, his conversations with the author remain privileged at his request.